Dog Tags

The History, Personal Stories, Cultural Impact,
and
Future of Military Identification

By
Ginger Cucolo

Second Edition
2012

On the Cover: The Three Servicemen Bronze Statue from The Vietnam Veterans Memorial Grounds, a Spanish American War Identification Tag, Department of Defense stock photo on how to wear the Identification tags during WWII model soldier David J. Hyslop, Jr., the POW MIA Dog Tag US Stamp, my husband's (Tony Cucolo) US Army Dog Tags on his chest, my father's (H.K. Allen) US Navy Dog Tags and shoulder boards, stock photo of fallen soldier display, a section of the Harpers Weekly advertisement for identifiable company pins 1863, my husband's US Army Dog Tags laid out, woman's Dog Tags and knitted holders from the US Army Women's Museum, Ft. Lee, Va, Keifer Marshall's Dog Tags, a US Marine who served at Iwo Jima in WWII, from Temple, Texas.

Second Edition

Copyright © 2013 Ginger Cucolo

ISBN 978-098330572-9

Library of Congress Control Number: 2013930073

Published by Allen House Publishing

Printed in the United States of America

www.dogtaghistory.com
contact@dogtaghistory.com
www.allenhousepublishing.com

First Edition
Copyright © 2011 Ginger Cucolo

Dog Tags

The History, Personal Stories, Cultural Impact, and Future of Military Identification

Ginger Cucolo

Second Edition

Allen House Publishing

In Memory of

My father, H.K. Allen

USS Iowa in 1945
U.S. Naval Institute Archive

USS *Karin* (AF-43)
Adria Class Stores Ship
San Francisco Bay, CA., circa 1945-1946.
US Navy photo # NH 82220

You will not be forgotten!

Table of Contents

Acknowledgements

This would not have been a book researched and written by me had it not been for my husband, Tony, who thought it would make an interesting subject. He was right, and he knew my love of the military, history, and writing would be a wonderful way for me to combine those interests. He has been the best ally for me through it all. Listening, editing, reading…listening, listening, listening. Quilting, quilting, quilting…I am such a lucky woman.

Another supporter, and of no surprise, has been my mother. She believes I can do anything and is always encouraging whether she should be or not. If my dad were still here, they would be a strong team and be my best cheerleaders.

During my research, Luther Hanson at the US Army Quartermaster Museum was a wealth of knowledge. Had I not set time limits on myself, I could have stayed for days at a time listening to his stories and being amazed at his knowledge of everything. He is the Quartermaster Museum's Curator at Fort Lee, Virginia. I have told him he does not have permission to *ever* die because of his vast knowledge on everything having to do with the US Quartermaster Corps – goodness, the US Military. I recorded him often, but the details taken must be less than 1% of the knowledge he holds in his head – he was invaluable to me and the research for this book.

Another person of immense knowledge on the history of the American Identification Tag is Paul F. Braddock. I have never met him, but his book, <u>Dog Tags: A History of the American Military Identification Tag 1861-2002</u>, should be a field manual for his knowledge on different tags, their timeline, and images of variances. When I first bought his book and began reading it, I thought my subject had been covered. And while he is very thorough, it is a different focus on the Tag than mine. I am grateful he took the time to be so thorough and give facts on Tags throughout our history.

To my daughter, Mackie, for her support and patience. The first edition blatantly left her out of the acknowledgements. She did a wonderful job in photographing many of the images in the book and I am indebted to her for her work. My daughter, Abbie, for repeatedly fixing my headers and footers, and increasing my knowledge of

Photoshop. I must say thank you to my Aunt Evelyn Allen for her help with the book. And of course, family and friends for supporting me. To Greg Fontenot for reading the manuscript and giving me suggestions; to Melody Sexton for running over and helping at a moment's notice; to Richard Clayton for sharing his amazing collection and stories, and to the hundreds of people who shared stories, wrote to me, sent pictures, requested information, and allowed me to share in their lives. This has been a memorable and touching journey.

Thank you!

Preface

I have a personal and intimate connection with the military. My husband is a career Infantryman with more than thirty-three years of service in the United States Army. The Dog Tag has forever been a part of his extended self, wearing them whether he is on duty or not. This is not unusual, and like so many others, he has added to the chain that carries those Dog Tags throughout the years. This adaptation to those Dog Tags has now altered this identifying tag to mean more than just the pertinent information that is imprinted on its face. It has value beyond that. It, and the items added to that chain, have become his personal good luck charm. It is a weight that gives comfort and security in knowing he has this collection on his body.

Having been present as brand new soldiers receive their first imprinted tags, and also as friends and family members accept those tags as a lasting memory of their service and dedication has always been an honor. They hold these tags as dear and connected mementos which hung next to their loved ones. Appreciating this shared feeling about these tags help to understand their personal statements.

This is more than a piece of metal with words imprinted on it. This is a personal item that individualizes the human who wears it within the larger society. This society demands their obedience, commitment, and duty to a higher cause. However, society can't take away this Tag which hangs privately within their shirts, not only identifying their selves but comforting the soul who lives by their chosen commitment. If understanding you will be identified and not forgotten brings comfort to the fear of death, then what a simple thing to have.

I understand and am committed to bringing justice to such a small and seemingly trivial item. I am the daughter of a Navy Veteran, the daughter-in-law and the sister of an Army Veteran, and a niece of a Marine. I am a wife of an Army soldier, a mother and an American. My years as the spouse of an Army Soldier have involved me in the lives of other servicemen and women whose families have needed information and support.

The research required to bring justice to such a personal item should continue for years. Everyday a soldier, sailor, airman, or marine understands the necessity of being identified and the reality that comes with understanding its importance. It is each individual's story that makes this small piece of metal so important and poignant. It is difficult to limit the interviews. Each story is significant, and my personal wish is to have their voice be heard and be validated.

It is trite to say, but important none-the-less -- this is personal.

Husband's Dog Tags
Anthony (Tony) A. Cucolo, III

Father's Dog Tags   Father-in-law's Dog Tag
Henry Kiper (H.K.) Allen, Sr.   Anthony (Tony) A. Cucolo, Jr

Historical Setting

Fictional Stories with Identification
Civil War and Current Day

First recorded and requested use of identification in America, Civil War...

Battle of Cold Harbor, 1864

A thick cloud of dust surrounded Company H, of the 112th Regiment of New York Volunteers. They moved forward, shoulder to shoulder, each man quiet in his own thoughts. The dust reeked with the stench of dead men and dead horses and it floated like a morbid veil allowing them to only see those marching to the left and right of them.

Two lifelong friends, Albert Jones and John Freeman, marched together knowing all too well what waited for them amidst this shroud. Within moments shot and shell ripped through the air. Their adrenaline pumped.

"Let 'er rip!" Someone yelled.

In unison those up and down the line yelled, "Hurrah!"

Jones and Freeman, still shoulder to shoulder, picked up their pace over uneven and broken ground. They heard muffled curses as many stumbled, but kept going. These men moving forward with them were like family and all took pride in the way Company H continued to fight even when exhausted. Their senses in overdrive, they never felt more alive. In the near distance, the unmistakable sound of a rebel yell and bursts of guns and mortars.

John heard a shell burst near him and looked left to see Albert fall backwards.

"Albert!" Freeman yelled and dropped back, kneeling beside his friend. Minie balls whizzed by him.

"John, I'm all right," Jones said with a strange calm. "Get back to the line."

Blood spurted from Jones' neck. Freeman knew he would not be all right.

"Freeman!" Yelled Sergeant Keyes. "Toe the mark! He's somebody else's darlin', now."

Freeman knew what the Company Sergeant wanted him to do, but he couldn't leave his lifelong friend alone to die. He pulled his scarf from his own neck and wrapped it around Jones' throat to try and stop the bleeding. Jones could barely speak, and Freeman saw him reaching for his chest.

"It's there, Albert. It's there." Freeman told him as he pulled Jones' arm across his chest so his hand could feel the paper that had his name and regiment, written before the battle so if he fell, he would not be unknown. When Freeman let go, Jones' arm slid back down as life left his body.

A sense of duty got Freeman back to his feet and he jogged forward to rejoin Company H. He was glad they had written their names on a piece of paper and pinned it to their blouses. He would come back for Albert, and make sure his family knew how he died. But as he ran, he instinctively felt for his own piece of paper, found it, and was reassured of not being lost and forgotten. He knew too well he could be next.

Current Day, Iraq

Alpha Company, 1st Battalion, 36th Infantry Regiment, "The Spartans"

Second platoon lumbered toward the city of Tikrit in the early morning sunlight. Sgt. Morales sat in the front seat of his Humvee knowing all too well what might lie ahead. His Platoon Leader, Lt. Decker, and his driver were severely wounded by an IED (improvised explosive device; the enemy's weapon of choice) the day prior and were on their way to Germany for urgent medical care. He was a good lieutenant, Morales thought to himself. Damn shame.

He glanced quickly at his side mirror and then looked to his right, his "three o'clock," for anything suspicious. As the lead vehicle in the four vehicle convoy, he knew his eyes and his gut feel for the battlefield could mean survival or death for the vehicles and his platoon-mates rolling behind him.

"See something Sarge?" asked Private First Class (PFC) Hanson, from behind the steering wheel. Hanson, in his second year in the Army, was from St. Cloud, Minnesota, and a darn good driver. The

Humvee carried two other members of Morales' squad, Specialist (SPC) Chris "Mongo" Strube from Mobile, Alabama, and PFC Tommy DiCarlo from Hoboken, New Jersey.

"No, just...checking." Morales answered, his voice trailing off. They were approaching a set of squat, baked mud and brick buildings in a small village. Only a few people were out, but those that were, were all military age males. No women, no children.

"Stay alert, Okita!" Morales barked over the intercom to his gunner, SPC Kier Okita, who hailed from Homer, Alaska. He was hunched behind a .50 caliber machine gun atop their Humvee.

"I got 'em, Sergeant, I got 'em..." Okita said calmly. They had been in Iraq fourteen months now, and there wasn't much that got Okita, or the rest of Second Platoon, excited.

Looking straight out their windows on either side of the Humvee, Strube and DiCarlo scanned for trouble or suspicious debris that could hide another IED.

"Deeds, Not Words, baby" Morales said back to Okita, smiling, repeating the motto of the 1st of the 36th Infantry. Everyone else in the Platoon nodded or smiled at his comment, too.

Morales noticed several men sitting on a curb up ahead. One of the men looked behind his shoulder, then back to the convoy as they passed. Morales grabbed the radio.

"White 4, White 2." Morales urgently spoke to Sergeant First Class (SFC) Burton, the Platoon Sergeant. He was in the last vehicle of the convoy, "Military age males, eleven o'clock, no weapons or cell phones...yet...heads-up!"

"2, 4, Roger...heads-up White," Morales heard Burton tell the rest of the platoon. At the same moment, Morales heard a "whoosh!" and a loud "bang!" Morales didn't see anything, but he heard a Mark 19 grenade launcher start its slow chatter. That was on the third vehicle, he thought. More explosions. Small arms fire.

"Contact right! RPG! Machine gun, second floor! White 3 is hit!" he heard Okita yell over the intercom.

"Contact right! Ambush! Weapons free! Gimme a casualty report!" Burton snapped.

Hanson jerked the Humvee right, Morales' helmet bounced off the heavy glass of the window in his door and Okita started to make the ".50 cal" sing. Hot brass fell around Hanson and Morales; dust kicked and human forms came apart where the group of men had sat before. Okita shifted fire to the building.

"Shit!" Morales yelled to no one in particular. Composing himself, he grabbed his M4 carbine in one hand and clutched the radio hand-mike in the other. He couldn't wait. He knew there had to be casualties in the vehicle behind him. He yanked the heavy door open and took a good firing position behind it. He couldn't identify any targets as a hail of combined machine gun and grenade fire reduced the mud building to a pile of smoldering brick and wood. Bodies and their dismembered parts littered the area.

"Cease fire, cease fire!" Burton yelled over the radio, "Give me three-sixty security; Red 2, check 3 and tell me something – I'm sending the nine-line!" "Nine-line" was short hand for the standardized message for the immediate call for dustoff, a medical evacuation helicopter.

"Hanson and Okita, security, nine-to-three; DiCarlo, three-to-nine; Okita, stay on the radio; Strube, we're going to get White 2!" Morales shouted. "Let's go Strube."

The two of them ran back to the second vehicle in their convoy, now torn in half on its right side. Bright pink tissue and bone fragments lay in the sand around them.

"RPG my ass – that was an EFP, damn it!' Barked Morales. "I hope Okita nailed those guys."

The gunner, Corporal Yung, had been thrown from the vehicle and lay motionless in the sand. Staff Sergeant Murray, who sat in the right front of the vehicle, was clearly dead. Morales motioned for Strube to check SPC Williams, the driver, as he bent down to check on Corporal Yung. Yung was gone. Morales moved on to PFC Travis, in the left rear of the vehicle. Shrapnel had torn his face open, but his eye protection and helmet had saved the rest of his head. He was bleeding badly, but still alive. Sergeant Morales tried to comfort Travis as he yelled to Strube, "What have you got?"

"He's bad. Working a tourniquet on his right arm and I'm slapping a hemcon on his hip…I gotta' stop the bleeding. Breathing ain't good, either"

"Work it Strube, work it, buddy…Burton's got dustoff on the way…stay with me, Travis, you're gonna' make it, bro', I know it…just stay with me…you hear helicopters, man? They're in-bound, dude, they're in-bound…we'll get you outta' here…"

Four Soldiers ran up with pole-less litters, and after Morales and Strube had tried their best to stop the bleeding, the six of them ran the wounded to a medevac chopper, one at a time. Morales turned away from the biting sand. The rotor wash blew up and turned everything brown for a moment. As the aircraft turned south, he knew there were combat medics on that bird working hard on Travis and Williams. He also knew the 86th Combat Support Hospital, or CSH -- called a "cash" -- would do the best they could to keep those two Spartans alive.

In the helicopter, the copilot was talking with the CSH, giving them a status report. Williams and Travis had passed out and could not offer any personal information. The medic in the back was yelling out their names and the info from their Dog Tags over the intercom to the copilot, who was relaying it to the CSH. Blood type would be important for both these men.

When they landed at the hospital helipad, two "gators" – small, 4-wheel, utility motor vehicles, were waiting with medical personnel to receive the litters from the aircraft. Transfer of the injured moved like clockwork as the CSH personnel ran with the gators moving the Soldiers into surgery. As they moved, a nurse huddled close to each body, further triaging the Soldiers, hoping to save time and get them in the best and quickest shape for the surgery that would be next. Time was critical.

Once inside, Dog Tag info was reiterated and checked to make sure information was correct. One of the Soldiers, Travis, had been in the CSH not two months ago, and they had his prior info in the system. As the nurses and doctors continued triaging the Soldiers, blood was ready, and IVs were inserted.

It's called "the golden hour." The time immediately following a Soldier being wounded. Timing and correct personal information are life and death for Soldiers like Travis and Williams, and no one knows it better than the incredible military medical teams.

Chapter One

History of the Dog Tag in America

Identity as defined by <u>The American Heritage Dictionary</u>:
The collective aspect of the set of characteristics by which a thing
is definitively recognizable or known. [1]

1

If we define identity for ourselves under this definition, then we understand the importance of being remembered. Selfless warriors have repeatedly stepped forward ready to give life and limb for our country. They pledge an oath to support and defend this great nation, understanding the consequences of such an oath. With this understood, we cannot deny them the human aspect of innate existence and fear of facing death: I do not want to be forgotten; I will not be unknown.

This fear is compelling not only in validating the emotional aspect, but also in acknowledging the practical aspect. Having no finality to a person's whereabouts leads to an inability for closure - closure for paperwork, closure for financial arrangements, closure for emotional well-being. Families are placed in a state of limbo.

We often hear statistics about our dead, but to give percentages or numbers, sound bites and reasoning, or even words of wisdom and condolences does little to family members who lose a loved one. Their loss is not a percentage. The injured veteran is not a number, and financial compensation does not take the place of a human soul or repair a broken body. War is incalculable to those who serve and to their family members. It is the toll that might be taken on these families that makes this individual story so important.

As individuals we assign value to things, especially items that have been a part of personal belongings. The value is not monetary, it is emotional, and however, it is the emotional aspect that makes it invaluable. We collect things because they remind us of something important to us, or we find comfort in having it around us. It fills a void or a need. This is the value of the Dog Tag in our most recent history.

2

The Tomb of the Unknown Soldier at Arlington Cemetery is one of the most visited sites in the world. Tall and majestic soldiers walk the carpet, protecting and honoring the tomb. They are a personal symbol to us that we respect all those who have died for our country. We stand in silent reverence for those who died without being identified. We stand there, watching, grateful for their service. We stand there knowing there is family somewhere who does not know about their loved one.

Identification of soldiers predates America. The most common known story is of Spartan soldiers who carried a shield and they were to come home with it, or be brought home on it. Each soldier had very individual designs on their shields which were often passed through generations. Identifying the Spartan soldier who fought with that shield gave the armor a special meaning and purpose.

Identification has many essential aspects, but the significance of identification in regard to the Dog Tag is not the same as identification for military burial. Internment needs its own reverence. It was during the Civil War that attention, time, and money was spent on making sure we took the proper respect to bury those who served and sacrificed for their nation. That is not the meaning addressed here. To be honored and buried might bring comfort to the thought of being left on an open field, but it does not comfort the person who is concerned about being unidentified. Identification for the military makes the burial process easier if Dog Tags are worn and recovered. A nameless body does not connect the soul that inhabited it, but a name and its identifying information make a connection to that human body. Consequently, it took the effect of war on American soil to put that desire into actuality.

3

During our Civil War, hardened soldiers were sickened by the inability to identify and bury those they fought so hard beside. They knew family members would not want to know their loved ones were left on the battlefield with exposed limbs and body parts sticking up from the ground. Or worse, eaten by hungry animals that ravaged them. [2]

"Human bones lying on the ground, unknown and
forgotten. Known only by their God,"
as quoted by Joshua Chamberlain,
<u>In the Hands of Providence</u> –
"Never to be found or known on earth again."

3

Knowing young boys would be left unknown on the battlefield might have been the hardest thing for family members to comprehend. "Every aspect of soldiering comes alive in their letters and diaries: the stench of spoiled meat, the deafening sound of cannons, the sight of maimed bodies, and the randomness and anonymity of death." After the battle of Shiloh in Tennessee, these were the image soldiers were left with, and thus supported the importance of identification and burial.[4]

Visual recognition is historically the most well-known means of identification. Having a relative or friend recognize the remains helped to establish identity, however this is not always possible. A comparison of identifying markers is used for more positive discovery. It was necessary to evaluate all facts relevant, when available. This included clothing, medical history, physical characteristics, personal effects, teeth, and of course, any written identification.

The inability to bury soldiers or retrieve the wounded from the battlefield in a timely matter led to erroneous identification and difficulty in marking the bodies. Not only did this difficulty occur for the Army on the battlefield, but the Navy faced complex situations, too. Frequently, ships sank and the Navy was unable to recover bodies for identification. Having seen these occurrences, individuals took it upon themselves to find ways to be identified.

In May of 1862, a New Yorker by the name of John Kennedy, wrote to the Army and offered to pay for all Union soldiers to have a disc with name and unit or place of birth. He drew the design on his letter and offer, and submitted it to Secretary of War E.M Stanton. This disc and its proposition were turned down with no discernible reason. Being a forefather of what is used even today, his letter, below, and their responses are held at the National Archives in Washington DC. [5]

Here is a copy of the original letter sent to Secretary of War E. M Stanton:

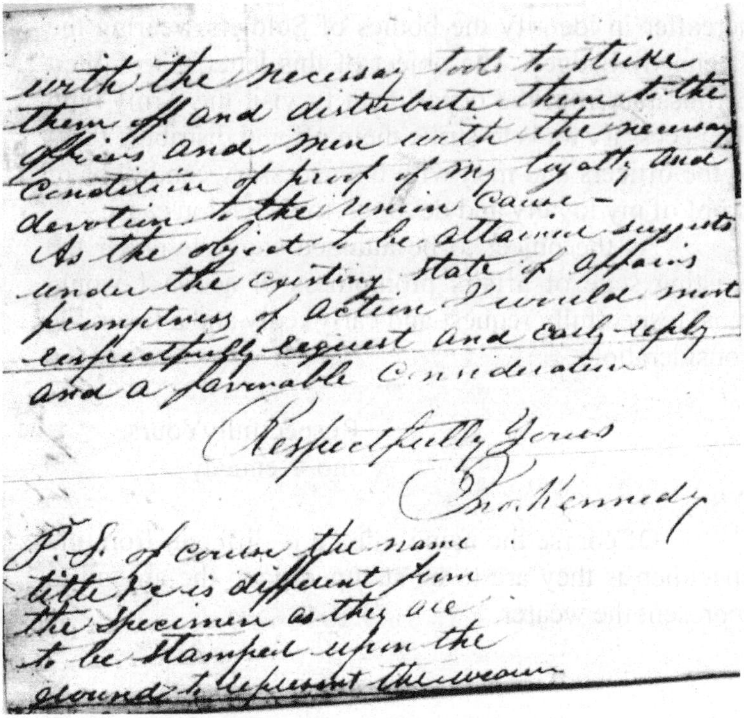
with the necessary tools to strike
them off and distribute them to the
officers and men with the necessary
conditions of proof of my loyalty and
devotion to the union cause –
As the object to be attained suggests
under the existing state of affairs
promptness of action I would most
respectfully request and early reply
and a favorable consideration

Respectfully Yours

Jno Kennedy

P.S. of course the name
title &c is different from
the specimen as they are
to be stamped upon the
grounds to represent the wearer

Now, transcribed as written:

15 South St

New York May 3d 1862

Hon E M Stanton

Sec of War

Washington DV

Dear Sir

Enclosed please find a plan of a badge or medal which I propose getting up for distribution in the Army for the purpose of obviating the difficulty already experienced at Bulls Run is identifying the bodies of the slain after burial – It is intended to be metal and worn by the Soldier under his clothing. It will simplify the record kept by the buriel squad and enable the friends of the Patriotic dead to identify their remains even in the after years – It has been highly affirmed by all the military men to whom I have shown it – It has also been endorsed by the Union Defence Committee of this city – I have no doubt Sir but your own intelligence will enable you to see at once that their case be no difficulty hereafter in identify the bodies of Soldiers wearing the "Kennedy badge." The object of this letter is to Solicit permission from the department to visit the Army with the necessary tools to strike them off and distribute them to the officers and men with the necessary conditions of proof of my loyalty and devotion to the Union cause –

As the object to be attained suggests under the existing state of affairs promptness of action I would most respectfully request and early reply and a favorable consideration.

RespectfullyYours,
Jno. Kennedy

P.S.

Of course the name title *c is different from the specimen is they are to be stamped upon the ground to represent the wearer.

Original drawing of the medal proposed for the Union Army by John Kennedy

There is not a signature or office designation on the first acknowledgement of his letter as to who read it, summarized it, and then passed it on to the Secretary of War's office, but the following note was written back to Mr. Kennedy in response.

Transcribed as written:

75 South St. New York May 3/62
John Kennedy

Enclosed specimen to be worn by every soldier to aborate the difficulty of identifying the remains of those who fall in battle. – Asks that permission may be given to him to visit the army, with the necessary tools to strike these off. That he may make and distribute them

May 5, 1862

One day later, a response is written from the War Department, but not from the Secretary of War, E.M. Stanton.
Transcribed a written:

War Department
Washington DC

May 6, 1862
Sir,
I am directed by the Sec of War to acknowledge the receipt of your letter John 3on with asking permission to visit the Army for the purpose of making badges to be worn by the troops, and to inform you in reply that your request cannot be granted.
Very L,
PAW
ASW
  Mr. John Kennedy
     15 South Street
     New York

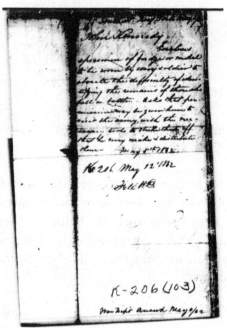

Summary of Kennedy Letter

Response from War Department to John Kennedy

What is quite amazing is the straightforward solution offered here to soldiers and family members. This simple offer would have helped to account for many of the unnamed dead, and at no cost to the Federal government. Since there is no record for the reasoning behind its ungranted request beyond the response from the War Department, we can only guess. Perhaps it was out of caution for safety of the soldiers and not wanting to take the time to find out about this man and any agenda he might have wanted to pursue. Perhaps it was a feeling that such an item was not needed. We had fought before and not had such a thing, why was it needed now? Perhaps it was too much to bother with, or, so many people were illiterate at the time that reading or writing their own names made it debatable.

There were alternatives available during this time period to identify one's self after injury or death. Those wealthy enough to purchase copper, brass, silver, or gold, had their items inscribed. These were the best and most permanent ways for identification. Variations included medallions, watches, combs, bracelets, neck ornaments, and rings adorned with their names and possibly their home towns or units.

In the many Civil War Collector's Encyclopedias, there is shown a wealth of information and images on various ways soldiers kept their items identifiable. Possibly only for personal identification and safety in the case of loss of the item versus identifying items that would identify them in the case of death. Whatever the reason, there are innumerable items shown and marked for identification. In these books you can see that if it was possible to mark items, soldiers did it. For example, cigarette cases, housewives (discussed in Chapter 5, Urban Myths and Legends,) mess equipment, trenching tools, canteens, buckles, belts, buttons, stencils, and instruments just to name a few.

Offering more specific identification items, Harpers Weekly offered disks for sale in their publication for "Soldiers Pins" which could be mail ordered. They listed pins for sale with name, Company, and Regiment. It was available for Infantry, Cavalry, Artillery, Engineer, Signal Corps, Monitor, National Battle Pin, Army or Campaign Badges. For sell in the amount of $1.50, it was made out of coin silver. Harpers Weekly also advertised a Soldiers Badge or Charm, for $1.00, with Name and Unit marked on it. This badge was also made of silver, and could be attached to any piece of clothing.

Identification tags worn by Union soldiers during the Civil War

6

7

The same quest to have known the wearer's identity did not stand on ability to afford precious metals. Different ways to record their information were considered, and those savvy enough to realize money could be made from this desire was sought. Sutlers and campsite traveling salesmen made disks, tags, and coins with a soldier's name and unit for them if they wanted. Sutlers might take a coin the soldier had, flatten it some, smooth it out, and then imprint the information.

If they did not have a coin, cheaper metals like lead or tin were sometimes available for purchase. Soldiers could buy an inexpensive tag that was used as a stencil. Their info was cut out and they could repeatedly use this stencil on any of their personal items.

More commonly used during this time period were examples like our lead story about Jones and Freedman at the battle of Cold Harbor.

Soldiers recorded their information in much less permanent ways. Many wrote on their uniforms, wrote on pieces of paper, and scratched names and personal information onto metal objects they carried with them. Wood was a common personal identifier, and many scratched their names and units onto a chunk of wood. They would often bore a hole through one end so that it could be tied to them.

These less permanent objects were easily lost or ruined during battle and after. Even the permanent identification pieces were often separated from their owner, so proper identification was not always assured. Having nothing officially issued by the military through this time period, these early practices led to the eventual plans for items and techniques employed by future graves registration and identifying procedures.

4

Quartermaster Officers and Graves Registration Units have been in charge of recording and burying deceased soldiers since the 1800s. While their sincerity in accommodating this task is recognized, death on the battlefield in such as the Mexican War and the Civil War proved too much to handle. Almost 58% of those who died were not identified during the Civil War.[12]

Amazingly, it is recorded that at one time in 1864 at the Battle of Ft. Stevens which was by Washington DC, Captain James M. Moore effectively identified all of the remains. With his team from the Quartermaster Cemeterial Division, they painstakingly went onto the battlefield and matched bodies with personal effects. A huge feat at any time, but during this time period it was unheard of. It would be over thirty years before Graves Registration accomplished such thorough practices again.[13]

918. Collecting Remains of the Dead.
[FOR DESCRIPTION OF THIS VIEW SEE THE OTHER SIDE OF THIS CARD.]

.14

While citizens wanted to have such accomplishments, it remained a highly unorganized event. Different organizations tried to coordinate practices, but it took the efforts of many to bring about assistance in different areas. The United States Sanitary Commission was assigned the duties of recommendations of all matters pertaining to the wellbeing and hygienic conditions of Union forces. Though originally composed of wealthy woman and the upper class in New York and known as the Women's Central Association of Relief, Lincoln realized the importance of their ability to raise money and bring attention to needed efforts. [15]

16

On June 18th, 1861, their organization, now to be known as the United States Sanitary Commission (USSC) became an official agency under specific legislation. Their interest extended beyond the medical care of soldiers in the field, camps, or hospitals. They helped with collection and distribution of supplies and began to administer field relief to soldiers and their families. Through their medical reports, they were successful in improving methods for recording information for military hospitals. They printed standardized forms to help with collected information and thus helped to record a person's identity. Although labor intensive, this helped to record over 600,000 soldiers.[17]

As helpful as this was, the USSC realized identification had its difficulties. Service Members, who were unable to identify themselves, for whatever reason, did such things like enlisting under false names or deserting their units. This made correct identification difficult. There is also record of enlistments to gain access to bounty money, and enlistments of soldiers wanting to become another person and leave their past behind. Whatever caused the lack of ability to identify soldiers; this led to a higher level of disappointment for family members. "By 1862, frustrated citizens were asking why "a nation of shopkeepers" could keep track of its parcels, but not its soldiers."[18]

Understanding the importance of and caring for the individualizing of soldiers, other organizations such as the United States Christian Commission (USCC) and the Maryland Bible Society created Identification cards to give to soldiers. While not recorded, there must be multiple instances of groups who assisted soldiers in various ways.

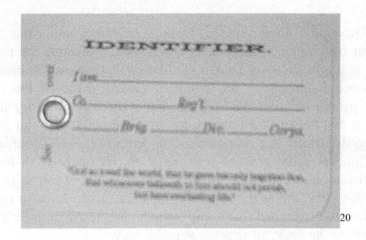

As the war continued, the USSC was the largest organization to realize the importance of correct identification. Through this, men and family members would be able to request back pay, be issued benefits, and show proof of service. This was not only an emotional issue for families, but also one of finances and economics.

5

Historical Setting

Fictional Story with Identification

USS Maine, Cuba 1898

Captain Sigsbee sat at his desk in his cabin, penning a letter home to his wife. He glanced up at his porthole which was open, and watched the shadows of seagulls flying by reflecting against the dim lights in the sky. He listened for a moment as the comforting noises of the harbor lured him into adoring thoughts of his family and home. He looked back down at his paper and continued to write. He wrote about the success he believed was forthcoming, and how America should feel hopeful about the situation there in Cuba. He told his wife of the evening and the warm response he had received from the Spanish Officers who had joined him for dinner.

The ship's bugler started "Taps," and the Captain put his pen down, sat back against his armchair, and looked towards the porthole, relaxed. A bright shooting light, a loud boom and the sudden heaving of the massive battleship – up and then down, shattered the reverie. Slipping from his chair, CAPT Sigsbee ran to the window. Forgetting for a moment that he was the Captain, his first instinct was to run from his cabin and depart the ship. He grabbed his letter to his wife, stuffing it in his coat pocket as he grabbed it to put it on. He opened the door, and then turned around, remembering *he* was the Captain of this ship. He ran back to his desk and grabbed his pistol, then turned back to return to duty. He now assumed from the sounds he heard and feeling the movement of the deck, an attack was under way.

He leaped into the passageway and ran towards the stern, the ship began to list to one side and he could feel the bow sinking into the water. Immediately he began to think through procedure, and turned to head towards the bow to check out the situation. Marine Private William Antony ran smack in to the Captain. The Gunnery sergeant of the battleship's Marine Detachment had ordered Antony to find and protect the Captain.

"Sir!" shouted Private Antony above more explosions, "Excuse me, but you must not come this way. The Maine is going down and I must get you to the quarter-deck."

"The sailors?" Asked Captain Sigsbee. "Can we get to the sailors in the aft?"

"No, Sir. Chief Gunner's Mate Brofeldt has gone to secure the area. Please, sir, the quarter-deck!" The Captain of the ship and young Marine stumbled and moved together towards the quarterdeck, not knowing history was at hand.

The Captain and Private Antony made it topside. The smoke of multiple explosions hung so heavily it was difficult to see any damage. But the Captain knew. He instinctively knew from the feel of the deck under his feet, his sensing of the water line, and the sounds his beloved ship was making, what a bad situation they were in. The ship would be lost, and much of his crew along with her.

Tomorrow would only bring dire news for hundreds of family members, and days of uncertainty. All that could be done would be to undertake a process of checking the names of the living against the crew's roster. Knowing who was alive was the only way of identifying who was dead. And what of those recovered? Could it be guaranteed that the body pulled from the waters of this Cuban harbor could be identified against the crew's roster?

It was imperative to try because America would want to have a full accounting of those that were lost. For whatever reason the ship had sunk, bringing the bodies' home to their families and their homeland would be a top priority. And, any recovered remains would be necessary to help fulfill identification of those lost.

Back to History

Many of the dead during the Spanish American War were buried in Cuba or Puerto Rico, and it would take a very determined and committed Graves Registration Organization to record and identify the remains of those buried. It is also important to note that this same organization was to disinter the war dead and bring them back to American soil for reinternment. The wisdom gained from concisely coordinating death, burial, and grave registration was the way to successfully identify remains. The US Army put this into practice during the Spanish-American War.

9075 General View of the Wrecked Battleship, Maine, Havana Harbor, Cuba, 21

As discussed before, many organizations tried to record names. The San Francisco Red Cross supplied many service members with identification tags. These tags were mainly given to those who lived close enough to receive the tag by the organization. While some were given after the fact, the Red Cross understood the importance of each soldier having identification. Unfortunately, like so many other organizations, they did not have the wherewithal to get them to everyone who needed them. [22]

23

The military sought direction of identification and death services with the establishment of two organizations. They operated out of the Philippines with similar and yet different tasks. One, led by D. H. Rhodes, was Chief of the Burial Corps. The other unit was the United States Army Morgue and Office of Identification established by Chaplain Charles E. Pierce. Both organizations were largely civilian.

Mr. Rhodes proved that fewer soldiers were left unknown if burial and registration happened as closely together as possible. It was also Mr. Rhodes who promoted the idea of a remains' bottle to collect and transfer records of identification. His bottles and their basic purpose became a part of the future Army regulation in 1913.[24]

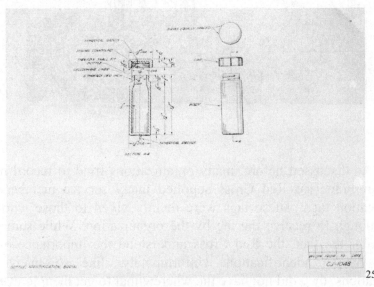

25

Image of remains bottle sketch

However, it was Chaplain Pierce who believed the identity of War dead should be practiced on a more scientific basis. He suggested a central collection agency where mortuary records would be gathered, and more importantly, the addition of an "Identity Disk" in the combat field kit. Much like the original disk suggested by John Kennedy, it was this "Identity Disk", in 1899, that is recorded as being the first Identification Tag for our military service members. [26]

In his final report to the Adjutant General for his thoughts on how identification worked during the Spanish American War, he stated:

"In order to facilitate identification, I recommend the issue to all officers and men of a small tag of aluminum, bearing the name, rank, to be worn constantly around the neck. This method was followed largely by the organizations comprising the earlier Philippine expeditions, and it is better that all men shall wear these marks as a military duty than that one shall fail to be indentified..." [27]

Finally, in December of 1906, the Army officially authorized an identification tag as part of the uniform to be kept in the possession of the soldier when not in uniform. This is the first time the War Department does so officially. The tag was to be of the following description:

"An aluminum identification tag, the size of a silver half dollar and of suitable thickness, stamped with the name, rank, company, regiment, or corps of the wearer, will be worn by each officer and enlisted man of the Army whenever the field kit is worn, the tag to be suspended from the neck, underneath the clothing, by a cord or thong passed through a small hole in the tab. It is prescribed as a part of the uniform and when not worn as directed herein will be habitually kept in the possession of the owner..." [28]

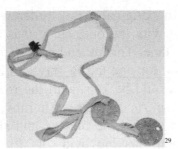

29

Understanding the importance of these ID tags led to a new regulation in 1913. It required that Aluminum ID tags, like those first suggested by John Kennedy and then Chaplain Pierce, were to be a required part of the field kit. The wooden field kit contained metal letters and numbers, a hammer, an anvil, metal pieces, and a notch for holding the tag in place. A soldier would hand stamp his information on the tag. Carrying this wooden box with him, the soldier could at any time, stamp his or anyone's name on a piece of metal or additional ID tag.

30

Similar to the Army, the Marine Corps authorized the use of Identification Tags in October 1916. In almost the exact same wording as the Army Regulation, the tags were to always be worn by officers and enlisted marines, or kept in their possession. The information on the tag would be as follows:

"Officers - full name and rank at date of issue; enlisted men - full name and date of first enlistment in the Marine Corps." These tags were regarded as part of the field kit and were to be suspended from the neck under clothing." [31]

That same year, the original Army order was amended to add a second tag to go along with the one, but it was to hang below it on a second chain, cord, or tape. This amendment carried the belief that the second tag would allow for one tag to stay and be buried with a body while the second one would be kept with the records. This second tag was often called a toe tag. As can be seen in movies and TV shows, this second tag was looped around the big toe and shipped along with the body to its destination, staying with it at all times for proper identification.

As in other countries identification tags, it was seriously considered that the tags should be made of different material and colors. With each having a separate meaning, the material and color differences would make separating them and using them a much easier process. However, over time, the United States chose to keep both tags of the same metal and color.

In 1917, the U.S. Navy authorized identification tags. Their tags made of monel, were oval in shape. One side of the tag there was noted personal information while on the other was a print of their right index fingerprint. Officers and enlisted men had slightly different information imprinted on the front. [32]

A very interesting feature of the Navy ID tag design is the use of a fingerprint on the back of the tag. Using the right index finger, the print was etched onto the monel metal. Making sure the finger is clean, they wiped a mixture of printer's ink and turpentine or gasoline on the tag, and the sailor rolled his finger across like you might see while being booked at the police station. They then sprinkled finely powdered asphaltum, heated it, and let it cool. The final step was to put the tag in a nitric-acid solution to set. After this process, it could be cleaned and dried and given to the sailor. The process worked well, but it was very important to do the steps correctly. [33]

Monel was named after Ambrose Monell, but formed by Robert Crooks Stanley who worked for the International Nickel Company (INCO) in 1901. The new alloy was named in honor of the president of the company, Ambrose Monell. An "L" was dropped because family names were not allowed as trademarks at the time. [34]

Monel was blended to withstand the worst of conditions. Knowing that it was a highly non-corrosive blend, it was thought to be a perfect metal to be used as an identification tag. There are different types of Monel, but it must be at least one part metal and a combination of nickel, copper, iron, and other elements. It is highly resistant to rust. Its commercial strength made it a desired choice in the making of future ID tags for all services.

The next authorized tags for a short time period were square tags to be worn on soldiers serving overseas. They were one inch square aluminum tags with rounded corners. These Dog Tags are rarely seen today since not many were made towards the end of 1917.

The Marine Corps also issued square tags in August, 1917 with an amendment to it which provided that:

1. Two aluminum identification tags, to be furnished by the Q. M. C.
   (Quartermaster, Marine Corps), will be habitually worn by all

officers and enlisted men, and also by all civilians attached to the American Expeditionary Force.

2. Both tags will be stamped with the name, rank, company and regiment or corps to which the wearer belongs; and the second tag will be worn suspended by a cord one inch long from the bottom of the first tag.

With the commitment of proper identification being taken under War Department Regulations, the identification tag was now an item recognized from past lessons learned. General John J. Pershing, the Commander of the American Expeditionary Forces in World War I, knew the benefits of a Graves Registration Service. Chaplain Pierce, having retired as a Major, was called back to duty by General Pershing to head up this unit under the Quartermaster Corps. He trained soldiers in Philadelphia, Pennsylvania, then took his unit and positioned them in Tours, France. The people trained under Pierce were sent to all areas of combat during the next year and a half. [35]

Event: WWI Graves Registration Service
Date: 27 September 1917
[36]

With special attention being given to the burial process and proper identification of soldiers, the War Department took another step forward during World War I by issuing all military personnel a unique serial number. Issuing a serial number helped distinguish personnel who shared like names. Rarely do you find anyone who served during this time period who does not remember his or her military serial number as easily as their Social Security number or their phone number. Learning this was better known than family member's birthdays by some.

These numbers were assigned to units in numerical blocks and put into effect on March 16, 1918. The individual serial number was added to each ID tag. Understanding the system helped in differentiating the component and corps area, thus allowing individuals to understand who they were assigned to, when they entered the service and how, and other personal information.

37

Non-combatants were also issued identification tags. Even though they often were forced to use weapons, most were not trained to use weapons, or to use weapons in their job descriptions. While in the service of the military, they technically were non-combat, military personnel. One such use of non-combatants was the American Ambulance Service.

38

7

Historical Setting

Fictional Story with Identification

WWI

Ed and I were lucky enough to remain together as the War wore on. I think it was the Major who allowed it. He seemed to make sure we were always on the same ambulance team, whoever we were assigned too. Our French was good and we worked well together. Today we were on our way to the Marne Valley from Paris. They needed us. All of the Allies seem to need the Volunteers of the Ambulance Field Service, especially the French.

Here we are, on our way, going up and down hills in this beautiful country. One moment you see a lovely field or woods, then the next thing you see are huge holes in the earth or blown out buildings. It is almost surreal. Even the noises and the people are surreal. One moment they are sharing a cigarette and the next they are running for their lives.

I am glad we are here because we can make a difference. It is such a worthy and satisfying job. Well, satisfying for the soldiers and people we can save. The Major reminds us that if we were not helping, many more would be lost. We know he's right, it's just hard to lose someone - anyone.

We can hear shell fire in the distance and Ed looks over at me as we acknowledge its direction.

"How much longer you think?" I asked Ed.

"I don't know, maybe a half hour?" he answered.

We drove on and I rolled a cigarette with some papers I got from Sheldon. Ed hit a bump and my hands dropped the tobacco and paper.

"Jeez, Ed, need a driving lesson? I got tobacco all over me."

"You wanna drive?" Ed said rather perturbed. "I think the rounds are getting closer and they're's some soldiers up ahead."

"Really?" I sat up a little straighter to look down the road. "You're right. Allies?" I asked.

"Yeah, looks like French." He said. We pulled forward slowly, as two of them started motioning for us to get off the road. They spoke to us in French.

"We think the Germans are about 2,ooo meters over that way." The Sergeant pointed. "Park over there. I'm sure we'll need you shortly."

"But…" I began.

"Angelo, we can't leave 'em now. Anyway, they'll be better for our protection right now, too. You try to radio and let them know where we are." Ed told me.

We parked the ambulance behind some trees and headed over to where they told us to come. We got down on the ground and listened as the artillery got louder.

"Hey, got any more of that tobacco?" Ed asked me.

"Yeah, but only two papers." I told him, as I handed him one. One of the French guys by us asked if he could have one. I told him I only had one, and he shrugged his shoulders. Ed and I looked at one another, and I handed him mine.

"Here, you need it worse." I told him in French. He thanked me and finished rolling it. I took out my matches and lit both of theirs for them.

One of the other guys in the trench with us motioned that we were to be quiet. The French guy who had my cigarette calmly smoked it, but Ed put his out and placed it back in his pocket for later. The firing was so close I could hear the action of the front lines engaged in battle. Ed and I started to look over the edge, but the French guy held out his hand and he started up. Cigarette still in hand. His helmet lay back on his head in a relaxed position. Ed and I looked at one another again, thinking this guy was too nonchalant for the situation. As he raised his head, a bullet hit him in the face and he was thrown back down in the trench beside us.

We jumped into action trying to assess the situation. There was yelling all around and the noises were all too familiar of hand to hand combat, much too close for comfort. Our guy was still alive and we worked on him with the items we had with us. We knew that for him to have a chance, he needed to get to one of the field hospitals. We placed his flaps of skin back in place across his face and wrapped it the best we could. He was alive but unable to talk, and for some reason we had not gotten his name before as we counted our cigarette papers. He had no identification.

We stayed there until the fighting ceased, and then I peeked out over the edge to check out the situation. There was moaning and other bodies we needed to check, so with our guy stable, we slipped out and wandered the area, looking for wounded and trying to take care of them the best we could. Almost a quarter of them were dead. The wounded were our interest and getting them to the help they needed.

None of the dead had identification and we had no idea how the French would be able to know who was who unless they had a letter or something else on them. Even as non-combatants, we were all given ID tags and ordered to wear them. It was during times like these that we knew just how important those ID tags were, and Ed and I were grateful we wore them all of the time. We just wish these guys had done the same. We could get the injured to help, but the dead would have to wait. It was beyond our control.

Back to History

Marines were assigned serial numbers while in France. In 1918, the Marine Corps stated, "The numbers assigned to all men present will be stamped in identification tags." [39] They were to keep these tags until the supply was exhausted, according to their manual in 1921. They would then follow Navy Regulations until their next change which was in 1940.

Towards the end of World War I, the Army Quartermaster Graves Registration Service claimed that if they had one hundred bodies, less than three were unidentified of the ones they were able to recover. Roughly thirty thousand bodies were buried overseas, while an additional forty seven thousand were sent back home to the United States. [40]

Realizing they still had a percentage of unknown, Congress approved a Resolution on March 4, 1921 to make available a burial place for an unknown and unidentified soldier from World War 1. Assigned to the Quartermaster Corps by the Secretary of War, they took the utmost care in selecting and honoring a fallen soldier.

41

Well known to all now as Arlington Cemetery and the Tomb of the Unknown Soldier, it was a necessity that this very special person would not ever have any indication that their identity could ever be established.

"Over in peaceful Arlington, across the historic Potomac, he rests - our Soldier Unknown - his last fight fought, his last journey ended. Within hallowed stone his tired body sleeps, safe for all time, but his lofty spirit quickens with the years in the responsive hearts of all Americans, symbol of sacrifice and of service. There the Army laid him in our National Shrine overlooking the fair Capital of the Nation - unknown, yet known, the first soldier of them all, typifying the soul of that mighty host which fared to France, only such a little while ago, that civilization might survive and our own land continue on their apportioned destiny."[42]

43

"It is a simple, sweet story - the selection of one of our own Unknown Dead, thus to be brought home in glory. This war-wracked frame, so slender and so still - whose identity shall never be disclosed until the last trumpet shall sound and the dead shall be raised - this has been the very one selected as representative of the 77,000 American soldiers who made the highest and the last sacrifice, in a cause which the world knows to have been right and just." [44]

As before, after World War I, the push for ID tags subsided. It was popularly believed that ID tags were only needed in combat areas.

In the *Bureau of Naval Personnel Manual*, 1925, it stated that, "in time of war or other emergency, or when directed by competent authority, individual identification tags shall be prepared and worn by all persons in the naval service, suspended from the neck or from the wrist on cotton-sleeved Monel wire. Monel-metal chain could be used at the individual's expense." The information remained the same on the tags as during WWI.

Similarly, the Army continued with the same set of ID tags of aluminum or other metal. In 1926, they were to "be worn by each member of the Army when in the field, when traveling on transports, and when the field kit is worn in garrison." It was still to be worn around the neck by a cord or thong passing through the hole in the tag with the second tag hanging from the first with a short tape or string. The officers were to have the following stamped on theirs: US, name, rank, and branch of service. Enlisted men were to have USA and their name on one side, with their serial number on the other. [45]

Identification tags basically remained the same up until World War II. It was during this time that the ID tags became known more commonly as Dog Tags. In World War II, these Dog Tags had a variety of personal information on them.

[46]

Photo taken March 22, 1942, David J. Hyslop, Jr.

Many GIs wore them with metal chains instead of the cloth tie around their necks. This lent itself to be most like dog collars with a tag on them. Never being called such in regulations, the Dog Tag has forever imprinted itself on the serving individual's mind and the tag they wear. A much more in-depth story is told in the Chapter 5, Urban Myths and Legends. While there are quite a few urban myths, if you read through the Chapter, the information given lends itself to a most appropriate reasoning as to their labeling.

As America entered World War II, the Navy ID tag remained oval shape, the Marine Corps had square and oval shapes, and the Army instituted the oblong shape which can be seen today. The Navy and the

Marine Corps had basically the same information imprinted on their tags: Name, rank, religion, blood type and tetanus dates, and their corresponding service acronym – US Navy (USN) or US Marine Corps (USMC)

47

New Navy tags were made of 17 percent chrome (stainless) steel. A new braided plastic and steel-wire cable, with a 24-inch loop and an attachment for both tags, was made for newer personnel. The wire was designed to withstand a temperature of 2,000 degrees and was made to retain at least a 5-pound pull even after heat has burned the plastic composition. The wire was designed to break at 21 pounds, when unburned, to prevent accidental injury to the wearer, and could be cut readily with a knife. In addition, a jump ring could be added to be opened to facilitate detachment of tags. [48]

Often called a tooth tag or wafer, Comdr Frank E. Jeffreys of the US Navy developed a technique in which a person's personal data would be inscribed on the wafer just like the ID tag. The information was typed onto onion skin paper, and then before the plate of the false teeth is completed, a carbon copy of the information is placed on it. [49]

For the Army and the Air Corps, their ID tags had five lines with name of wearer, serial number, tetanus immunizations, blood type, name of person to be notified, address of notification, and religion. Blood type was simplified during this time as A, B, and O. If you were Positive it listed as Pos, and Negative as Neg, but there was no Rh positive or negative, yet. Religion was possible for all the services, but the only choices given during this time period were C for Catholic, H for Hebrew, and P for Protestant.

50

There were not options at this time for other religions, but you could leave it blank if the wearer chose to do so. This became an important option for the American Jewish wearer. It is understandable that one might fear their Nazi captors if Hebrew was imprinted on their Dog Tag. While the concept of placing so much information on the Dog Tag was thought to be helpful, this is an instance where life or death was decided upon because of too much information. Many US Jewish soldiers were taken captive and separated from the other GIs because of their religion.

In the New York Times, June 22, 1994, Victor B. Geller (in an earlier letter, June 14) offers as explanation of the scarcity of Stars of David in D-Day cemeteries in Europe, that the families of fallen Jewish servicemen *chose* to have the remains shipped home for reburial, but he believed there is a more likely explanation. Many Jewish G.I.'s omitted from their dog tags the indication that their religious identity was Jewish for the prudent reason that in the event of falling into German hands, their lives would be at greater risk if they were identifiable as Jewish.

Consequently, fewer American D-Day casualties were grave-marked with the Star of David than would have been justified. "As a combat veteran I know that my dog tags and those of many of my Jewish companions were religiously anonymous." Paul Lippman Hoboken, N.J., June 14, 1994.

"The radio operator, Archie Mathosian, says that Gitlin bailed out ahead of him through a hole in the fuselage made by cannon shell from the jet. From that time to my knowledge he has never been seen or heard from. It is my suspicion that, if his chute did open he may have been killed by the Germans for he was a Jew, had it on his dog tags, and didn't seem to care who knew it. That may or may not have happened. Nonetheless that was the last seen of him." [51]

9

Many soldiers believed one of the toughest duties was escorting a body back to family members. Having trained to fight an enemy they were not trained to handle the emotional side of death and losses. Here is one example of a soldier facing this duty.

"Most of the people had left, and the area doctor and I were in the kitchen chatting when she came, drew me to the casket and said, "Henry, please open it. I want to see if that's really my boy." We had been briefed to "expect anything," but this was unbelievable. Rather than comply, I assured her that it truly was her son because a soldier's remains were required to pass fourteen different tests in order to be certified for return to the family. Quietly, but firmly, she said, "My boy broke the little finger of his left hand playing football in high school. It didn't heal right, and that kept him from being accepted into West Point. I want to see his finger, then I'll know that it's him for sure."

"Earlier, others had shown me newspaper clippings stating that he had died in a fiery B-24 crash. Furthermore, my visit to the warehouse and a scorched dog tag nailed on the shipping case left me with no illusions as to what was in the box. Gently, I held her hands to hinder her attempts to open the casket. The doctor had been watching us, and I gestured that she needed a shot. He gave her a sedative and the coffin stayed closed. She and I remained on Christmas-card terms until her death nineteen years later."

"The four-month assignment taught me that it is easier to lose a friend in combat than to bury a stranger. During the war, a fellow may have slept next to you, but when he went down, there were no card, flowers, wakes or funerals. He disappeared to some nebulous place you did not care to think about, another guy replaced him, and you carried on. It was not until I helped all these bereaved families that I began to truly understand the enormity of war." [52]

Supporting three divisions each, a typical Graves Registration Company had 260 men and five officers. Facing more advanced weapons and covering a vast amount more of ground, these companies faced difficult condition and many totally unrecognizable remains. Each company was to collect, evacuate, identify, and supervise the burial of remains in cemeteries wherever they were in support of their divisions.

There is record of a "Quartermaster Graves Registration Company that scrambled ashore on D-Day with the First Army. There they gathered bodies from the beaches, in the water, and inland, actually cutting many from wrecked landing craft submerged in the shallow water. By the end of D-Plus-2, one platoon alone had buried 457 American dead; by working day and night, the three platoons had been able to clear the beaches of all remains." [53]

In 1949, Army and Air Force Regulations made a change to the Dog Tags. Imprinted on the metal, oblong tag was now the name of the wearer, the serial number, tetanus immunization, blood type, and religion. It held the same letters for the following religions, C for Catholic, H for Hebrew, and P for Protestant with one addition. **X** could be added for any other group that would not be included by one of the original three. Also allowed would be a totally separate tag that was the same size or smaller than the issued tag provided by his or her own religious group to identify them as a member of that group.

The oblong style tag was issued by all services in the 1950s. The same standard information as stated above for the Army in 1949 is now listed on all service's Dog Tags. However, each service lists their own acronym: Navy (USN), Marine Corps (USMC), Army (US, RA, WA, AF).

It is surprising that the importance of maintaining a unit large enough to take care of unforeseeable conflicts and accidents was repeatedly played down. The history of Graves Registration Units up until now was thought to be a wartime necessity, and was dissolved after Victory over Japan. The ill-advised dissolution of this service was readily profound as the Korean conflict conceded the need for emergency deployment of a Graves Registration Unit. There were only a limited number of combat experienced personnel, and supporting the Korean War in 1950 was extremely difficult.

The Korean War was the first time a mass evacuation of combat dead took place during hostilities. Towards the end of 1951, every effort was made to recover and reduce the number of personnel listed as missing in action, and continued throughout the war. The proficiency and competence of the Graves Registration Units helped to identify more than an estimated 97% of those who were recovered during the Korean War. [54]

The ID tags had other revisions in the year 1952 and the mid-1960s. In 1952, there was an addition to the religion of the wearer: C for Catholic, **J** (instead of H, Hebrew) for Jewish, P for Protestant, X for any other group, and **Y** for prefers not to designate. In the mid-1960s, the notch was removed from the end of the tag opposite the hole, and the tetanus shot date was removed. It was also during these years that the serial number was replaced by the social security number of the individual.

The Vietnam War was a time period where changes were made to the information on Dog Tags. They were often associated with body bags and the dying, but it was during this time period that the wounded had a much better chance of getting medical help. The Dog Tags went from the earlier 8 digits with their prefix, to the current day 9 digit Social Security number. You could have both stamped on your tag if you wanted, but from this point on, the Social Security number was the main identifying number.

The Marine Corps Tags had a variety of digits including 5, 6, or 7 digits, plus the size of their gas mask. They, too, added the full name of religions, with many more to choose from than before. It was very common for the Marine Corps to put one of their tags on their boots, laced up with their shoelaces.

Even with slight variations, one could see how service members might have kept their older Dog Tags. Issuing units used a wider range of religions as designated. It was during this time period that religion was spelled out completely, and "No Preference" was given as a choice.

After Vietnam, the Dog Tag became a highly recognizable icon. Being used as the symbol for POW/MIAs, this icon represented more than its original meaning. It continues to show itself in all aspects of our society, with little acknowledgement of its actual personal connection by the majority of our nation.

Through the years, all services have made hundreds of changes. You can see issued varieties that are different, and you can also find personal varieties with differences. Dog Tags range from rolled or smooth edges, different sizes, shapes, and materials used, embossed or debossed information, differences in information printed, and more. What must be remembered is the importance of the Dog Tag and the highly valued importance of those who are assigned to take care of those who have served their country and make sure they are remembered.

It was almost fifty years before regulations forced the proper identification of military service members. The realization and foresight of a few, led to the establishment of a simple item the American Armed Services call, the Dog Tag.

Chapter Two

In Life and Death

Historical Setting

Non-Fiction

The Vietnam War –

"On June 23, 1966, the crew aboard the AC-47 "Spooky" gunship flew a nighttime armed reconnaissance mission over southern Laos. At about 9:25 p.m., the aircraft radioed, "we have a hot fire," and another radio transmission was heard to order "bail out." Witnesses reported the aircraft was on fire then crashed into a heavily wooded area 30 miles northeast of Tchepone, in Khannouan Province, Laos. No parachutes from the crew were observed and no emergency beepers were heard. An aerial search of the site found no evidence of survivors."

"In October 1994, a villager directed a Laotian and American search team to an area where personal effects, aircraft wreckage, crew-related materials and a crew member's identification tag were found. In May-June 1995, a joint U.S.-Lao team excavated the site where they recovered human remains as well as identification media of other aircrew members. The U.S. recovery team members were from the Central Identification Laboratory, Hawaii (CILHI). CILHI scientists applied a wide array of forensic techniques to the recovered remains, including comparisons of dental charts and x-rays, as well as the use of mitochondrial DNA sequencing. The DNA sequencing was done by the Armed Forces DNA Identification Laboratory, whose results aided the CILHI scientists in identifying the remains."

"The six servicemen missing in action were identified and buried as a group at Arlington National Cemetery Friday with full military honors. They are Air Force Colonel <u>Theodore E. Kryszak</u> of Buffalo, New York; Air Force Colonel <u>Harding E. Smith</u> of Los Gatos, California; <u>Air Force Lieutenant Colonel Russell D. Martin</u> of Bloomfield, Iowa; Air Force Chief Master Sergeant Luther L. Rose of Howe, Texas, and Air Force Chief Master Sergeant Ervin Warren, of Philadelphia, Pennsylvania." [55]

1

The Quartermaster Service has historically done superbly with supplies, transportation, and pay as far back as June, 1775 when General George Washington accepted Command of the Continental Army. After the turn of the century, it was Quartermaster Officers who were assigned to outposts and designated to handle cemetery plots, burying the dead and recording burials. Through the 1840s, Commanding officers sought to care for their war dead, but often improper procedures and inexperience led to improperly collecting the dead. The resulting efforts during this time period had little success.

In the early years of the Civil War, much of the identification and collection of remains was done by burial "squads". These squads were groups of soldiers who were often POWs or unwilling soldiers who were forced to have burial duty. In July of 1864, the Quartermaster General's Office was assigned the task of "supervision of burials and preservation of internment reports." [56] This act began the proper procedures and concern for the current and future disposition of all American war deceased. It was during this War that "American soldiers made efforts to ensure that their identities would be known should they die on the battlefield. Their methods were varied, and all were taken on a soldier's own initiative. Still, despite the fact that fear of being listed among the unknowns was a real concern among the rank and file, no reference to an official issue of identification tags by the Federal Government exists." [57]

In 1898, the Secretary of War under President McKinley instituted the Quartermaster Burial Corps. Quartermaster General Marshall I. Ludington believed that the Burial Corps was successful in transporting and caring for what was then the challenge to exhume our buried dead from foreign soil and bring them home to family and friends. As discussed in Chapter 1 about the Spanish-American War, it was General Ludington who assigned D. H. Rhodes to be Chief of the Burial Corps. During this same time period the Commander of the Pacific Department, Major General F. S. Otis, assigned Chaplain Charles C. Pierce to organize the United States Army Morgue and Office of Identification at Manila.[58]   Along with his identity disk or identification tag, it was Chaplain Pierce whose suggestions laid the foundation for improved identification of deceased personnel for all future Graves Registration and Mortuary Services.

Through both men's dedication and concern of the complete burial process, their guidelines led to the improvements in identification and graves registration. In August 1917, The Secretary of War directed through War Department General Order No. 104, that the Quartermaster

General was to request a Graves Registration (GRREG) Service for the Quartermaster Corps during the period of the existing emergency (WWI). It was Chaplain Charles C. Pierce who was to run this unit. Having retired and brought back to serve on active duty, Chaplain Pierce was now a major and sent to Tours, France to train and prepare his people.

Pierce stands on the far right as you look at the picture

Through these trained and dedicated individuals, they applied a more scientific approach to identification and burial. It was during WWI that the thought of burying the soldiers where they fell became important to many family members, even if on foreign soil. When Teddy Roosevelt's son, Lt. Quentin Roosevelt was killed, he requested that, "Where the tree falls, let it lie." Thirty thousand American's from this war are buried in one of eight cemeteries in Europe, while forty-seven thousand were returned to the United States.[60] The Identification Tags which became mandatory for all services in 1917 became a major influence in the identification process during this time.

2

Graves Registration Companies were again assigned to units during WWII. They regularly collected, evacuated, identified, and supervised the remains of those killed during the War. Once again, they oversaw the selection of cemeteries and the collection of personal effect. ID Tags were part of those personal effects.

61

62

Hoping to identify and recover what remains they could from the Bataan Death March route, the Army's 601st Graves Registration Company faced a difficult mission. The road they walked on held the unidentified remains of Americans, English, Dutch, and Filipinos. It had been nearly four years and time had taken its toll. The Company found a Master Sergeant Abie Abraham still in the Philippines who was a participant of the Bataan Death March. He knew the route and was willing to work with the locals and this company to try and identify any remains possible.

Americans wearing Identification Tags, Bataan Death March

"In attempting to locate the graves of service dead, search teams entering a town or territory sought out all available records of burial." [64] Even with the help of Master Sergeant Abraham and local natives, they were able to identify only a few single graves and a few common graves. There were many difficulties besides the passage of time. It was quite common for Filipino natives to remove objects from the remains. Considered as souvenirs, personal items were taken from soldier's bodies on the ground and kept by the locals. This made identification impossible. The Graves Registration Company told the people they could keep the souvenirs, if only they could show these souvenirs to them to help with identification of the remains. It takes ingenuity, determination and sleuthing skills to work through such situations as presented to this company, and most Graves Registration Units.

Regulations requiring identification tags to be worn were sometimes evaded; tags were lost, or in some instances, destroyed by the manner of death. To this cause may be traced most of the unidentified burials. Where no tags were found, bodies were searched for other means of identification, such as letters, photographs, lockets, et cetera.

Bataan Media

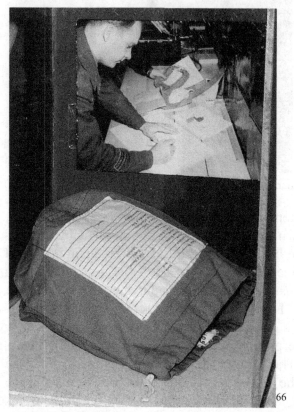

Media Bag

3

Identification today is a huge part of our forensics world, but before the science was so refined, search and identification was an intensive procedure to ensure the correct identity of all remains. Some of the cleverest minds have been a part of Graves Registration. For instance, one might look for a ring on the finger and track down the jeweler. Perhaps look at the clothing and find a laundry mark. "The search team then had the clothing of the dead soldier carefully cleaned in gasoline. Then, portion by portion, it was dipped in water. Ultimately a laundry mark was revealed, and from the mark identity of the soldier was established." [67]

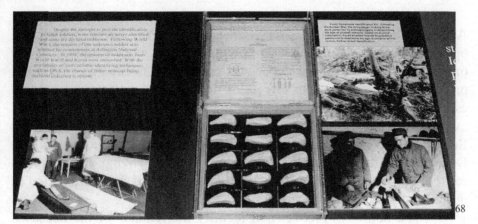

Identification Process

Other such sources considered might be "watchmakers who have contributed a great deal of help in establishing identity by tracing the serial numbers of watches found on deceased soldiers." Or maybe "the handwriting on scraps of letters. No matter how many hours of tireless searching are required, a case is never closed until positive identification has been made."[69]

Having downsized greatly after WWII because foresight did not see the importance of sustaining the units, Graves Registration was thrown into an emergency build up for the Korean War. Even with the difficulties they faced with shortages of manpower and supplies, they remained committed to caring for and supervising the situation for our American deceased.

As part of "Operation GLORY," deceased enemy personnel were exchanged with North Korea on "Glory Railhead." For our own soldiers, Graves Registration organized refrigerated railroad cars, temporary cemeteries were built, and remains were shipped back to the United States. "Unless remains of men listed as "missing in action" are recovered, the change in their status to "killed in action" may be long delayed. Next of kin, anxious about the fate of their missing loved ones, find it extremely difficult to accept such a finding unless the remains are recovered and positively identified."[70] Graves Registration worked endlessly to find, identify, and recover remain of those listed as Missing in Action (MIA).

From 1961 through 1965, the US Air Force provided mortuary services on Temporary Duty (TDY) by a mortician assigned to the Air Force with a two-room mortuary at Tan Son Nhut Air Base, Saigon. Once again, mortuary services were caught short because of the increasing need and Army Graves Registration were assigned to the unit to increase the staff.[71]

Believing most of the losses in Vietnam were Army losses, the Army assumed mortuary services and the Air Force transferred operational control of the Base. Having a better understanding of the process, a personal effects depot was established to receive, inventory, process, package, and ship effects of deceased. More mortuaries were established to handle the numbers of deceased, and the depot was eventually moved. Simultaneously, the Army identified the remains and flew them to "entry mortuaries in Oakland, California, or Dover, Delaware. Following reprocessing, to include cosmetizing, dressing, and casketing, the remains were forwarded to the place of final disposition as designated by the appropriate family representative."[72]

The ability to recover and identify the remains of the deceased helped tremendously when accounting for the dead. Once combat units were trained in procedures for our wounded and dead, the units helped immensely in shortening the time that both could be accounted for. In Vietnam, the use of communications and helicopters helped in removing remains more quickly and bringing those remains to MASH units or mortuaries. Identification methods were also improved from the usual methods of visual, ID Tags, dental records, and fingerprints with more laboratory procedures. [73]

By the end of the Vietnam War, of all Americans recovered, only twenty-eight were unidentified. Then by May, of 1984, all but one was identified and those remains were interred at the Tomb of the Unknown at Arlington National Cemetery.[74]

"The remains of the Vietnam Unknown were exhumed May 14, 1998. Based on mitochondrial DNA testing, DoD scientists identified the remains as those of Air Force 1st Lt. Michael Joseph Blassie, who was shot down near An Loc, Vietnam, in 1972. It has been decided that the crypt that contained the remains of the Vietnam Unknown will remain vacant."[75]

[76]

4

Military Field Manual 1954-1962, FM 10-63 Handling of Deceased Personnel in Theaters of Operations. This field manual provides technical assistance to personnel of the Army, Navy, Marine Corps, and Air Force engaged in graves registration activities during major military operations. It is designed for use by all commanders (including combat commanders) and by personnel and units concerned with, or responsible for, search, recovery, and evacuation of deceased personnel, location and layout of temporary cemeteries, identification and burial of the dead, and preparation of reports and records in connection with these activities.

Supporting troops in Somalia, Mortuary Affairs personnel's "main objective was to completely recover, positively identify and transport (in a dignified and respectful manner to the final destination determined by the next of kin) the remains of deceased U.S. military personnel. Also, our mission included separating non-U.S. dead, processing and returning the remains according to existing international agreements or Central Joint Mortuary Affairs Office (CJMAO) guidance. Statements of recognition and incident reports with identification tags and photographic identification cards were sent by the unit with the remains to the Theater Mortuary Evacuation Point (TMEP). The mortuary affairs personnel at the TMEP received, processed, completed identification records and ensured a completed death certificate before shipping remains out of theater. In most other countries, we rely on host nation support to process their dead. However, Somalia had no agencies, no established police force, limited hospital support and no host nation relief agency to process remains."[77] This meant Mortuary services needed to work with the senior Judge Advocate General (JAG) officer, the International Committee of the Red Cross (ICRC), the Somali Red Crescent, officials from Digfer Hospital, a local Somali hospital, and other local agencies.

During the Peace Implementation Force (IFOR) in Bosnia-Herzegovina, theater plans for Mortuary Affairs Support became a bigger responsibility than was planned for. As part of the North Atlantic Treaty Organization (NATO), nations were not as experienced as our own service. Thus, a Joint Mortuary Board was organized to help the supporting nations.

"Mortuary affairs facilities in the tactical and operational areas would receive and process all US deceased personnel. On a case-by-case basis, mortuary affairs personnel would provide reinforcing support to other NSEs or TCNs. Processing included completion of many tasks according to procedures outlined in Joint Tactics, Techniques, and Procedures for Mortuary Affairs in Joint Operations (JTTP-4-06)." These tasks included:

"Completes two evacuation tags for each remains received. Records on the DD 1077. Moves the remains to the X-ray station where remains are X-rayed for unexploded ordnance. (Note: TMEP task only.) Initiates an original and duplicate individual case folder file. Creates an alphabetical index card with basic information on the deceased. Fingerprints all remains using DD Form 894 (Record of Identification Processing). Takes footprints of all pilots recovered from air crashes using AF Form 137 (Footprint Record). Gathers and inspects all official military and personal identification media and records on DD Form 890 (Record of Identification Processing Effects and Physical Data). Completes DD Form 1076 (Military Operations-Records of Personal Effects of Deceased Personnel). Takes two sets of pictures of each remains using a self-developing film camera."

5

Realizing their expanded duties or accomplishments in many areas of peacekeeping, war, and accidents, Graves Registration is now called Mortuary Affairs. While they still have Graves Registration, it is now "temporary burial of the war dead" subsequent to their return to the Continental United States. A new concept, Operations Other Than War (OOTW), is part of the new terminology for Quartermasters. All are assigned anywhere there are American soldiers, and they have multiple duties to undertake and be concerned with. They have proven themselves to identify, take care of, and recover remains in all situations.

They have lost fellow members themselves, as acknowledged in Operation Desert Storm. The 14th Quartermaster Detachment suffered the greatest number of casualties during this War. In their memory in Greensburg, Pennsylvania, "the 69 names of the Detachment soldiers who deployed to Saudi Arabia are featured on two bronze plaques on the front of the right and left stones. On the rear of the left stone is an etching of a female soldier's hands holding the American flag. On the rear of the right stone, an etched map of the Persian Gulf, indicating the locations of Dhahran, Saudi Arabia and Kuwait. To the left front of the monument is an actual size bronze casting of the boots, M-16 rifle and helmet, symbolic of the fallen soldier. To the right front are two life-size cast bronze figures; a kneeling male and a standing female in desert battle dress uniforms, reflecting on the loss of their comrades. On the cement wall surrounding the monument is a bronze plaque listing the names of the 28 soldiers killed in action. Behind the wall are three flagpoles bearing the flags of the United States, Pennsylvania and the United States Army. Behind the monument are 13 hemlock trees, the Pennsylvania state tree, planted as a living tribute to the 13 soldiers of the 14th Quartermaster Detachment who lost their lives in the war. The monument faces 90° due east, toward Saudi Arabia."[78]

[79]

During Operation Desert Storm, 47 American military personnel were listed as Missing or Duty Status, Whereabouts Unknown. Twenty-one were captured and released after the cease-fire. The remaining 26 individuals were determined to have been killed in action. However in 2001, the status of one service member was changed to Missing In Action, and in 2002 changed again to Missing-Captured. An active effort is ongoing in Iraq to account for this individual.[80]

The Armed Forces DNA Identification Laboratory is an important part of identifying remains, today. It is known as the Joint POW/MIA Accounting Command (JPAC). Its "mission is to achieve the fullest possible accounting of all Americans missing as a result of the nation's past conflicts. The highest priority of the organization is the return of any living Americans that remain prisoners of war. To date, the U.S. government has not found any evidence that there are still American POWs in captivity from past U.S. conflicts. JPAC is manned by approximately 400 handpicked Soldiers, Sailors, Airmen, Marines and Department of the Navy civilians. The laboratory portion of JPAC, referred to as the Central Identification Laboratory (CIL), is the largest forensic anthropology laboratory in the world."[81]

The Armed Forces make every possible effort to eradicate discrepancies and remove doubts about casualties, not least those doubts that families may hold concerning the demise of their loved ones. In recent years, a near perfect record of identifying service members who have died in the line of duty has been achieved, a far cry from the 58% rate of identification that stood during the Civil War. The ID tag has been and remains a major part of the reason for this record.

"The sole purpose of the identification tag when it was invented was to affirm identification in the event of death. During WWI and WWII, the ID tag was a far more important piece of identification media than it is today." [82]

If ID Tags are found hanging on the neck of a deceased soldier, then those and only those tags around the neck, are to stay with the remains at all times.[83] If ID Tags are found anywhere else but around the neck, a note is made of this and the tags are placed in the Record of Personal Effects of Deceased Personnel, and placed in an effects bottle.[84] This bottle was eventually replaced by the current effects bag. "When it was required to bury the deceased in the field, one tag was left around the neck of the remains, the other was affixed to the grave marker," said Tom Bourlier, "or placed on a wire ring in the sequence of the temporary cemetery plot. This enables Graves Registration personnel to make positive identification of remains during disinterment procedures; when the remains are disinterred, the tag on the wire ring is removed and placed with the matching tag around the neck." If there is only one tag present, another is made to match the first. If the remains are unidentified, two tags marked "unidentified" are made.[85]

"Technically, the ID Tag is government property and not considered personal property. They are not removed from the remains during processing, or transportation. Even today though, it is not recovered by the government, but often treated as sentimental effects and given to the family," Tom Bourlier said. Understanding the sentimentality of these small metal tags, the government allows the family members to keep them as part of the personal effects. Another set of tags is made by the morgue for the body to be buried with for proper identification.

86

6

Until recently, all US military services have relied on the Army to bring back the fallen servicemen and women. Believing that they should take care of their own, the Marine Corps has instituted their own Mortuary Services, having been trained under the Mortuary Affairs Army School. They now serve in combat and, and take care of their fallen. Not just for themselves, but for their buddies, friends, and family.

Department of the Navy Provides for the Navy and the Marine Corps:[87]
- Search, recovery and identification of remains.
- Preparation, casketing & inspection of remains.
- Transportation of remains.
- Military escort for the remains.
- Payment/reimbursement of funeral claims.

An example of this was explained to me in an e-mail sent to me in January, 2008. John said:

> Ginger,
> …doing recovery in combat for Marines. Dogtag recovery can be graphic, they are usually mixed in with remains portions and remnants of uniforms. They do survive extreme heat, we chipped one out of a pool of cooled aluminum armor under a APC. They are not a dependable means of ID, I have seen them blown off and

embedded in other remains giving you two identities for a given remains. Also, the habit of placing packs on the outside of armor vehicles confuses things, gives you way more infomation/tags than the occupants of a vehicle. Tags are useful to corroborate other identification media, also to put the medical examiner on to a smaller pool of DNA samples to consider. Included with the dogtags are the medical alert tags, similar info and worn with the dogtag.

John

Knowing that a Dog Tag may be the only thing identifiable, they understand the importance of painstakingly going through burned out vehicles or debris. "Dog tags always seem to make it. I don't know what they're made of but they seem to survive through anything," said Staff Sgt. Ralph Patterson, Acting Company Gunnery Sergeant, MA Company. "One of our Marines was looking through the wreckage of the Amtrak and found a melted glob of metal that was a rifle. There was a chain hanging out of that metal glob and when we cut it open there was a dog tag inside."

"Patterson said he spent two days in a pile of debris that used to be the driver's area of an amphibious assault vehicle that was hit by a missile. He almost quit, but something inside told him to keep looking

A few hours later, he found the dog tag of the last Marine left to be identified from the vehicle. He unexpectedly saw that name again later. "There was a story in the Marine Corps Times about a woman who was left at home caring for her children while her husband was fighting in Iraq," said Patterson. "It went into a lot of depth about the family. At the end of the story it said, 'In memory of (the Marine's name)'. That is one of the many parts of the job that make it worthwhile."[88]

"The Marines of the mortuary affairs company follow strict rules and military traditions when handling the bodies of fallen service members." We go by the old traditions of handling bodies of a fallen brother," said Smith. "You don't stand over the remains. You don't walk over the remains. That's for friend or enemy. "We give the dead Iraqi soldier the same respect we would give our own Marine. They are warriors, just like us."[89]

7

The Fallen Soldier Display that is so well known to military forces and family members is a loving tribute and a visual reminder of the fallen soldier. Being displayed at the front of a unit or group of people, it stands there proud and tall, representative of that soldier. The boots, the inverted rifle, the Dog Tags, and the helmet or beret gives final tribute to their sacrifice.

Having a historical significance from World War II, the items were displayed as a visual marker for units coming behind other ones to know where the fallen had been temporarily interred. The rifle's firing pin was removed, and the rifle was turned upside down and stuck in the ground with the helmet placed on top of the rifle. This allowed the units following them to easily find and take care of the fallen soldiers.

Because the memorial services are normally for the unit of the fallen, this same display has come to represent the fallen. The actual Memorial Significance is explained in Army FM 7-21.13, Appendix C-6:

> "The helmet and identification tags signify the fallen
> soldier. The inverted rifle with bayonet signals a time for
> prayer, a break in the action to pay tribute to our comrade.
> The combat boots represent the final march of the last
> battle. The beret (in the case of soldiers from airborne
> units) reminds us that the soldier has taken part in his
> final jump."

The items connected to a fallen comrade are of special significance to those they fight beside. Often, even with the most sincere of actions, "there seems to be something about identification tags that make Soldiers close to the deceased, want to take them off their deceased comrade, in the field. Whether it is for accountability purposes, or whether they have watched too many John Wayne movies, I do not know. But once the ID tags have been removed from the remains, they are absolutely worthless for identification purposes. During the Vietnam era, often service members would lace one ID tag into the lace of the boot. This was to help ensure that it did not get lost," said Tom Bourlier.

The Department of the Army and Department of Defense have come a long way in successful identification of soldier remains. Identification remains the key step in the mortuary affairs process. Identification is achieved by pre- and post-death medical and dental records, examining personal effects and, more recently, DNA analysis.[91] When Dog Tags are found around the neck of the person, they are recorded as personal media, and still used for identification purposes. Other forms of ID media considered today are things like "ID tags, ID bracelet, wallet, watch with inscription, rings, credit cards, and driver's license," said Tom Bourlier. "Wearing your ID tags is one of the easiest actions you can make towards achieving total readiness, so take those tags out of your dresser and put them around your neck. Remember -the simple information contained on that small aluminum tag can speak for you if you can't speak for yourself; it could mean the difference between a positive identification and an uncertain future for those who survive you, should your identity be "...known only to God."[92]

8

Area 60 of Arlington National Cemetery is that part of the cemetery where casualties from Iraq and Afghanistan are laid to rest. During a recent ceremony, a mother clutched her son's dog tags, the chain hanging over her clinched fist, as rifles were fired and Taps was played. Those pieces of metal gave her comfort. The tags hung beneath her son's shirt, against his skin and over his heart while he was alive. When she holds them, she feels close to him.

The Dog Tag is forever connected to the life and Death of our military service men and women. Its image conjures up the most personal of memories, whether good or bad. The following images are the most representative of how these memories are associated:

"George Blake was awarded the Silver Star Medal for gallantry in action against the enemy on 9 December 1944. His Silver Star Medal citation describes his courageous actions, stating "George C. Blake...Private First Class, Infantry, Company "D", 761st Tank Battalion, for gallantry in action against the enemy on 9 December 1944, in the vicinity of Norville Les Vic, France. Private First Class Blake, seeing many of his comrades wounded by artillery and small arms fire, dismounted from his 1/4 ton truck, and under intense artillery and mortar fire, carried the wounded to his truck and evacuated them to a medical aid station. Private First Class Blake returned and remained in the field during the night to administer first aid and evacuate the wounded. Private First Class Blake's courageous action and devotion to duty exemplifies the highest tradition of the Armed Forces. Entered military service from Worthington, Ohio." He served in the 761st Tank Battalion, which was the first African American tank unit of the United States Army. The first image shown here displays the Silver Star Medal, Good Conduct Medal, World War II Victory Medal Ribbon, other medals and ribbons awarded to Blake, and his military id "dog tags".

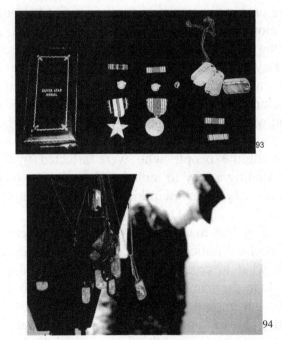

Dog tags left by visitors hang from a memorial plaque atop Mt. Suribachi here Jan. 17 as Lance Cpl. Joseph Ballard, 23, an infantryman with 2nd Fleet Anti-terrorism Security (FAST) Co., 7th Platoon stands solemnly.

95

Boots, rifles, dog tags and helmets stand as a solemn reminder of the sacrifice of 3d Infantry Division soldiers.

For those who have a connection and want to share it, the image of the Dog Tag or its representation can be seen at Memorials, Exhibits, Statues, and more. In Chicago, Illinois, there is an exhibit where thousands of Dog Tags hang as a statement in themselves. It is called the "Above and Beyond Memorial," which hangs in the atrium of the National Vietnam Veterans Art Museum. "Richard Steinbock and Ned Broderick developed the idea to create a piece that would commemorate all the men and women who died in the Vietnam War. Their goal was to make people comprehend how many lives were lost, all the "wasted potential," and all the people who were affected by the loss. They struggled with finding a way to include all the names of the soldiers in the artwork. The only other memorial with all the names listed is the Vietnam Wall in Washington D.C."

"Although they had many ideas, not one idea seemed appropriate. Then one day Richard noticed Ned's dog tags on his desk and that was when he knew what to create. They would make a dog tag for every soldier and include the name, date when killed, and branch of service. Ned created the design and the tags would be arranged as if they were soldiers standing in formation, shoulder to shoulder. The sculpture would start with the dog tags of the first person killed and end with the dog tags of the last person killed. There would also be space reserved for veterans who would die later from diseases or injuries resulting from the war."[96]

97

(Dog Tags are represented in memorials quite often, and a more in-depth look at their representations is written about them in Chapter 4 about Icons.)

This is a brief history of a long and valiant branch of the Army Quartermaster Corps. They have quite a varied amount of assignments and tasks which are much too numerous to list. They began a service that has surpassed its original intent, and will forever be a necessary service to our military servicemen and women. The publications cited are only a short representation of their listings and references. My focus has been on their role in identification of remains and the connection those remains have with Dog Tag history.

Chapter Three

Personal Stories

This chapter honors those who have shared their stories. There are veterans, family members, active duty service members, historians, anthropologists, authors, journalists, and more that give an emotional depth to this simple identification item. They have shared these memories in recorded interviews, in handwritten testimonials, and in e-mails. They are young and old, coming from all walks of life; service does not matter, and yet share a very basic connection – the Personal Side of Dog Tags.

While there were various ways the stories could have been organized in the chapter, they have mostly been collated in time periods of conflict. This might seem an obvious assertion, but the difficulty came when generations of family members shared their thoughts, or stories arose out of a time period when a conflict was not the driving force for the story. Those stories are grouped in the Miscellaneous Section of this Chapter.

Because of the varying ways people shared their stories, I have tried to use their own words as often as possible. If they wrote something down, I have taken it and shared their words as they wrote them. If they told me their stories, I have taken much of what they told me verbatim. The stories written that are from various sources are compiled to the best of my understanding of the subject matter. My main goal was to have those that have served our country to be remembered. Enjoy their memories…

My husband's Dog Tags

World War I

Elsie Robbins - Taken from the Questionnaire filled out by Tim Robbins:

Whose Dog Tags do you have?
Name: Elsie Robbins
Relationship: Great Aunt (she raised my father)
Under what circumstances did you receive the Dog Tags? She gave them to me.
Where do you keep them? In a frame with her burial flag, WWI Victory Medal and Nurses' Pin
Do you know how the family member felt about the Dog Tags?
This is the only military issue item she saved from her military career which spanned from 1917-1933.
What are your feelings and thoughts concerning the Dog Tags? They are my most prized family heirloom and a proud reminder of the military career of the woman I called "Grandma". P.S. I also have her diaries from her two years in France which are very interesting.

Anything else you would like to share:
She had an interesting military career for a small town Indiana girl who never went beyond the eighth grade. She went to nursing school in Indianapolis and graduated in 1915. In 1917, she enlisted for overseas service in Army Nurse Corps in France. She served in France and Luxemburg until the end of the war. From 1919 to 1928, she served in the Army at Walter Reed in Washington, Schofield Barracks in Hawaii, Letterman Hospital at the Presidio, San Antonio and at Fort Leavenworth. From 1928 to 1931, she served as a nurse in the Philippines at Sternberg Hospital in Manila and on Corregidor. While on Corregidor, she started to go deaf. As she lost her hearing, she taught herself to read lips. It wasn't until she was transferred to night duty that the Army discovered that she couldn't hear. On night duty, she had to shine a light in soldiers' faces to read their lips. After complaints from the soldiers about the night nurse shining the flashlight in their faces, she was questioned by her commander. She confessed that she had been deaf for quite a while but did not want to leave the Army. She was discharged from the Philippines by Douglas MacArthur who was General Governor at the time. She was officially retired from the Army in 1933 as a lieutenant.

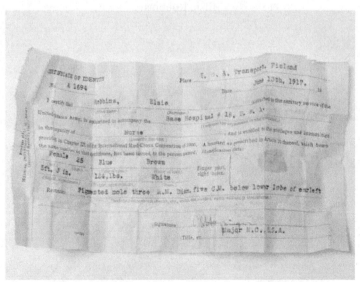

Elsie Robbin's Certificate of Identity and ID Locket

Elsie Robbins

Victory Medal, Nurses pin, and ID locket with Identity Papers

From Charles F. Edler:

Here is a picture of my Dad's unit – Co G 353rd Infantry. They sailed for France, June 4, 1918, returned to US May 22d 1919. The photo #335 Levin, PO building Patchogue, NY, all of that is on the picture. Also here is picture of my Dad's Dog tags, also here a picture given to him when he was wounded in action it has Woodrow Wilson on the bottom.

I hope this will help you.

Ethel Gray

Ethel Gray, a World War I nurse (or Reconstruction Aide,) who helped U.S. Soldiers recuperate in military hospitals. The cape in the image was worn by Ethel and was handmade. Many of the uniforms women wore during this time period were handmade because no uniforms were issued.

Her uniform and personal items, including her Dog Tags are in this image and have been donated to the US Army Women's Museum at Fort Lee, Va.

Ethel Gray's "dog tags" worn in France during World War I

World War II

David J. Hyslop, Jr., Stock Photo Image identified

From his son, David Hyslop, III, in an e-mail:
Hi Ginger:

It was great hearing from you. Talk about being stunned!! I was watching one of my favorite TV programs on PBS, the History Detectives. Anyway, as part of a story they were doing, they focused on how, during and after the Civil War, how difficult it was identifying the war dead left on the battle-field. They went on to describe the WWI effort to have the round aluminum ID tag for the soldiers, finally adding serial numbers in 1918. This commentary followed-up with photos of them and then describing the progression to the WWII "dog tag," with THE photo of my Dad; the very same one you have on your website. It was a very emotional experience for me. I emailed the producers to ask where they obtained the photo; they have, yet to respond.

Anyway, my curiosity got the best of me the next day. I "googled" history of the dog tag, and was directed to your website, among others. There was Dad's photo prominently displayed on your site, with the citation, from the QM Museum at Ft. Lee. I've already contacted the director, and we've exchanged emails; he sent me a high resolution photo of same. I provided him some detail of the circumstances and where it was taken.

Added information regarding the photo: Dad was ordered by higher authority to have the photo taken. He was a PFC at the time, (mistakenly, I told you he was either a 2nd or 1st Lt.) and was finishing commissioned officer training school, at Ft. Hayes, in Columbus, OH. The date of the photo is 22 March 1942. The authority for the photo at the time was the 5th QM Corps, also there at Ft. Hayes. The remainder of my earlier information is correct.

From an earlier e-mail: (The G.I. in the photo is my father, David J. Hyslop, Jr., of Geneva, Ohio. At the time, early 1942, he was assigned to the Quartermaster Corps, as a either a 1st or 2nd Lt. I cannot, for the life of me, recall whether Dad volunteered for that photo, or whether he was randomly "volunteered" by higher authority. In any event, he saved a copy of the newspaper where this photo appeared in 1942. It is contained in his WWII scrapbook which the family still has. Dad served in the CBI (China, Burma, India) theater of operations, and was in the first convoy of supplies that travelled over the storied Burma Road into China. He survived the war and was Captain when he was discharged. He died in 1989. Thanks for letting me tell his story about the dog tag.)

Back to e-mail begun at top: As you can probably determine in the photo, Dad was not happy about being photographed at the time. He had only been recently married to my mother. He felt, if the photo was released openly, he was not given time to properly dress/groom for the photo op. The authorities assured him at the time, the photo would only show him from the shoulders down, no facial photo. When the photo showed up in the media he was quite upset, to hear him tell the story, many years afterwards.

So now, to have that photo on a nationwide televised program, and being on the worldwide web, he must be "rolling over," in his grave. If only we could kid him now!

Best regards,

David J. Hyslop III

Green Valley, AZ

Arlington National Cemetery Website

29 September 2001: Mack Sparks, 2d Lt. Unites States Army Air Corps, co-pilot on a B-24D named "Cold Iron," took off from his base in New Guinea with nine other men in March 1944. They never returned.

Knowing that his remains were found more than a decade ago, it took almost 60 years for a conclusive test to identify 2d Lt. Mack Sparks. His B-24D bomber, called "Cold Iron" flew into the side of a mountain. The family had always wondered what happened to the crew and their loved one. The tail section, miscellaneous artifacts and Lt. Sparks Dog Tags were found at the crash site. Once DNA was done years later, they were able to finally identify him. The family felt that by seeing his Dog Tags, there was some comfort in knowing there was closure.

Joseph R. Beyrle
Sergeant, US Army
As told to me by his son, Joe Beyrle...

Sgt. Beyrle in Ramsbury, 1943
Released into the public domain by beyrlejr

If you didn't know any better you'd feel safe placing a bet on the fact that this story was made for the big screen, and not a true one. His story begins like so many other young men's. This youngster graduated from Saint Joseph High School in Muskegon, Michigan. Honored by his classmates as Best Dressed, Best Informed, Most Obvious Temper, and the Class Shark, he volunteered to serve his country and became known as "Jumpin' Joe" to his Paratrooper buddies.

But the twists and turns of what happened to him while he served not only the United States, but Russia as well, are more than most can imagine. It is understandable that a book was written about his life. With this in mind, you'll need to recognize that a few paragraphs about him do not do him justice. This is a short version of his military service and life,

Packing gold for the French Resistance in a bandolier strapped next to him, Joseph R. Beyrle parachuted as a member of the 101st Screaming Eagles into Normandy. Then on June 6, 1944 at 0015, he along with others of the 101st were the first allies to touch down on Nazi occupied French soil. The Normandy invasion began.

Deep into enemy lines, Joseph Beyrle landed on the roof of a church in St. Come-du Mont. He jumped from the rooftop into a cemetery, then onto their mission through gulleys and over bushes.

Hiding as they went, and fighting the Luftwaffe. The Germans were waiting and willing to fight at all costs. And costs there were.

Joe Beyrle and other paratroopers were captured by the Nazis. While being led to another area, he was hit by machines gunfire of Allied planes and even with schrapnel he escaped, only to be captured again a short time later. A soldier within this German unit took his Dog Tags from him, who in turn put them around his own neck.

Beyrle was transferred from prison camp to prison camp, and transported by train to various places. Like other prisoners, he withstood torture, interrogation, and starvation. In January 1945, he escaped and joined a Russian unit. This unit was not well led, and he observed them killing an elderly couple, feeding them to their pigs, and then eating those pigs days later. Trying to get back to an American unit, he stayed with the Russians, fighting alongside them as a machine gunner for at least a month.

This Russian unit helped destroy the prisoner of war camp he was in, and during this siege, he was terribly wounded by German bombers. He was taken to a hospital, and eventually made his way to the US Embassy in Moscow hoping to return home. However, not knowing what had occurred while he was a prisoner of war, no one in the embassy believed he was who he said he was. While missing, the German soldier who had placed Beyrle's Dog Tags around his own neck was killed while wearing an American uniform. Thus, a telegram was sent to Beyrle's family in the states telling them he was dead.

It was not until they could prove who he was through his fingerprints, that he was finally identified as Joseph R. Beyrle. On September 14, 1946, he was able to return to Muskegon. He married Joanne in the same church they had his memorial service years before. They spent 58 years together and had three children, and numerous grandchildren.

Having been awarded medals from both countries for his service, Sergeant Joseph R. Beyrle is believed to be the only World War II veteran to serve the United States and the Soviet Union during the same time period.

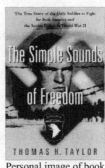

Personal image of book

Side Note: When the Beyrle children lost their mother, the son, Joe Beyrle, invited me to their Mother's funeral at Arlington Cemetery where she was buried alongside her husband, Joe Beyrle. I remain touched by their consideration during a difficult time.

From: **Dan Robinson** <xxxxxxx@charter.net>
To: stories@dogtaghistory.com
Date: Wednesday, February 03, 2010 02:32 pm
Subject: Re: Dog Tags
Ginger,
My dad was stationed at Torretta Airfield, Cerignola, Italy in Nov/Dec 1944. His last mission was #151 to Ordertal to bomb the oil fields there. He was attacked by Luftwaffe, shot down, landed in small town of Kokory, Olemuc region of Czech. Picked up by farmers, taken by German soldiers to another town and eventually to Stalag Luft 1. That is the last he knew of war. I found pics of his plane crash, mission reports, missing aircraft reports, pics of his plane parts, and pics of his dog-tags, held all of this time and now in a museum in Cz. He was floored. I have narrowed down the Luftwaffe pilots to one of 14, so it is getting interesting.
Dan Robinson

Donald Mitchell Briscoe
Where were you first issued your Dog Tags?
Camp Pendleton California, June 1944

Did you wear them when you were off duty? Yes

Where on your body did you wear your Dog Tags?
Around my neck.

Reason for wearing them where you did. It was ordered.

How did you feel about your Dog Tags during your service?
It's who I was. I was ordered to wear it.

How did you feel about your Dog Tags after you got out of the service?
Forgot about them.

Where do you keep your Dog Tags? My children framed them with my medals.

Anything else you would like to share:
I am a survivor of Iwo Jima. First wave Fifth Division.
Donald M. Briscoe
November 1020

Name of Dog Tag Owner: Donald Mitchell Briscoe
Name of Family: Carol Briscoe – wife

Under what circumstances did you receive the Dog Tags? From his mother who kept all his letters and personal items from his Marine Corp service during WWII.

Where do you keep them? In a framed box hanging on the wall with his Purple Heart and other military theater service chevrons.

What stories do you remember about your family member wearing them?
I have a complete story of his military service from his first letter to his mother on train going from Chicago at age 18 to Camp Pendleton California June 1944. He wrote graphic letters to his parents and his mother kept them all. But he did not talk about his experiences for many, many years. At my urging, he closed himself up in a room with

his sons and related all he could remember—at great emotional cost. He was wounded on Iwo Jima March 1945. Was sent to Hawaii for 4 months recovery, and then redeployed to Japan and the Palao Islands until May 1946. It is a wonderful family history for his 3 sons and 1 daughter and 13 grandchildren and 4 great grandchildren. It has been a hard life for him because he came out of Iwo Jima and the islands with bad PTSD, which was not recognized then, and it plagued him all his life (multiple marriages, behavior problems, relationship problems) but we have been married for 53 years. His age in 2010 is 84. He was officially diagnosed and is being treated in 2009.

Do you know how the family member felt about the Dog Tags? Yes. Like all military subjects, he does not wish to discuss them.

What are your feelings and thoughts concerning the Dog Tags? I remember them as a child on my father who never left the states. It was just a part of his attire.
Carol I Briscoe
November 2010

Larry Rosen
Hi Ms Cucolo,

In response to your request in the Rainbow Reveille for dog tab stories, following are some stories I have heard from Jewish American prisoners of War captured by the Germans, and their connection to this identification.

I joined the 42d Rainbow Division in 1943, and was a member of the 542d Field Artillery Battalion. If you research the Rainbow history, you will find that our infantry units were sent to Europe before the arrival of the artillery, engineers, quartermaster, and other non-infantry units.

In the battle of Nordwind the infantry units went into combat in the Alsace section of France without artillery support and other units during which time there were many fatalities and many prisoners captured by the Germans.

As a Jewish American, I have always questioned former Rainbow prisoners of War, at our many reunions, if to their knowledge, were Jewish American POW's treated differently than non-Jewish Americans by their captors.

I have heard different stories-like those Jewish American prisoners who had knowledge that the German government was hostile against Jews, threw away their dogs tags that were imprinted "H" for Hebrew, and in some cases those Jewish Americans who had no knowledge of their potential danger and retained their "H" dog tags, were separated and marched away, and not seen again. One former Rainbower related that he was questioned for a long period of time, even though his dog tags were not marked "H". When I mentioned that he did not look Jewish, he replied that he wasn't, but because his first name was David, he was suspected of possibly having Jewish relatives, or not telling the truth.

I recommend a book entitled "Soldiers And Slaves" by Roger Cohen that relates the following story, and probably involved dog tags. as a method of identifying certain soldiers. : In February 1945,350 American POW's captured earlier at the Battle of the Bulge or elsewhere in Europe were singled out by the Nazis because they were Jews or were thought to resemble Jews. They were transported to Berga, a concentration camp in eastern Germany and put to work as slave laborers mining tunnels for a planned underground fuel factory. Twenty percent of these soldiers - more than seventy of them perished.

Also the Berga story is available on a DVD entitled "Berga Soldiers of Another War", documentary by Charles Guggenheim and is available from public television--www.pbs.org.Another book on the Berga story is "Given Up For Dead" by Flint Whitlock, a former U.S. army officer, military historian who served on active duty from 1965 to 1970.

Without a doubt, dog tags with the imprint of "H" served as a easy means of identifying Jewish Americans by those German camp commanders who sought to inflict severe harm to Jews even though they were American soldiers.
Sincerely,
 Larry Rosen
Rockville, Maryland

Norman Brust's story of his Brother-in-Law, Jerome Bach
Dear Mrs. Cucolo,
I served in Korea in 1952 with the 40th Infantry Division. I still possess my dog tags, but this story is about my brother-in-law, Jerome Bach. Jerry's parents were Jewish immigrants from Eastern Europe. His father was an army veteran of World War I. His parents spoke Yiddish in their home, which is 85 or 90 percent German. Jerry was with the army in Europe during World War II. He single handedly captured eight German soldiers, convincing them in his poor "German-Yiddish" that they were surrounded and why die when the war is almost over. He was awarded the Bronze Star for this service. However, in the Battle of the Bulge,

Jerry was captured by the Germans. He feared that he would be killed if they knew he was Jewish. Therefore, he threw away his dog tags with the letter H stamped on them. When questioned by the Germans he claimed his family was German. His blond hair and his name "BACH" was convincing. When they spoke to him in German, he informed his questioner that he did not speak the language. He knew they would easily pick up the Yiddish accent. When the Americans retook the battlefield, his dog tags were found. His parents were informed that he was missing and presumed dead. Jerry escaped from the Germans three times, recaptured twice. The third time he and two fellow American escapees hid in a forest for three weeks until they spotted American units passing by the forest. The three weeks of exposure however caused Jerry to collapse and faint from pneumonia. He was put in a plane and flown to England, where he awoke to hear English nurses speaking English. They informed him where he was and he asked for a telephone. He telephoned his mother and that is how she learned he was still alive. Jerry passed away in December of 2004. He is buried in the Veterans Cemetery in Jacksonville, North Carolina. Because of all the veterans who have fought for our freedom and liberty, Jerry's family did not have to hide his background, as Jerry did when he was captured by the Germans. There is a Star of David on his tomb stone. God Bless all veterans. Jerry, you did well.
Rest in Peace. Norman Brust

Medic, 3rd Infantry Division, Rock of the Marne!

Joseph E. Gunterman, Waterbury, CT
On 30 June 1943 I was a crewmember on the USS Zane (DD-337 to DMS-14) a WWI destroyer converted to a high-speed mine sweeper. During the invasion of Sasavele Island off the coast of Munda, New Georgia, Solomon Islands, while we were helping to deploy U.S. Army Companies A&B of the 169th Infantry, we ran aground and had to jettison our anchor.

Some 40 years later my island friends found that anchor and used it to construct a monument to honor those who had fought there during WWII. I sent them a bronze plaque along with a U.S. flag to mount on the monument that now rests on a hillside overlooking the Blanche waterway.

James D Connor

The Following newspaper article was sent by e-mail from L. Terry MCD. His cousin, Loretta found it in the Marion Chronicle in Marion, Indiana.

Michael Conner honors his grandfather, James D Connor, a WWII Veteran. It carries that strange feeling an eerie story might have in fiction, but this is true. His mother was browsing in an antique shop when her eyes glanced over a dog tag. She noticed the name was similar, and after holding it and reading the information imprinted on it in its entirety, she could not believe that such a coincidence could be the man she knew as her father. She thought maybe this was a relative. She purchased the Dog Tag, took it home and they did some investigative work of their own. Matching the information to her childhood address and personal information, the realized this Dog Tag was her father's Dog Tag. This was a connection, if written in a story, would be too coincidental to believe.

Chance find connects veteran, grandson

Bob Levine, email submission

I'm sure you're not lacking for stories about dog tags with the letter "H" on them and it hardly fits into the concept you mention of a dog tag bringing comfort to a soldier, but you might be interested in the story of Bob Levine, a veteran of the 90th Infantry Division who was wounded and captured on Hill 122 in Normandy.

Levine's leg was amputated by a German surgeon, and for many years Bob wondered if the doctor had cut off his leg because of that H on his dog tag. Many years later, in the pocket of his uniform jacket which he had kept, he discovered a note from the German doctor explaining that the amputation was necessary.

To make a long story short, Bob went to Normandy on the 40th anniversary and, because the note was signed, the Perier historian Henri Levaufre was able to locate the family of the surgeon, who had since passed away. Bob became the head of the New Jersey chapter of the American ex-POWs, and the surgeon's granddaughter, who was visiting America, spoke to the chapter on POW day. It was quite an emotional experience, at the center of which was Bob's concerns about being identified as a Jew by his dog tag.

You can find my interview with Bob on my web site at www.tankbooks.com I have some other stories related to dog tags on my web site and in my archives. I'll see if I can locate some of them.

Sincerely, and best of luck, Aaron Elson   (E-mail)

Members of the "Royal Flush B24J Crew

(Arlington National Cemetery, News Releases from the United States Department of Defense)
408th Bomber Squadron, 22nd Bomber Group, Heavy

As part of the Army Air Force's greatest non-combat aviation loss, more than 37 planes were lost during a terrible storm while flying back from a mission during World War II. Known from then on as "Black Sunday", the B-24J, called "Royal Flush" and its crew were one of those planes who fought valiantly against the Japanese, and yet were now to be listed as missing. They were told they had gone down in the ocean. It was April (16th or?) 20, 1944.

Many of the family members did not forget their loved ones and wanted them returned, but it was not until 2002 that a villager was hunting and found the wreckage of two B-24s. Looking untouched except by time, the rusted pieces remained in their places because of the fear of ghosts and bothering of remains.

The military recovery team spent months unearthing various parts and remains on the site. Still in his bomber jacket with sunglasses in his pocket, a team member saw the Dog Tags of First Lieutenant Frank P. Giugliano still around his neck. Having gone to Public School 63 in Queens, and then was a printer before the war, he was like so many other young men. Notifying the cousins of Lt. Giugliano brought tears and goose-pimples to know he was coming home.

As the recovery team continued to sift through the remains, they found other objects undamaged. They were able to use these objects, like rings and watches to help with identification. And, the tail of the bomber still had the serial number on it.

Able to now inform other family members, Staff Sergeant William Lowery's nieces and nephews were sad and at the same time glad they now knew what happened to their uncle. Since Lowery's dog tags were recovered from the wreckage, his niece, Norma Golembiewski said she was also glad the family could have something that belonged to her uncle. They knew that other family members, who had passed on, had hoped for closure.

Identification tags were also found for Staff Sergeant Elgin J. Luckenbach, Staff Sergeant Marion B. May, and Captain Thomas C.

Paschal. The Department of Defense POW/Missing Personnel Office (DPMO) - the remains of eleven U.S. airmen, missing in action from World War II, have been identified They are Captain Thomas C. Paschal, El Monte, California; First Lieutenant Frank P. Giugliano, New York, New York; First Lieutenant James P. Gullion, Paris, Texas; Second Lieutenant Leland A. Rehmet, San Antonio, Texas; Second Lieutenant John A. Widsteen, Palo Alto, California, Staff Sergeant Richard F. King, Moultrie, Georgia; Staff Sergeant William Lowery, Republic, Pennsylvania; Staff Sergeant Elgin J. Luckenbach, Luckenbach, Texas.; Staff Sergeant Marion B. May, Amarillo, Texas.; Sergeant Marshall P. Borofsky, Chicago, Illinois; Sergeant Walter G. Harm, Philadelphia, Pennsylvania; all U.S. Army Air Forces.

Signal Corps photo, 1942.
All pictures during this time period were taken by the US Army Signal Corps

Note the Dog Tags on these two soldiers from the Signal Corps Photo. The top one carries two on a leather looking strap. The bottom one looks as though it hangs with cotton cord and with a cross.

Family of John Rigapoulos, with permission and submission from Catherine Metropoulos
August 28, 2007

Relationship: Brother to my mother (Diamondo Rigopoulos Pergantis)
Where do you keep them? I wear it around my neck all the time.
What stories do you remember about your family member wearing them?
None. I am the first and only recipient of this tag. No one in the family even knew that it existed after John Rigapoulos' death in 1944.
What are your feelings and thoughts concerning the Dog Tags?
I am both privileged and honored to be the owner of this dog tag. My Uncle John was killed in action on September 20, 1944 – 16 years before I was born. Even though I've never met my uncle, from the first time that I saw and touched his dog tag, I felt like I've known him forever. He is a huge part of my life in ways that I cannot comprehend nor describe.

Story

When I was a young girl, my mother would speak often and quite proudly of her brother John. She told me how her big brother had promised her nylon stockings and a ride in his military jeep when he returned home from the war. She would tell me stories about how he was a parachute jumper and how he had been shot and killed while jumping out of an airplane during WWII.

Over the years she purchased many books about the war, always searching through them hoping that one day she may find a photo or something about her brother. Real late one night I remember finding her up, sitting very close to the television screen. She was watching actual black and white footage from WWII which showed our men being shot at and killed while jumping out of military aircraft. She told me that she was looking for her brother…

I was raised in Massachusetts, and we would visit my grandparents in New Jersey on holidays and whenever we could. During our trips there, I would occasionally sleep in their one spare bedroom. Hanging on the wall in that room was a frame that contained a flag which was neatly folded into a triangle and with it, a medal which read "purple heart." I remember staring at the framed items while I laid in bed, never truly knowing and understanding then what it all really meant.

When my grandfather died in 1977, per his request he was buried with his son's flag and medals. He never, ever recovered from the loss of his eldest son who never returned home and is buried in Holland.

In the late 1990's I started researching Rigopoulos family history on the Internet. In October of 2000 I was contacted by an historian by the name of Dave Berry who asked me if I had an uncle who had been killed in WWII. He said that he had a photo called a "stick" picture dated June 5, 1944, of a group of men who had volunteered as members of the Pathfinder's team. Dave had been on a mission for 18 years wanting to fill in all the names in that photo. He told me how he was unable to locate the family of John Rigapoulos, not knowing for many years that the military had misspelled his last name – Rigapoulos vs. Rigopoulos. Someone had suggested to Dave that he change the "a" to an "o," and finally, a connection to me and the Rigopoulos family was made…

In 2003 Dave Berry contacted me about a new book entitled, "All the Way to Berlin," in which my Uncle John was quoted. The book had been written by a man named James Megellas, who is the most decorated officer in the history of the 82nd Airborne Division. During a book signing of Jim's book that May, Dave called me saying that he had a surprise for me. He then handed the receiver to Jim Megellas so that I could speak with, and meet by telephone a man who personally knew my uncle during the war. In half Greek-half English, Jim shared with me stories about John Rigapoulos that our family never knew. I was shocked to discover that my uncle was not shot and killed while jumping out of an airplane like my mother believed, but on the ground by sniper fire after he had crossed the River Waal during Operation Market Garden.

Jim told me that being of Greek decent like my uncle, he and John Rigapoulos had formed an instant connection. Due to this bond, when John was killed Jim took one of his dog tags with the intentions of one day finding his family back in the states. He wanted to personally meet John's immigrant parents and share with them exactly how their son had been killed, one fellow Greek to another. Unfortunately, due to the misspelling of the name Rigapoulos (Rigopoulos), Jim Megellas was unable to find any of John's relatives and unable to give them John's tag. Jim then told me that he still had that dog tag after 60+ years and that he would be honored if I would accept it…

A month later in June 2003, I received John Rigapoulos' dog tag in the mail… it has hung around my neck ever since. Even though I have never met my uncle, he was killed years before I was born, from the instant that I saw and touched his dog tag, I felt like I have known him forever. He is a huge part of my life in ways that I cannot comprehend nor describe. I just wish that my Mom had lived long enough to have known the real truth about her brother.

In March of 2005 I had the incredible opportunity to meet James Megellas in person at a book signing in Connecticut. To me, I felt like I was taking my grandmother's place in meeting him. I brought along as a token, a basket full of homemade Greek cookies (my grandmother's secret recipe), as I knew she would have served him something like this were they to have met back in the 1940's.

I also had the privilege and honor of meeting a number of men who personally knew my uncle as well. Albert Tarbell, a full-blooded Indian, who was my favorite, had known John since "jump school." Albert was a radio operator during the war and shared with me some incredible stories. He is a wonderfully warm and genuine man.

You might like to know that a few months ago I learned that a movie is being made about the Pathfinder's mission in 1944. You can find information about this film on their website at _www.pathfindersfilm.com_ (http://www.pathfindersfilm.com/). I have chatted numerous times with the writer/director of the film, Curt Sindelar, and he tells me that John Rigapoulos is a war hero. He is also one of the main characters being portrayed in this film. I am very proud of my uncle, and honored to be wearing his dog tag!

Images of John Rigapoulos, and with family... John is #1, or 2d row far left, standing.

Earl H. Spredemann
Sergeant, U.S. Army
718th Air Force Base Unit

Having made it through WWII, Sergeant Earl H Spredemann was on his way of Queensland in Australia heading to Biak Island It was believed that the plane and all its passengers were lost at sea. In fact, that's what the family was told. Then in 1995, a helicopter pilot for a mining company saw what he thought was the wreckage of an airplane. This proved to be true, and the results of his DNA tests proved that the Dog Tags found with his name on them, were in fact those of Sergeant Spredemanns.

When he was brought home to be buried, members of his family were there to attend his service. His niece, Sharon Dryer, remembered growing up and hearing people say, 'Uncle Earl isn't in there. Uncle Earl is in the ocean ... And I would tell them, 'No, he's in the jungle.' She was given the only item that remained of her Uncle Earl's belongings, a small, black velvet bag which held his Dog Tags.

Francias A. Brogan
Name of Family: Bevis/Brogan
Whose Dog Tags do you have?
Relationship: Grandfather
Under what circumstances did you receive the Dog Tags?
I received the Dog Tags after he passed away in the summer of 2005.

Where do you keep them?
I keep the Dog Tags in a box with his other military items and hope to soon display them in a shadow box.

What stories do you remember about your family member wearing them?
I remember him talking for the 1st and last time about his time over in Europe as an Army Air Force Officer. His stories rarely centered on the fighting itself, but on the ways in which he kept busy during his free time.

What are your feelings and thoughts concerning the Dog Tags?
To me my grandfather's Dog Tag is not just a piece of metal. It represents a part of his life that he rarely ever talked about. To me it represents his courage, commitment, and patriotism in a time when his country asked for his help. His Dog Tag has helped me to better understand a man and a generation of men who risked everything and asked for nothing in return. The possession of his Dog tags has made me feel more connected to that part of his life. It has also given me a deep found respect for the servicemen and women who have served and who are currently serving
Zachary J. Bevis
8-29-07

The search for Uncle Angelo
From: Francesca , 2/16/2007
I started asking my parents questions about him. My dad remembered some pretty intense stories that Angelo had told him after they'd been hunting together. He remembered them so clearly because Angelo never talked about the war and when he opened up to my dad, it was something my father would never forget. He felt honored that Angelo was willing to tell him what he had done to earn his DSC and the rest of his medals. Lucky for me that my dad has such a good memory. My mom remembers when Angelo received his Silver Star, Bronze Star and two Purple Hearts in the mail. He'd been awarded the DSC right after the war, but no other medals. So my mom was over to visit when she was in college. She says it must have been around 1960. This brown envelope arrived in the mail. Angelo opened it, read the letter and pulled out this whole mess of medals. The Army had sent the medals along with a letter of apology saying the records had been reviewed, there'd been a mistake and he should have been awarded these medals years earlier. He showed the letter and medals to everyone, then shrugged it off, put them back in the envelope and stuck them in a drawer. My mom says my Aunt Annie was completely appalled. She said to him, "Angelo, I worried about you for 4 years, and I'll be dammed if these medals are getting stuck in a drawer. You earned every single one of them and I'm taking them down to get them framed tomorrow." And sure enough, she did. They hung on the wall in the living room until his death. I remember them vividly. She donated them to a museum after his death. Annie and Angelo are both buried in Arlington National Cemetery. He rarely talked about the war at

all because it was too painful, but I know that it was always a part of him. When he found out he was dying of cancer, he requested and received permission to be buried in Arlington. He'd more than earned the right to sleep among heroes. He was in the 25th I.D./161st "Tropic Lightning". He fought on Guadalcanal, New Georgia and the Philippines. The 25th saw 165 days of continuous combat on Luzon, Philippines. He earned his DSC near Kapintalan on April 2, 1945. If you want to read the citation, I'll be glad to send it to you, but don't put it on the web site.

After talking to my dad on December 12, 2006, I put Angelo's name into Google and got a single hit on his name. Imagine my astonishment when I found an article while doing some research on his time in WWII. It had a list of 18 dog tags that had been found on New Georgia, in the Solomon Islands. I'm not sure if I can describe the feeling I had. Shock, hope, joy, disbelief, amazement, disbelief again! Have you ever felt like a moment in time has been set in stone for you since the day you were born? One of those magical days that God gifts us with every once in a while. When it seems like miracles are just raining down from Heaven? Just so you know, I was raised Catholic, but I haven't been to church in about 20 years. I still pray, though. Going to Church just isn't my thing, however. The reason why I said it was mystical is the way it all played out. If I hadn't wanted to share pictures with Alex, then I would have never met Joey. If I hadn't met Joey, I would have never been inspired to learn more about what happened to Angelo during WWII. If I hadn't started researching him, I never would have found that article and started on this whole "Journey of the Dog Tags!" I truly believe it all happened for a reason.

I called the WWII veteran, Mr. Gunterman, who'd written the article and found out that I was the first person to call him in the 2 years since he'd written the article. I sent him confirmation that I was a relative. I also told him that I would try to find more veterans or family members on the list so I could put them in touch with him. I found 4 veterans/families in total. I had a really great conversation with one of the veteran's sons, Joe, and he reminded me that the dog tags might not still be there since it was a while since Mr. Gunterman had written the article. So rather than get people's hopes up, I stopped contacting them until Mr. Gunterman heard back from his friends. In the meantime, Mr. Gunterman had expected to get letters of confirmation from the 4 families I'd contacted. Joe and I were the only ones who wrote to him. So he waited about a month to give them a chance. Then he gave up on them and sent money and gifts in exchange for my Uncle's dog tags and those of Joe's father. So far we haven't gotten any response from New Georgia yet. But I've asked Justin Talyon of the Pacific Wrecks website to make inquiries for me. I have faith that I'll eventually get the all 18 dog tags on the list back to the veterans or their families.

After I found the article and contacted Mr. Gunterman to find out if it was for real, I called my entire family. Angelo passed away in 1995. His wife, Annie, passed away in 2001. My 3 sisters and I had spent a lot of time with them and their 3 Granddaughters when we were kids. They'd come out to our ranch for the summer and for deer hunting season and we'd faithfully go to their house every Easter. They were always my favorite extended family members growing up. Then my parents divorced in 1988 and we all drifted apart because we moved away. I didn't see them for many years and then someone in my family told me that Uncle Angelo had died. I hadn't even known he was sick and I didn't get to say goodbye. But Aunt Annie came to visit me a few days after my son was born and I was so happy to see her again. It was great. She passed away 3 years later. I'd lost touch with their son, daughter, and granddaughters, but my Uncle Jerry gave me everyone's phone numbers and email addresses and I called and wrote them for the first time in 15-20 years to tell them the good news. So finding that article reunited our entire family. Even if we never get the dog tags back, I will always be grateful for that. I had this image of Angelo and Annie looking down at us from Heaven and saying to each other "Look! It worked, we finally got them all back together again!"

"There are no atheists in fox holes"
The phrase "There are no atheists in fox holes" originated in WWII and had a double meaning that made it such a popular phrase, one is what NG Romano is alluding to, and the other referenced the fact that dog tags had a field that listed a person's religion and atheist was not an option that could be selected. "No preference" could be selected but then

nothing was printed in the religion space...so according to the dog tags, officially there were no atheists in fox holes.
Sidewalker
March 20, 2007

Transcribed from A handwritten letter from, Morris (Ike) Eisenstein, written by his wife, Lorry 5/12/07:
Dear Ginger,

This is an experience that my husband, Morris (Ike) Eisenstein, 2d Bn 222 Reg had during the early part of January 1945 north of Strasburg, France. His squad had a strong position on the Moder River, when the germans threw 6 or 8 divisions at our regiment and overran our position. He and his squad of 6 or 8 GI's took off into a wooden area where the germans were and ran towards Strasburg. When they saw an abandoned farmhouse who an 81 mm mortar and amo. He and his buddies stay there and jumped to the motor position and fired about 100 rounds three-bursts and stopped the germans in their positions.

About 3 or 4 days later my buddies said "Ike, we're going to have to surrender. We have no food, no amo, and don't where our forces are." I told them that the germans in front of us were SS and they would be given PW status but the SS would kill me because I was Jewish and therefore I would not surrender. They turned away and came back to say, "we have the solution." They said they know I was from Chicago but do I know anything about Milwaukee. I said yes I had been there any number of times.

Okay, we will find to the end but if we have to surrender you keep your mouth shut and we will tell them that you are a dumb American german from Milwaukee. Also, and this is important, we want you to cut off the "H" from your dog tag 'Hebrew-Jewish' This I did and when we were relieved a week later I searched and found my dog tag which I had thrown away and wore my dog tag with the "H" missing until the end of the war.

My dog tag is at the Jewish American War Veteran Museum in Washington where it is on display.

Yours in Rainbow – Good luck for your book.

Shalom!!!

Signed,
Morris (Ike) Eisenstein

Eric Mailander
March 28, 2007

The Marine Corps dog tag found on the invasion beach of Peleliu belonged to a Marine Sgt who was critically wounded in the chest by rifle fire during the invasion. He survived only to take his own life years after the battle. His son was informed of the discovery and was very excited that the tag was found. That's where the story ends. I'm not sure if the island guide (who had the dogtag) sent it to the son or not. The Japanese dog tag (identity disc) that I found on skeletal remains belonged to a soldier in the 2nd Inf Regt (artillery). The tag has a code number that symbolized the unit he served in and ID number. Unfortunately I have not been able to access that ID number in Japan (Ministry of Health & Welfare) to put a name to the tag. I have another dog tag in my possession but have not researched it yet (also found on Peleliu).
A contact of mine living in Australia and who has explored the island of Guadalcanal many times found several US dog tags and successfully researched their former owner's in an attempt to return them but they have all since passed away. He also collects German dog tags from soldiers killed in Russia and has quite an extensive display. I will forward this to him since I know he will be an excellent contact for you!

I know of a veteran of the Peleliu campaign who killed a Japanese soldier and took his dog tag as a souvenir. He returned it to family in Japan in the early '90's along with a samurai sword. That event made headline news in Japan.

I work with a co-worker who visited Viet Nam and purchased handfulls of dog tags from the war there. She has since researched alot of those names in an effort to return them to the former owners. I remember reading the article in our local paper but have not talked personally with her.As a side note, I found a canteen on Peleliu with the former Marine's service number and was able to return the canteen to him after 55 years!!

B-24 Liberator
News Release from the United States Department of Defense
From the territory of New Guinea in November, 1943, a B-24 Liberator and its crew took off on a mission. They sited some Japanese ships, and successfully had three direct hits. However, shortly thereafter, radio

contact was lost. In 2002 airplane data, remains and Dog Tags were given to US officials. The site was excavated in 2003, finding more remains and items for identification. The following men were identified: They are 1st Lt. William M. Hafner, Norfolk, Va.; 2nd Lt. Arthur C. Armacost, III, Cincinnati, Ohio; 2nd Lt. David R. Eppright, Warrensburg, Mo.; 2nd Lt. Charles F. Feucht, Reynoldsburg, Ohio; Technical Sgt. Raymond S. Cisneros, San Antonio, Texas; Technical Sgt. Alfred W. Hill, Temple, Okla.; Technical Sgt. James G. Lascelles, New York, N.Y.; Staff Sgt. William C. Cameron, Los Angeles, Calif.; and Staff Sgt. Wilburn W. Rozzell, Duncan, Okla. All were members of the 63rd Bombardment Squadron, 43 Bombardment Group. 1st Lt. Hafner's wife gave him an ID bracelet with a heart drop from her own bracelet before he went to the Pacific. As stated in an article from the News-Observer and Jay price, "Honey, you will never know how much the identification bracelet and the little heart mean to me," Hafner wrote on Oct. 29, in one of six letters the 24-year-old sent home. "I never take them off and they are a constant reminder of you; not that I need a reminder as I think of you always. Hilliard points to her own case as reason that all those families shouldn't lose hope of finding an answer. "To know, to actually know, is something special," she said. Recently, she got a small package in the mail. She opened it to find the bracelet and turned over the little dangling heart. After six decades in New Guinea's soil, the words engraved on the back of the charm were still clear: "Forget Me Not.""

Neil C. Morrison

Soldiers want to be remembered for their deeds and passing so it is not in vain. This practice of identifying ones passing and not being forgotten still rings true today. In our museum from Iraq I began noticing the large amount of cell phone images being sent back to family. Individual photos of... "me in my tank", "me standing guard", "me, me , me, why, so that those back home will remember them as shown in the photo as the most recent image. Images have replaced gold ear rings, written names and metal "Dog Tags" for family members. Now days the "Dog Tag" is more for body identification purposes, but it is the last photo of the soldier sent home that sets next to the cassette, then on the mantel at home.

A few years back a local prospector (yes we still have them here in the desert) was out walking about, when by chance found what appeared to be a hard packed dirt area that had impressions of what could have been a cooking area with what was determined to be a well packed surface with a 10-12" whole (sump) at one end. What the miner determined the hole was a garbage sump where they must have poured out the garbage/dirty water into the pit to evaporate. Apparently he dug into this sump to see if anything still remained of interest. He pulled up a set of early WWII "Dog Tags". Eventually a friend of his along with the tags ended up at out museum activity. Long story shorter, I was able to get a copy of his DA 214 (military records) located his next of kind and we made contact. Apparently he made it through training out here under Gen. George Patton early in the war and went to North Africa. He survived the war and reenlisted to go to Korea but did not make it back. His daughter came out to California and wanted to see the area. The prospector took her out and they spent the day walking and looking over the terrain. She thanked him for the tags and returned home back east. I am very sorry for over the years I no long have any POC's etc. for her. Just a case of helping someone out and then moving on. Sorry.

Very Respectfully,
NEIL C. MORRISON
Museum Director
Your history, then and now.
Fort Irwin, CA 92310-5029

Alvin MacLeod's WWII dogtags An email exchange sent to me regarding Dog Tags...
February 9, 2008

Dear Miss Cucolo,
I composed a book 2006 on the history of Camp Tophat in Antwerp/Belgium. The camp was set up at the end of WWII to

repatriate the American forces and some 270.000 men used between June 1945 and April 1946 this gate home. The men waited for their ship varying from a week to two months. They camped in tents and of course a lot of equipment was lost during these days. Three friends of mine have searched the area with metal detectors, which is still unhabited, and found an amazing collection of wartime souvenirs among a handfull of dogtags.

For the book I made some research and found back 3 of the former dogtag owners. (Surprisingly one married an Antwerp girl!!) I'll send also a copy of my correspondence with the daughter of Alvin Macleod.

Kind regards from Antwerp/Belgium

Sent: Saturday, February 18, 2006 9:35 PM

Subject: Alvin MacLeod's WWII dogtags

Hello,

Recently while visiting my mother in St. Augustine Florida, I was contacted by Michael Isam regarding my father's dog tags. Mr. Isam said that you had found them in Belgium. What an incredible surprise. He had some wonderful memories of being in Europe during his youth despite the war. He often talked about how kind the people in Belgium and France were to the soldiers. My dad died 4 years ago, but I know my mother would love to have them. Please contact me at the above email address.

Thanks

Diane MacLeod Runkle

From: "Jean Dillen"

Sent: Sunday, February 19, 2006 12:06 PM

Subject: Re: Alvin MacLeod's WWII dogtags

Dear Mrs MacLeod Runcle,

I do not own the dog tag . He is in the possession of Mr. Jean-Pierre Ost who found it and whom I will inform of your interest by sending a copy of this mail and I am sure that Mr. Ost will respond the right way. Camp Top Hat in Antwerp/Belgium was an American repatriation camp which operated from June 1945 till April 1946. It processed more than 272.000 home going American service men on their last stop home. The former camp site is a park now but many long lost artifacts, left by the military, turn up once in a while. One of them being your father's dog tag. Pity he passed away before it was found.

I am preparing a book on Camp Top Hat. It will be a photobook which shows every aspect of the soldiers, waiting to go home after a successfully ended war. Your dad was probably here only for a short period, ranging from a few days to a few weeks, depending on the arrival of the ship to bring him home.

I wonder if you can spare a portrait of your father in uniform and one of him in the last part of his life. Also a few words of his involvement in the war are appreciated. I intend to have a chapter on those lost & found dog tags in the book. Included a picture of the tag.
Kind regards from Belgium,
Jean Dillen

Bill Holton

Your upcoming book on the history of the "Dog Tag" is a uniquely esoteric subject, especially because of their enforced use by millions of us former military vets. I was seventeen when I volunteered for the US Navy and served in the Pacific Theater during WWII. To me and my fellow young recruits who saw them more as a nuisance, we felt that we were invincible and never thought of needing tags for our own personal identification, as we had seen in the war movies. We wore them around our necks, never to be removed even in the shower, merely to comply with regulations and avoid punishment. We would never need such a trivial trinket for personal identification at some future time. And the fact that I am still here and responding to your mail proves that our bombastic comments to each other were in fact, true. However, privately, everything you said concerning the individualization, personal and humanistic aspects personified by the wearing of the dog tags, were an intrinsic, though nonverbal part of my consciousness, less it exposed my real fears and lessen the heroic patina implied by the uniform I was so proud to wear in the defense of my country.
Bill Holton

Robert Van Auker

This story being postal letter exchanges...

I was sort of just scanning as I was reading the August issue of Reader's Digest, and only gave a passing glance at the story on page 34, "Giving back", a story of the work of a Miss Stacy Hansen of Santa Cruz, California, in the returning of lost dog tags to Vietnam veterans.

But I had reason to remember it and go back to read it more carefully after getting a phone call from a pair of volunteers here in the states who offer their time and talents, at no cost, to help find missing Vietnam POW's.

They told me a gentleman in Australia, who is a member of a club called "Treasure Hunters" had contacted then for help in tracing me down. His hobby is to hunt for lost articles with a metal detector, and he had contacted them to see if they could find me, because he had found one of my lost dog tags in the ruins of an old hospital in a long ago deserted camp just outside Brisbane, Australia, a hospital where I was a patient after returning to Australia from the Buna Campaign in New Guinea. They asked me if they could send my phone number to him, and I said yes.

Two days later I got a phone call from this gentleman who asked me if I wanted the tag back. Of course I said yes. He told me he had run across it in a dig where he found four U.S. and five Australian tags. As far as the American tags goes he has already returned one to an 83 year old man from my division who lives in Grand Rapids, Michigan, with the help of these two fine people here in the U.S.

My address on the tag was of my old home in Wyandotte, Michigan, the home I had left in 1957. As a matter of fact I had even left the state to go to New Mexico. Yet they were able to trace me to here in Globe, Arizona, through 47 years which has since passed. Amazing, I believe.

I was in this hospital in the summer of 1943 when I lost the tag, so it had been buried for more than 61 years, and like with Stacy Hansen, it was lost before this man who found it was even born.

It turned out that he has a home computer and we have been in constant touch by e-mail since that first phone call. Two weeks ago my tag arrived here in Globe, Arizona. He sent it by registered and insured air mail at quite an expense. I have insisted on paying all his expenses
Robert Van Auker

Hi Stan,
I hope you do not mind me sending you an email. I am the Niece of Bob Van Auker, the man whose dog tags you found. I just wanted to tell you, that I think what you did was a WONDERFUL thing. Finding my Uncle's dog tags was one thing, but to take the time to find him and return them to him, is entirely another thing. I am so happy for both of you. My Uncle Bob is a wonderful man, and I am sure the two of you

will become Great email buddies. I think this is so very exciting; I can't wait to hear more news about you from my Uncle. Thank you again Stan for making my Uncle so happy.
Best Wishes,
Edie,..A Niece who loves her Uncle very much.
Donald Dencker

I still have my World War II Army dog tags which I wore through the Battles of Leyte and Okinawa while a member of Company L, 382nd Infantry Regiment, 96th Infantry Division, a Rifle Company. However, I do not have any unusual stories related to these dog tags. I sure kept them on though as my Company L suffered a few over 300 Battle Casualties, and by the grace of God I wasn't a casualty.

I also have my Korean War dog tags where I was a Engineer Officer building airfields for the Fifth Air Force.
Donald Dencker
L/382/96

POW Ralph Rodriguez

http://www.pbs.org/wgbh/amex/bataan/sfeature/sf_mail.html

Bataan Rescue producers David Axelrod and Peter Jones found many veterans -- former POWs and their rescuers -- with indelible memories of their wartime experiences. "That death march was just plain murder," remembered ex-POW Bob Body. "...As you walked along you could smell, the odor was terrible from guys that had been left a day or so ahead of time, and laying in the sun, you know, and they left them people laying there. It's still hard for me to believe that this actually happened, and it is still hard for me to believe that I went through that."

"One of the duties that I had in the morning was to walk down through the [prison] barracks and take care of those men that had died, recalled former POW Tommie Thomas."...One of my obligations was to remove his dog tags and put one dog tag down his throat as far as I could get it and I had a little forked stick that I used to push it right down to his throat. And the reasoning for that was for purposes of identification at a later date."

"Sometimes I wonder how I did it," said former POW Ralph Rodriguez of the 30-mile march after the rescue. "You have to remember, [the Japanese] were behind us, we could hear them shooting, they were trying to break through."

Seymour Lichtenfield - Questionnaire
April 24, 2007

Did you purchase more than one set?   No
If so, where did you purchase them? Was issued a replacement set

Why did you purchase another set? Originals were destroyed during combat

Did you wear them when you were off duty? Yes
My outfit was surrounded for three days at the beginning of the Battle of the Bulge in Dec 1944. We were without food and ammunition and the end result was obvious if we were not killed. I am Jewish and my dog tag had a Capital H on it for religion (Hebrew). Knowing the circumstances in Germany at that time regarding Jews, I removed my tags and ground them into the dirt at the bottom of my fox hole just prior to being captured. I had no means to identify myself as an American GI until after I was liberated by the Russians and returned to US Army control. It was then that a new pair of dog tags were issued to me for the remainder of my stay in the service.

Where do you keep your Dog Tags? I have given them to my children

I have written an account of my combat and prison days and it is in the Library of Congress. It is entitled "KRIEGIE 312330 – A PRISONERS STORY" by Seymour Lichtenfeld

Korea

Sharing the joy of such a meaningful collection has made this research all the more significant. Richard Clayton began his service to this nation at the age of seventeen. It took a signature from his mother to allow his service, but he and four other gentlemen signed up to support their country.

Korea was on the brink of war as they enlisted and went their basic course. Richard served with the 5th Regimental Combat Team which was in transition during the Korean War going from the 25th Infantry Division, then the 1st Cavalry Division, then the 24th Infantry Division in tight succession. After serving, Richard came home and shared his life with his wife of 50 years. He found an interest in the Dog Tag and began collecting this memorabilia with a fervent interest. He has many that he has researched, found their families, enlarged individual collections, and donated others. He especially enjoys the ones he has acquired a photo or other personal media to include with its history.

- He has a set of Naval Reserve tags, from 1944, which he was able to retain the Appointment slip for a Donald Miller Doctor.

- Another set of Naval Reserve Tags from 1944 of James John Garrity with an ID bracelet.

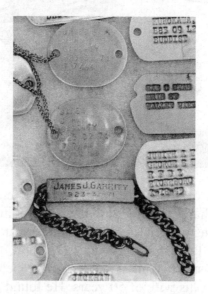

- Edward J. Betts, U S Army, dog tags with a locket engraved and pictures of loved ones inside.

- A Pennsylvania Volunteer Regimental Dog Tag from the Spanish American War, with JW scratched on the back.

- 759th Rwy Opn Bn, , William Parker, Algiers, 1943

- Foreign Tags:

German

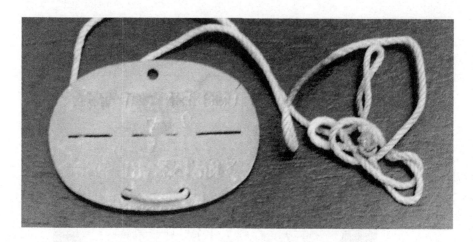

Japanese

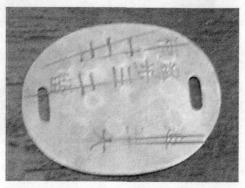

- Miscellaneous Tags, Trench art

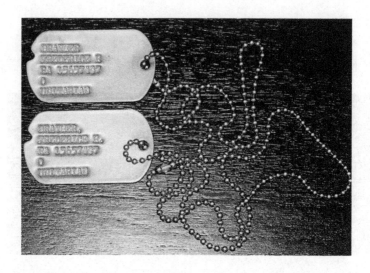

While religion is not unusual to be shown on tags from this time period. Richard does have a few that are less likely to be seen in the general population. Thus, this Unitarian one is an example. He also has a Buddhist tag, and an Indian one.

- His favorite and most cherished has a story all its own...
  While searching to increase his collection, he went into an antique shop and asked for Dog Tags. The shop owner said he had one, for $30.00. Richard thought this to be a bit much, but asked to see it. To his surprise, this tag and bracelet was the man who had raised him. His father left their family early on, and this gentleman helped to raise Richard. He believed fate had intervened, and Richard purchased the tag and the bracelet.

Robert Van Layton, Master Sergeant, U.S. Army
Hamilton, Ohio
Born 1924 - Died December 2, 1950 in Korea
Missing in Action - Presumed Dead
News Release from the United States Department of Defense

While no soldier wants to leave the fallen behind, sometimes there is no choice. This is what happened to those who fell along the Chosin Rive, North Korea November-December, 1950. Master Sergeant Robert V. Layton, U.S. Army, of Cincinnati, Ohio was one of those men. He was assigned to Company A, 1st Battalion, 32nd Infantry Regiment, 7th Infantry Division. When the unit had to pull back, he was listed as missing in action, and then Presumed killed in action under the circumstances.

The area where his remains were found was discovered in 1998, and then it took two years 2002-2004 to excavate the 225 members buried in the mass gravesites. The men had been buried there by their own comrades before they left. Dental records, physical records and DNA were used to identify the soldiers and marines. It is modern science that can help these families find closure, if closure is at all possible.

The personal items carried by Master Sergeant Layton were given to the family to remember him by. These items were personal. Whether they were complete in their previous form or not, they were his. From another time and place. "The rotted remains of a left boot. A beaded chain. Some buttons. Crumpled foil from a pack of Lucky Strike cigarettes. A key manufactured in Lancaster by Slaymaker Lock Co. A moldy canvas-and-leather wallet holding a faded photograph. A single military dog tag."

Layton was laid to rest at Arlington National Cemetery with full military honors on November 28, 2006, — 56 years, possibly to the day, that he died. Finally knowing her father's fate has eased a burden for Saylor. "To know that he died in combat, that it was quick, that he was buried with some respect, that he was not tortured, and to have him buried at Arlington with respect," she said, "that means a lot."

Army Corporal Homer L Sisk - Not knowing about a brother until you are told they are dead is a vacuum left unfilled. At seventy-five, William Sisk found out just such a thing. In a mass grave in North Korea, the remains of Army Corporal Homer L Sisk, his brother, were identified by laboratory tests. He served in the 8th Cavalry Regiment of the 1st Calvary

Division, when nearly 400 men of the unit were killed near Unsan in November, 1950. When Sisk was found in 2000, the excavation team found roughly ten other soldiers. They found multiple items including Sisk's Dog Tags. At the burial in Arlington Cemetery, "Sisk said he was given his brother's casket flag and medals -- including a Purple Heart, Combat Infantryman's Badge, campaign medals and unit citations -- and his dog tags."

Transcribed from a hand written letter by Gerald A. Wiley
June 15, 2007
Dear Ginger,

I was an official US Army Correspondent for the 3d Infantry Division, and especially the 65th Puerto Rican Infantry Regiment in 1952-1953. I also wrote articles for Stars and Striped – Korean Edition, and for Army Hometown Newscenter, and El Imperial and El Mundo of Puerto Rico.

I volunteered for active duty in Ohio Reserve Division 83d Infantry Division (Thunderbolt Division). I was promoted to Corporal in December 25th, 1952 after we soldiers told President elect Dwight D. Eisenhower we all wanted promotions during his visit to Korea in December 19..

I have had a ministry of helping people find jobs, income, scholarships, and clothes for many years.
Very Faithfully yours,
Gerald A. Wiley

"THE BORINQUENEERS "a documentary on the history of the all-Puerto Rican 65th Infantry Regiment. This compelling film chronicles the never-before-told story of the Puerto Rican 65th Infantry Regiment, the only all-Hispanic unit in U.S. Army history. Through the vivid testimony of the regiment's veterans and rare archival footage, the film traces the unique experience of the Borinqueneers (pronounced Boh-rin-keh-neers), culminating with their impressive performance during the Korean War. In the fall of 1952, though, the fate of the regiment would take a dramatic turn when more than 100 of its soldiers were arrested. Narrated by Hector Elizondo" For educational / institutional sales, contact The Cinema Guild. El Pozo Productions P.O. Box 302 Crompond, NY   10517 contact@borinqueneers.com

Lou Palumbo

I served in the Navy aboard the USS Missouri in Korea from October '52 thru mid '53. The ship was award 5 battle stars during that period. After fifty years of carrying my Navy dog tag, it was lost a few years ago, and I would like to replace it, if possible.

Regards
   Lou Palumbo

Patricia A Faull
Dog Tags and Army Photo, August 1949

TheSSSNAKE@xxx.xxx
April 30, 2007

My memory of Dog Tags dates back to Jan. 1951 Being issued my tags I noticed an X stamped on the lower right side i question this and was told it meant all others. All others meaning not Catholic or Protestant. I failed to mention that i am of the Greek Orthodox faith

Samuel K. Toomey III
Major, United States Army
News Release from the United States Department of Defense: March 26, 1990

"Until we see a body, it will be difficult to convince us that he's really dead," said Samuel K. Toomey Jr., a retired Army colonel. This is not an unusual statement to be made by family members because no one really wants to believe their loved one is dead. Colonel Toomey had a history with incorrect information from his own years of service. He was a battalion commander in the Korean War and at one time period was attacked by a Chinese unit. He believed one of his company commanders to be dead, even though they did not find a body, they did find the company commander's dog tags and watch. Roughly five years later, Toomey was in the Pentagon and walking down a hallway when he recognized a familiar face. It was the Company Commander who told him he had been captured by the Chinese, but was later released. Seeing a body and positive identification is what he needed for the confirmation of his own son's death.

Lavon T. McDaniel,

Hello, Ginger. Not being a story teller, I will probably leave out the important stuff which will cause the story to fall flat. But here goes ....I was draft in 1943 by the Indiana Draft Board and immediately reported into Fort Benjamin Harrison, Indiana for my initial duty. Following the normal in-processing activities, I settled down and waited for my first assignment orders. I had taken typing in high school and when a call went out for a typist, I volunteered for this duty. I found out that for the next two weeks I was going to sit and type dog tags on this electric dog tag making machine for the new "in-processing" soldiers. Naturally, while I was cutting dog tags for the new soldiers, and a couple of friends, I also made a set of dog tags for my brother, who wouldn't enlist until about two years later.

I was a faithful wearer of my dog tags. The same set of tags that I made for myself in 1943, I wore all through my first 6 1/2 years of service. Let's say they protected me for those 6 1/2 years.

In 1950, when the North Koreans invaded South Korea, my unit, Charley Company, 23d Infantry Regiment, 2nd Infantry Division, was called to go and stem the red tide in the little country of South Korea. While my unit process for this movement, new items were prepared for each of the deploying soldiers. That identifying item, DOG TAG, was once again prepared for each departing soldier. Assuring that each soldier was wearing his two tags. I decided I would wear the new dog tags to Korea and leave my World War II dog tags at home.

Following about a month of combat, my unit was almost annihilated on the 31st of August 1950. I was wounded and captured on the 1st of September 1950. During the first few hours of my captivity, my dog tags, amongst many other personal items, were taken from me. Never to be seen again, by me! For many years I have harbored the thought that some Korean native would find my tags and they would be returned to me. No luck so far!
When I was liberated in October of 1950 and returned to Allied control, I shunned the new dog tags that were made for me and elected to wear my old World War II dog tags.

Today, I still have my old dog tags from when I first entered service, as well as the set that was made for me upon my liberation. I belong to different military associations and when attending these meetings, I will always pull out my "old" dog tags and wear them to these meetings.

The picture on the left Sgt Bona and PFC McDaniel was taken in a small town named "Budberg, Germany." This town sits on the west side of the Rhine River and was taken just days before the crossing of the Rhine in March of 1945.
Story ends............................. Terry
Lavon T. McDaniel, CSM US Army Ret

George F. Drake,
Here is one for your book. You can entitle it **"Revenge for the Whore Inspection."**

I was stationed north of Seoul living in a tent in the middle of a stinking rice paddy fertilized with night soil. This was in 1952 or 1953. We had a new second lieutenant, the youngest graduate ever of West Point and he was an arrogant SOB. One night when he was Captain of the Guard a woman from the nearby village came to the company gate and claimed that a GI had beat her up in her "comfort house" and she wanted to file charges against him. LT. A.S. told her to go away. She, in turn, called him 'less than a man' and many other such terms. His manhood was challenged so he thereupon called a full company inspection, at 3 a.m. so this whore could inspect the troops and identify the one who assaulted her. Everyone was roused out of sleep to stand inspection. The woman, with Lt. A.S. at her side walked up and down the line of soldiers standing at attention. She failed to identify the soldier who committed the assault, probably for fear of her life. We were all allowed to go back to bed after what became known as "the whore inspection."

Not many weeks later my house boy said he had something for me. It was Lt. A.S.'s dog tags. I asked him where he got them and he said that the woman who filed the complaint at the gate and inspected the troops at 3 a.m. took them from the Lt. when he visited her bed and now she wanted us to decide how we wanted to return them to the Lt. The guys in my tent discussed the matter and we decided to secure the dog tags around the neck of our company dog. Finally the company commander learned that the dog had Lt. A.S.'s dog tags and called the Lt. in to enquire if he had his dog tags and wanted to know how they got on the company dog. How he explained his way out of that matter we never knew but the entire company, and probably the C.O. finally knew the true story.

George F. Drake, (Sgt.) Korean War Veteran

From a letter by Stanley J. Serxner
June 5, 2007
He wrote to me about a Dog Tag he had found and wanted help in finding the owner. Then, "My Dog Tags just hang there around my neck, one of them waiting for the notch to be inserted in my mouth if I came back horizontally one day in 1951 or 1952, and infantryman in Korea who carried his M-1 without too much bitching."
Sincerely,
Stanly J. Serxner

Vietnam

John Huebner, US Navy
Found by Tanna Toney, and submitted with an email trail to its owner.
http://lostdogtags.bravehost.com/

Searched For 8 Years And Found Him!!

In the Summer of 1995, while taking my dog "Chruble" for a walk along the Southernmost shore in Calif., I noticed a rusty piece of metal sticking out of the side of a palm sized rock. It was a Military I.D. tag, A-K-A "dog tag". It was embedded in sediment after being on the ocean floor for 30 years! It seemed to be attached to a key ring, as there were a few other items embedded in the rock also, a key, fingernail clippers and a small screwdriver. Much to my amazement, I could make out his name, I.D. #, branch of service and his religion.

My first thought was that this Sailor had perished at sea and I held his last farewell to this world in my hand. All I could think of was how much I wanted to return this brave Sailor's Dog Tags to his family and I wasn't sure how to go about doing that. So for the next 3 years, they sat on a shelf with other treasures that I had found on our many walks along the beach. I thought about getting in touch with the Navy, but I didn't want to become a "number in a file". Then, I discovered the "Internet". The only problem was, I was spelling his last name WRONG!

Thankfully, a friend pointed that out to me. So off and on for the next 5 years, I searched the internet for ANY information on a "*John Huebner*" that I could find. I don't remember which site I was on at the time, but I clicked on a link that took me to a Website called "Operation Just Cause". I emailed the website with the information that I had, along with 2 pictures of "the rock". While on the same website, I clicked on another link called "The Circle of Life". That is where I read Diane Moore's story about her father, who is STILL listed as MIA since 1965. I signed her guestbook and also asked her for any help that she could give in helping me find John Huebner's family.

The following are the actual emails that I sent and received from this wonderful group of folks, devoted to their Cause from the core of their being. Thank you all at OJC.

The most AMAZING thing has happened!! About 6 or 7 years ago, I found some Military dog tags on the beach at Imperial Beach, Ca. I have been searching for this man's family, so I could return his dog tags to them. Through COUNTLESS websites, and WAY TOO MUCH TIME ON THE COMPUTER, I found the Man himself!!! He lives in Milwaukee, WI. The last time he was in southern Calif. was in 1969. 34 years ago!!! I just received an email from him this morning. Attached is a picture of what I found. What a TRIP!!! Miles and Miles of Smiles PanTanna

From: John Huebner
Sent: Monday, August 04, 2003 5:52 AM
Subject: dog tags.
yep that's me. I would sure like to know how you found them, where etc., the last time I was in Southern Calif, was in 1969, thank you for taking the time to find me. please keep in touch, I suspect by the sdharleyrider.com website you're a Harley Rider???? I live in Milwaukee, WI. HOME OF HARLEY hope to hear from you John My email to EVERYONE in my address book after finding him

John aboard the USS Pledge

yep that's me. I had forgotten that I'd sent almost all the pictures on one of the Pledges Wed sites, It's about a year before I lost my Keys/dog tags. I even had hair back then, and was about 185. that's a British Submariners hat I'm wearing, We traded hats in Hong Kong. Friends always, John ---

Buck
Wed, January 19, 2008
Hello Ginger,
I read about your project at Lex's place. Here's my dog-tag story, which includes a picture. I've carried, and still carry, my dog tag on my key ring. While it ain't part of the original set of tags issued to me at Lackland AFB in 1963, it's close enough. I'm very, very fond of my dog tag...it's just a small memento of 22 years of service, but an invaluable and irreplaceable one.
Buck
Exile in Portales

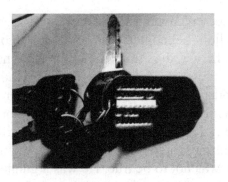

Pennington
My USAF-issued dog tag. I'm Buddhist, by an official act of the US Gub'mint. The story behind that lil bit of trivia goes like this... Once upon a time while I was still on active duty it came to pass, via directive, that all personnel had to have Official ID tags in their possession, at all times. Those of us who had lost their ID tags were ordered to report to the CBPO and get re-issued. So, I took my ol' self down to the personnel shop, found the ID-tag foundry and presented my ID card to the airman in charge. He looked at it in a bored manner and asked "What's your religion?" "No preference," sez I. "No go," sez he, "You have to choose a religion...pick one from this list..." and he shoves a list of about 25 religious denominations across the desk to me. I scan it quickly, and he's right: there are no "No preference" or "Agnostic" categories. So I said "I'm Buddhist." The airman didn't bat an eye and proceeded to pound out my dog tags. Ten minutes later I walked out of the personnel shop with my newly-minted dog tags and a brand-new religion. The Second Mrs. Pennington was most impressed when I got home, she being a closet Buddhist and all.

Kenneth Lloyd Crody, Corporal, United States Marine Corps
Date of Birth: 3 August 1953 - Date of Casualty: 11 July 1972
Home of Record: Griffith, Indiana
Branch of Service: Marine Corps
Rank: Corporal
Casualty Country: South Vietnam
Casualty Province: Quang Tri
Status: MIA (Until 2004)
News Release from the United States Department of Defense

His body had not been recovered since July 11, 1972, when the Sikorsky CH-53D Sea Stallion helicopter was shot down by a ground-to-air missile. Kenneth L. Crody, from Griffith, Indiana, was a Marine Corporal among a crew of 56 lost that day. He and another member, Sergeant Jerry Hendrix, were identified 32 years after their crash. Three weeks short of his 19th birthday and only one month in country, he promised his mom, "Don't worry, Mom," he had told his mother just weeks earlier. "Marines aren't ever sent into Vietnam. I'll be fine." Unfortunately, this was not to be true. He was a gunner for the Sikorsky, when a missile hit one of the engines and their fuel ignited.

His remains were identified by bones and personal items, including pieces of a razor, nail clipper, comb, watch, and fork. The only thing completely intact was his dog tag. On the return of his Dog Tags, his mother stated. "It will be so comforting to know our Kenny will be finally buried right," said Wilma Crody, who's in poor health and will not attend the burial. "It's OK, I guess. At least I have his dog tag and his class ring."

Carl Frederick Karst, Colonel, United States Air Force
The symbol on the Wall next to Carl's name was changed from a cross (MIA) to a star (KIA) April 30, 1994. Remains were identified.
Unit: Pleiku, South Vietnam
Date of Birth: 27 October 1930
Home City of Record: Galatia Kansas
Loss Date: 16 November 1968
Country of Loss: South Vietnam
Status (in 1973): Missing In Action
Acft/Vehicle/Ground: O1F
Source: Compiled from one or more of the following: raw data from U.S. Government agency sources, correspondence with POW/MIA families, published sources, interviews. Updated by the P.O.W. NETWORK in 1998.

Flying an O1F over South Vietnam, the pilot Major Carl F. Karst and his observer, Captain Nguyen X Quy, left Plieku at 1640 on November 16, 1968, but lost radio transmission shortly thereafter. A Vietnamese informer reported the plane had been shot down, and while Karst tried to escape, he had been captures and killed. In 1983, a refugee turned in some bone fragments and a rubbing of a dog tag to officials in Malaysia. He told US officials that a Buddhist monk had given him the items, and that up to seven other remains were from the same location. The rubbing had the name of Karst on it. By 1984, four other informants reported on the find, and US officials changed his MIA classification on the Vietnam Wall to POW once he was positively identified.

In 1989, Two Vietnamese were looking for incense wood, when they came across what appeared to be a crash sight. In 1994, The Air Force began recovery of the area, Quang Nam-Da Nang province. The F-4 was rumored to have been seen crashing in the area, but was never found. Captain Mason I. Burnham was the navigator and Major Thomas H.

Amos was the pilot from the 366th Tactical Fighter Wing based at Da Nang. In April, 1972, their plane went down. While the excavation of the site in 1994 was a slow process, they were able to identify the two men by bone fragments and other items, including the men's Dog Tags. Captain Burnham's tags were returned to his daughter who has worn them ever since, and she stated, "because he wore them next to his heart when he was killed."

Gordon Rottman

I'm a Vietnam vet and know quite a few other vets, including those of other conflicts.

I've never heard anyone mention anything special about dog tags, especially in regards to bringing comfort or security. You're told from the day you were issued them that they were part of the uniform and never to be taken off. That kind of stuck and most did just that. Just another habit of many one picks up.

I don't think there was much sentimentality attached to them by most men, at least not at the time. If they retained them or had not lost them after they left the service then at some point they might become a memento. I'm more attached to the P-38 can opener I carried than my dog tags. You might mention that a P-38 was often attached to the dog tag chain. Mention too dog tag silencers of different types.

Something else to be mentioned is the red medical warning tags that were issued in the 1980s I think. The attachment of dog tags to boots is another point to address.

I carried a third tag, a much prohibited "gag" tag as did a few others. It said:

If you are recovering my body...fuck you.
There may have been other such tags.
One thing I do recall now that I'm thinking about it. During a noon break on an operation I ranked out in a hammock without a shirt (it was really hot). The sun shifted and I was no longer in shade. When I came to my chest had reddened and you could make out the tags and chain. One of my Cambodians shot a pic of me with my camera napping at the time I still have the photo.

Gordon Rottman

Lewis Herbert Abrams, Colonel, United States Marine Corps
Born on August 17, 1929 in Montclair, New Jersey, he was a regular
Marine Corps Flight Officer.

He began his tour of duty in Vietnam on November 25, 1967 and
became a casualty of that war on February 9, 1968 when his fixed-wing
aircraft was shot down over the land in Vietnam. His body was not
recovered until 1997.

On July 9, 1997, he was buried with full military honors in Arlington
National Cemetery.

Lt. Colonel Lewis Abrams was not identified until they recovered his
remains in 1997 at the bottom of a water-filled crater on a farm in
Vietnam. He was killed when his plane was shot down in February,
1968. The near thirty year difference can be difficult for any family
member, not knowing exactly what happened. DNA, a piece of an ID
card, and a few other things helped to identify him. Buried with a host of
Marines standing by to honor him, he was finally laid to rest. "What
most people can do in three days, it took us 30 years to do," his widow,
LuEllyn Abrams, said. "It was just so perfect today. It finalizes a long
period of time for us, puts a cap on things. They gave me a little pile of

stuff, wouldn't fill a shoebox. It's miraculous the things that survived. I was handed my husband's dog tags today."

Raymond Thomas Heyne, Lance Corporal, United States Marine Corps
Full Name: RAYMOND THOMAS HEYNE
Date of Birth: 7/15/1947 - Date of Casualty: 5/10/1968
Home of Record: MASON, WISCONSIN
Casualty Country: SOUTH VIETNAM
Casualty Province: QUANG TIN
Status: MIA
News Release from the United States Department of Defense

Heyne had been at the American base of Da Nang for about two months when he and 43 other members of Platoon Delta X-Ray were ordered to the forward operating base of Ngok Tavak near the Special Forces Camp of Kham Duc to counter a North Vietnamese push against Kham Duc. In he battle that followed, described by those who were there as one of the most ferocious of the war, both Ngok Tavak and Kham Duc fell to overwhelming numbers. The small force at Ngok Tavak held out for more than 10 hours until they were forced to abandon the position. In the fight, a dozen Americans, including Heyne were killed. Because of the ferocity of the battle, it was impossible to recover their bodies. The battles of Ngok Tavak and Khum Duc remain as one of the most heroic stands of the entire Vietnam War.

In May, 2005 remains positively identified through mitochondrial DNA matching, confirmed that Heyne had been killed on the battlefield. The DNA evidence was found in three teeth that were discovered during painstaking archeological digs on the battlefield. In addition, a single stainless steel dogtag belonging to Heyne was also found. He is among 11 Marines and one Army Special Forces soldier whose remains have been identified. The announcement ends nearly four decades of not knowing what happened to their brother for Kostello and Nabozny.

According to Kostello, one man who has had much to do with the success of getting the effort organized is former Marine Corporal Tim Brown, who was a member of Platoon Delta X-Ray, but was medically evacuated with a case of pneumonia before the battle took place. "When I became a ranking member in Vietnam Veterans of America, I persuaded the POW/MIA committee of VVA to take up what later came to be known as the Khum Duc/Ngok Tavak project," he continued.

Brown took teams of veterans back to the old battlefield in 1994, 1995 and again in 1998, providing the U.S. Government with maps, videotapes of meetings with Vietnamese officials and veterans, and minefield locations. The work done by VVA led to the safe and productive recovery of the remains found at the battlefield in 1998 and 1999. Brown said the Veterans who made those trips had personal stakes in the effort. "Our friends, our brothers were left behind on the battlefield, and that is something that just troubled all of us for a number of years," Brown said. "But at the time, tactically, the remoteness of the location made it impossible to get them out at the time. Given that, plus the fact that the families were led to believe that they died in different fashions than they actually died, raised all the more the more interest to get at the truth."

Kostello said he news that her brother's fate was now absolutely confirmed was a relief.
"Finally the doubts were lifted. Finally, there is closure," she said. She said she especially prized her brother's dog tag, which was discovered at Ngok Tavak. "This means so much to me, that they found this. All these years we didn't know if they were captured, were they killed, were they taken alive for a while and then killed, we had no idea," she said. "There was doubt in your mind about what could have happened."

"It does resolve the questions that have lingered, for so many years," Nabozny said. Kostello said she and her sister plan to bury the dogtag at an existing empty gravesite memorial to her brother next to their parent's graves. Kostello said the ceremony will be both sad and a celebration. "He's finally going to be home," she said.

Mark Hartford
May 21, 2007 10:59 PM
Dear Ginger.
My dog tag story is brief. I wore the two tags around my neck. They said I was "a catholic, had A- blood type and my service number was RA 19xxxxxx."

I threw my Honorable Discharge and my dog tags away when I went to Dewey Canyon III, the VVAW antiwar event, Washington DC in 1971. I was never issued the three medals awarded to me at the end of my service, with them not coming to me until recently, almost 40 years later.

I am proud of my membership in my squad (1st), Bravo Company, 1/23rd Infantry Regiment, 2nd Infantry Division. I served 13 months north of the Imjin River and walked patrols, night ambush and OP duty in the Korean DMZ. My regiment lost 11 soldiers during my 13 month tour.

I returned my Discharge Papers and my dog tags in 1971 to show my solidarity with my comrades in VVAW and opposition to the war in Vietnam.
Mark Hartford
DMZ Vet
1966-1967

Ward Reilly
May 21, 2007
Greetings from Ward Reilly, SE contact for VVAW, and an Army infantry vet. (71-74)

Besides wearing my regular dog tags (one in each boot), I wore another one around my neck that had "FTA" carved into it. The FTA stood for "Fuck The Army". It was a play on the "official" FTA, being "Fun, Travel, and Adventure", and/or "Flying To America." You must remember that the military was in collapse at the time I was in, as the war in Vietnam was slowly ending... we were in rebellion, and I was part of a GI resistance to the war. So, my tidbit of a dogtag story. Attached is a photo of that tag, which I still have. The small book in the photo is my army-period address book.

Peace from Ward, Baton Rouge, La.
Gunner, First Infantry Division

Patricia Keefe (Patricia E. Keefe-Miyaji) – Questionnaire

Where on your body did you wear your Dog Tags?
Around my neck because I was in the Republic of Vietnam at the time and didn't want to be an Unknown soldier, it was bad enough for me, a girl, to have been over there but to have been Unknown would have been a tragedy to my family and my memory.

How did you feel about your Dog Tags during your service?
Just another thing to wear for my uniform.

How did you feel about your Dog Tags after you got out of the service?
They have been lost and they are something that I wish I could find. They were a treasured possession of mine.

I had them on my keychain for years and one day a gentleman asked me if my husband or son gave me their dogtags, and I said no, they are mine and he looked at me horrified and asked me if I was a WAC. I said yes and proud of it too. He was mortified and said they are all lesbians and walked away, so I called him back and asked him why he had said that. Did he get spurned by a woman in the military? Was his wife or daughter in the military? He turned red as a beet and then he laughed, no he said, not to any of those things, it was just what his Sargeant told him in boot camp and he never investigated to make sure he was telling the truth. He said he was at Ft. McClellan, AL for boot camp and I understood. I did boot at Ft. McClellan and we were told similar stories about the boys in boot, by our Sargeants. All that over a pair of dogtags. LOL

Also, I wore a dogtag to the Vietnam War that belonged to my father in WWII with the explicit instructions to return it in person to him on my return. I tried to give my son one of mine before he left for Iraq but I did not see him before he left.

Luther Fransen
2/5/2007
I received a call, months ago, from a guy in Vermont or New Hampshire who claimed that he had my dog tag. He proceeded to read the name on it, to include my social security number. He said that he has gone to Viet Nam several times and picks up dog tags on the open market. He

had my address and said that he would mail it to me. He thanked me for my service to my country during the Viet Nam era. I actually received my dog tag in a nice thank you card, again thanking me for my service. The explanation that I received is that (1) I lost my dog tag while over there or (2) extras were made by the military and given/sold to the local market for souvenirs. Mine actually looked used.
Luther Fransen

Vernon Cole
02-06-2007 06:40 pm
Sorry, I can't be of any help. My dog tags are still in Vietnam somewhere with my very first beret. Got drunk at the SFOB on my way back from R&R. Got kicked out of the NCO club. Woke up the next morning in a CIDG baracks next to the Mike Force. The beret and dog tags were gone.

Lonnie Shoultz
One of my more searing memories of Vietnam was when my Platoon Sergeant had us all gather around while he explained the process of lacing your second dog tag through the bottom lace of your boot.

USSYorktown.com
From an e-mail…
you said, "the human being who wears it within a huge and faceless organization. The armed forces demand obedience, commitment, and duty to a higher cause"

but the truth is; We saw our military service in a much smaller sphere. We worked with a small group of men and they became our brothers. We would do anything for our brothers, including give our lives to protect them. The Navy might have been huge and faceless but not your band of brothers. The armed forces may have demanded "duty to a higher cause" but we always thought of our friends. You might look at the USS Yorktown and see a giant deadly warship, but I looked at it as my home, where my brother, Phil, Kraig, Stretch, my older brothers Danny, Chief Relleve, Chief Herry and Lt. Jackson lived with me. This is the essense of military service-we love our brothers. We tolerate the Navy.

I put your email onto the forum page of USSYorktown.com

I remember my dog tag given to me in boot camp at Great Lakes Naval Training Center in Illinois. I felt like I was really part of the Navy and while I didn't "love" the Navy, I came to love it decades after I was out and remember all the commeraderie and great adventures (two tours in Vietnam coastal waters, picking up the first astronauts to travel to the Moon, NATO deployment in the North Atlantic searching for USSR submarines, etc.)

When I got my dog tags, there is actually one on the big chain and then a smaller chain and a duplicate there. Apparently if I was killed, they would have gone to different places.
I took the corner of one and scratched into the surface of the other, "MARGIE". I was 17 years old. She was 15 years and she was the girl I left behind in Detroit, Michigan. "Margie and Dan" didn't survive my year in the far east but I wore that dog tag with her name on it for the next 3 years because she was the world I left behind-the USA. I spent nearly 3 years overseas and whenever anyone talks about the Smothers Brothers, or some hit song from 1966 to 1970 I just smile and am completely ignorant of it. I missed all of American culture for those years as I was overseas on an American warship.
My piece of the United States, the women I left behind and the life I would return to was symbolized by my dog tag around my neck and next to my heart. (by the way, those things were VERY cold in the morning against your chest. Also, when they clanked together they were annoying at the least and could in fact be a danger out in combat. Most sailors put tape around them or had black plastic frames they put around them to remedy this.)
ussyorktown@xxxxxxxx.xxx>
Tuesday, February 27, 2007 11:46 am
Re: dogtag on USS Yorktown sailor

Semper Fi
Grunts are a superstitious lot, and I still am. In Nam we had one dog tag around our neck and one in our boot laces. This was because we suffered so many casualties from booby traps in Quang Nam province, where I mostly operated in "I" Corps. We had a lot of loss of limb injuries, many feet and legs. We figured it was easier to identify us if the worst happened. A good friend of mine tripped a 105 artillery shell and proved that it was a good policy. To this day, I still carry my two dog tags, and I

carry them separately. One is on my key chain and one is on my wife's key chain. Before I retired from the Fire Department, I carried one in my helmet and one on my bunker coat, along with my accountability tag. In Nam, I carried my P-38 on my dog tag chain and I still have it and carry it on my key chain. My most prized possession is my zippo lighter that has accompanied me since my arrival in Nam and still resides in my pocket. It still works, although I no longer smoke, and I still remember when we would refuse to light it up three times, only two. The third light was considered a sniper check and you were asking for it. Yes, we were a superstitious lot and I have to admit, I still am.

Semper Fi

03mfox2/1

Rodetripn@xxxxx.xxx,

2/14/2007

The nastiest safety photo I remember and I think it was in "Mech", showed the dangers of wearing a wedding band while working on aircraft. Apparently this guy slipped off the plane he was working on, the ring caught a fastener or some other protrusion, and neatly ripped all of the skin and muscle off of his ring finger, leaving nothing but bone -- the medical term is "de-gloving". I had two friends who had lost fingers because of rings and had learned long ago to wear my wedding band on my dog tag chain when I was around aircraft -- either maintaining or flyinginthem.

Regards,

Rode

Peter Commons

Dear Ginger,

I assume you want to use the part about me putting my wedding band on my dog tag chain, not the gruesome de-gloving part. I think it was relatively common for people to put rings on their dog tag chains, especially those working on electronics or mechanical stuff.

Just a little background on me... I was in the US Navy from 1977-1999. I was an Aviation Warfare Systems Operator (AW).... basically an airborne sonar and radar operator. For the first eight years I was a helicopter crewman and rescue swimmer. After that I was an instructor, then stationed in Iceland at an antisubmarine warfare command center, and finished out my career aboard an aircraft carrier.

Kind of an interesting coincidence. The other day my 13 year old was rummaging through boxes of stuff and found my dog tags. Of course he was fascinated by them. Now they are in the desk drawer right next to my keyboard. They bring back a lot of memories... some good, some bad.
Sincerely,
Peter Commons

Horace W Coleman
This is a different kind of dog tag story.

When I was having mine done everything was going smoothly until the question about religion was asked.

"Atheist" I said. Baptists were kind of short on theology at the time and I'd been force feed dogma ("Believe this because I say so!" and hectored into going to church and being baptized.
To me it was like being told to join up and sign on before I had an understanding of what this "religion" thing was all about. I wasn't a Doubting Thomas as much as an Inquiring Thomas. I'd see people doing the same dance steps when the Holy Ghost hit them on Sunday morning as they did on Saturday night. And, some of the biggest sinners seemed to be right in there with there with the biggest shouters. Plus, I never liked the story of the Prodigal Son ended. The one who was steady got no recognition at all.

One of my grandmothers was Catholic, as was the cousin the same age as me that she was raising. I used to read all the comic books he had about the lives of the saints. Catholics had a better rap but the only black saint they had at the time was Saint Martin de Porres--and he seemed kind of wimpy.

I didn't see much sense in joining a group where I didn't have much chance of reaching the top of the heap. Especially one about something as serious and important as God and eternity.

That didn't stop me from asking my Grandmother for a Crucifix that I wore to Nam. And lost.

Heaven always seemed to be an eternal drag to me, though. I'd know what to do in hell: Raise hell trying to overthrow the Devil. Didn't see why that couldn't done--the VC had taught me that if you took your losses and kept punching you always hands a chance.

My dog tags ended up saying "No religious preference"--which was true. Later on I refined that to what God was everything, every where, all at once that ever is, was and would be and how it all fit together and worked. Haven't gotten all the details on that--which doesn't bother me. If I did know, you know who I'd be.

I didn't need no stinking batches--or dog tags. Who ever was going to remember me was going to remember me and the tags really weren't going to confirm my death any way. About all dog tags could do for me was to save time for some medic, nurse or doctor as to whether I took high test, regular, unleaded or diesel.

God is what God is and does what God does and I get to deal with it. Seems like people are more worried about what your interpretation is and your practices are than God is.

By the time I'd left Nam, I'd finished breaking at least nine commandments. But if God was just I still had a chance. And any way, "God" has the whole universe to deal with and already knows who and what I am, supposedly. Which can't be all that much, in the ultimate scheme of things?

Believe, repent and be baptized seemed like too much of an easy cop out. No point in fearing that. Respect and enjoy the trip but don't fear. Scared or uncertain is okay, though. Why bull shit yourself or try to fool God?

Most folks can't even jive the Devil or time and God's all that and more. We'll just have to die and find out what the real deal is--maybe. I hear they've closed limbo--or was it purgatory? Die and find that out too, I guess. Just be cool doing it. By the time you figure it all out, it don't mean nothing--or at least not much.
Horace W Coleman, 22 May 07

James R. Jarrett

I was attending an NCO Combat Leadership School at Ft. Gulick, Canal Zone in October 1972 while assigned to the 8th Special Forces Group and the first day during inspection, it was pointed out to me that my dog tags did not meet current regulation, i.e. SSN instead of RA service number. I received demerits for this failure. There was to be another inspection right after lunch as there were two inspections each day of the 3 week course. We were not allowed to leave the training area. I had a buddy meet me at the fence during lunch and he went and had new tags made for me and returned before the afternoon inspection. Needless to say the cadre was surprised and impressed. I was honor graduate and it was that incident of initiative that broke the tie between myself and one other young sergeant. Added my P-38 to it.

James R. Jarrett, Feb 5, 2007

William Leondus Hutchison Jr, B Co, 1st Bn, 38th Inf Regt
June 4 2007
Veteran Questionnaire
Where were you first issued your Dog Tags?   Ft. Benning Ga

Did you purchased more than one set?   No

Did you wear them when you were off duty?   Yes

Did you add anything to your Dog Tag or its chain, while in the service?
Yes

If so, why did you add to it?   I added a rubber band to keep them from
making noise.

What did you add to it?   Also was given a red medical tag to show my
penicillin allergy

Where on your body did you wear your Dog Tags?
Reason for wearing them where you did. Neck and one inside my right
right boot. Everyone had to wear them around the neck as stated in basic
training.

How did you feel about your Dog Tags during your service?
I hated the thought of my family having another M.I.A. I always checked
and rechecked my tags out in the field.

How did you feel about your Dog Tags after you got out of the service?
I feel great about them and have one hanging on the wall over my
training platoon photo and the other on my key chain.

Do you have any special story about your Dog Tags?
Nothing really besides learning how to sharping the bottom of my med
tag and then using it to open MRE boxes :)
Where do you keep your Dog Tags?
one hanging on the wall over my training platoon photo and the other on
my key chain.

Anything else you would like to share.
Someday in the future, someone is going to find my uncle dogtag in New
Guinea. Even if they don't find his remains or the remains of the other 19
crew and passengers, I can hold the tag and know deep down in my heart

that it was near his.
Thank you,
William Leondus Hutchison Jr.

Iraq/Afghanistan

The first loss in Operation Iraqi Freedom
From President George W. Bush's Memorial Day Address to the Nation
Arlington National Cemetery, 26 May 2003:
Almost seven weeks ago, an Army Ranger, Captain Russell
Rippetoe was laid to rest in Section 60. Captian Rippetoe's father, Joe, a
retired Lieutenant Colonel, gave a farewell salute at the grave of his only
son. Russell Rippetoe served with distinction in Operation Iraqi
Freedom, earning both the Bronze Star and the Purple Heart.
On the back of his dog tag were engraved these words, from the
book of Joshua, "Have not I commanded thee? Be strong and of good
courage. Be not afraid, neither be thou dismayed, for the Lord thy God is
with thee." This faithful Army captain has joined a noble company of
service and sacrifice gathered row by row. These men and women were
strong and courageous and not dismayed. And we pray they have found
their peace in the arms of God.

PVC David J. Bentz III (DJ),   KIA 6/20/07
Thursday, August 09, 2007 10:32 am
Hello,
We are submitting my daughter's essay about her Brave Courageous
Brother **PVC David J. Bentz III (DJ),**   KIA 6/20/07
I am his mother and while we are still grieving heavily...my brother had
sent this site to us and since his sister Elle (16) had already did this I
thought it most fitting and personal about her brother's dogtag. The
picture of my son on the phone is his last day in America...he is on the
phone with his sister Elle. God Bless our
Soldier Angel and all the troops.
Thank you -
Kimberly Geonnotti

Name of Dog Tag Owner   **PFC David J. Bentz III (DJ)**
Name of Family   Kimberly Geonnotti (mother) and Elle Bentz (sister)
Whose Dog Tags do you have?   Name:_PFC David J. Bentz III (DJ)
*Relationship:___*Brother
Under what circumstances did you receive the Dog Tags?
Just before he deployed – about a month before deployment date
5/19/07.

Where do you keep them?   Around my neck
Do you know how the family member felt about the Dog Tags?
My brother gave them to my mother and I and his close friends so that
we all could wear them and be proud.

What are your feelings and thoughts concerning the Dog Tags?
"My brother passed away KIA on 6/20/07. I had written this essay soon
after receiving my dog tag from my brother DJ but before he went to
Heaven. God Bless Him and I miss him terribly.

   "David John Bentz III, that's my brother's name. I don't see him
everyday, not even once a week, more like a couple times a year if I'm
lucky. But I feel him. Not physically feeling him, but feeling his name.
Little punched out letters on a squarish metal necklace. This necklace,
his dog tag, is the most important thing to me. Everytime I feel it
dangling off my neck, or hearing the sound it makes when it squeezes
through the bumps on my chain, it reminds me of him, and how much I
miss him.
   A dog tag is such a small thing, but it represents something so
much bigger, my love for him. Just as we were kids, playing with toys
and sharing our ninja turtle t-shirts. But through it all I knew he would
one day get out of the loop and he proved it to me the moment he gave
me his dog tag. He didn't only prove how much I loved him, but how I
love his strength, his courage, his will to go on. He proved it to himself,
not just me that he could be the man he always wanted to be. There was
never a doubt in my mind that he couldn't be that person.
   Anyway, back to the dog tag. I don't wear it everyday. I just
never know how I'll be feeling that day. If I'm in a depressed mood and
I look at it, it will only make me break down and cry. My brother will
be leaving me soon for a year and a half, but his presence will always be
with me. Just knowing that I have touched something he touched,
smelled something he smelled, gives me the strength to believe. Believe
in just one more day, one more week, one more month, one more year. I
never imagined something so small could be such a big support system
in my life.

I love you DJ.
Proud Soldier's Sister
Gabrielle Bentz,   8-8-07

PFC David Bentz with sister Gabrielle Bentz

Kemaphoom A. Chanawongse, Corporal, United States Marine Corps
DOD ANNOUNCES CHANGE IN MARINE CASUALTY STATUS
The Department of Defense announced today that Marine Corporal
Kemaphoom A. Chanawongse, 22, of Waterford, Conn. was killed in
action during operations on the outskirts of An Nasiriyah on March 23.
He had previously been listed as Duty Status Whereabouts Unknown
(DUSTWUN). Chanawongse was assigned to 2nd Assault Amphibian
Battalion, 2nd Marine Division, Camp Lejeune, N.C.

Excerpt…
"If he knew that he would pass away, and if he had a choice — (this) is
his choice, I know that," his mother, Tan Patchem, said after the service.
Struggling to keep her voice steady, her son's dog tags still dangling
from her neck, Patchem said "everyone knows what Ahn is like and
everyone is very proud of him. Everyone has a feeling that, other than
sadness — and sadness is still there — but more than sadness, we're
proud."

David Mahlenbrock

Requested to share, from the following:
http://www.blackfive.net/main/2004/12/warriors_last_r.html

Specialist David Mahlenbrock was killed by an IED on December 3rd in Kirkuk, Iraq. I received this email via <u>Soldier's Angels</u>. It's from David's Squad in Bravo, 65th Engineers and they are forwarding a request from David. It appears that David had a special letter sent to his squad in the event of his death.

Dear 1st Squad,

If you're reading this, then I've died for our country. I just hope it wasn't for nothing.

After the IED went off yesterday, I wanted to write this in case something happens to me. There are a few more letters that I'd like you to give my wife and family.

I'd like to have a military funeral, but, if you can work please make sure that Toby Keith's "American Soldier" is played at the ceremony in addition to the bagpipes. If they won't let it happen, that's ok, thanks for trying…....

I know that all the belongings I have here will go to Melissa, but there are a few more things I'd like for you guys to make sure she gets. I have a dog tag w/ our picture on it along w/ some pictures and an American flag in my left breast pocket. There is also a can that says "Son" on it that Melissa's parents gave me that I'd like for them to have, and that angel stone should go to her grandma and grandpa Snow.

Now if I died w/ blue eyes (one blew that way and one blew the other way) and there's nothing really left of me, that's ok, I know you meant well.

Alright, enough with the dead guy's last request, there's a lot of thank you's I wanna say to you fellas……

Specialist David Mahlenbrock will be laid to rest at Arlington National Cemetary on Wednesday, December 15th at 10AM EST.

Leonard Mallonee Cowherd III, Second Lieutenant, United States Army WS RELEASE from the United States Department of Defense No. 468-04

May 17, 2004

Second Lieutenant Leonard M. Cowherd, 22, of Culpeper, Virginia, died May 16, 2004, in Karbala, Iraq, when he received sniper and rocket propelled grenade fire while securing a building near the Mukhayam Mosque. Cowherd was assigned to Company C, 1st Battalion, 37th Armor Regiment, 1st Armored Division, Friedberg, Germany.

Excerpt...
E-mail brings the war to the dorms. The night before the battle for Fallujah began, senior Mark Erwin got a message from his brother, Lt. Mike Erwin, West Point '02: "Markie -- I will be carrying your cadet picture in my right breast pocket with my prayer to St. Michael, dog tags and St. Michael's medal," the big brother wrote. "If by some chance something happens to me, you're the voice to the family."

Clay Patrick Farr, Specialist, United States Army
New Release from the United States Department of Defense

The Department of Defense announced today the death of two soldiers who were supporting Operation Iraqi Freedom. They died in Baghdad, Iraq on February 26, 2006, when an improvised explosive device detonated near their HMMWV during patrol operations. Both soldiers were assigned to the 1st Squadron, 71st Cavalry, 1st Brigade Combat Team, 10th Mountain Division of Fort Drum, New York

Farr, 21, of Bakersfield, California, died February 26, 2006, when a roadside bomb detonated near his Humvee during a patrol in Baghdad. Specialist Joshua U. Humble, 21, of Appleton, Maine, was also killed.
Excerpt...
Farr's mother said he was destined for the military. "We knew from an early age that he would be in the service," she said. "He was born with dog tags on."
In kindergarten, camouflage was his favorite color -- until his teacher told him it wasn't a color. In elementary school, he dressed as a soldier for Halloween with face paint from an Army supply store. Even as a youngster, Clay Farr seemed destined for the military life, his father said. In school, he liked to color everything in camouflage patterns.

"Clay was all Army from the time he was small," his father said, recalling a photograph of his then-4-year-old son wearing a camouflage ball cap at an air show. "That's when the Army got him."

Jimmy Lee Shelton
Corporal, United States Army
News Release from the United States Department of Defense
No. 1270-05
December 8, 2005

Corporal Jimmy L. Shelton, 21, of Lehigh Acres, Florida, died in Bayji, Iraq on December 3, 2005, when his forward operating base was attacked by enemy forces using mortars. Shelton was assigned to the 1st Squadron, 33rd Cavalry Regiment, 3rd Brigade Combat Team, 101st Airborne Division, Fort Campbell, Kentucky.
The Shelton's are clinging to vivid memories, trying to keep their son's spirit alive.

Excerpt...
Both parents are keeping a piece of Shelton next to their heart, both wear his dog tags. "I told him I'd take it off when he was home, done for good, I'll never take it off," says Burgess. The Shelton's say the Army was not only what Jimmy died for, but what he lived for.

We are stationed at Fort Hood and since my husband deployed to Iraq the first time, on my keys I carry a dogtag that says:

SGT Hardt
My Friend
My Husband
My Soldier
My Hero

It's a little worn as he is about to head out on his third deployment.
 Korin Hardt
www.armybloggerwife.blogspot.com

Min Hee (Andy) Kim, Lance Corporal, United States Marine Corps
News Release from the United States Department of Defense
No. 1113-06
November 02, 2006

Lance Corporal Minhee Kim, 20, of Ann Arbor, Michigan, died November 1, 2006, while conducting combat operations in Al Anbar province, Iraq. He was assigned to Marine Forces Reserve's 1st Battalion, 24th Marine Regiment, 4th Marine Division, Lansing, Mich.

Excerpt...
As she spoke, Mi Hea held the three possessions the Marines had sent in a red velvet pouch: a crucifix, his dog tags and a Timex watch, still ticking on Iraqi time. Someone suggested that she place the crucifix in the casket with Andy, but Mi Hea knew he would have wanted her to keep it. "I think Andy gave it as a gift," she said.

Ken Ballard
Karen Meredith, mother of **Ken Ballard**

Taken from profile:
On May 29, 2004, I was living what I thought was an ordinary life. I had raised my only child on my own and I was enjoying watching him make his way through this world successfully and happily. On May 30, 2004, Ken was killed in a war that I never supported brought to this country by an administration I never supported. While many people say that casualties for have been relatively low, any number more than zero was too many for this war. Very few people have actually met a Gold Star Mom. It is important that people know what it feels like to be in my situation. I know not all Gold Star Moms feel as I do, I speak for myself, no one else. You cannot or do not want to imagine the process that the military goes through when a soldier is killed in combat, or any other situation. This is not a journey that any family should have to make. Welcome to my world.

Excerpt from an e-mail: March 13, 2007, kensmomkm@xxxxx.xxx
When my son's body was returned to me, they gave me what was on his body when he was killed; his belt-buckle, his spurs (Cavalry), and his dogtags. I immediately put them on and have not removed them for

anything; not for airport security, not for a mammogram. They stay close to my heart where my son will always be.

Uday Singh, Specialist, United States Army
News Release from the United States Department of Defense

The soldier from C Company, 1st Battalion, 34th Armored Regiment, 1st Infantry Division, based at Fort Riley, Kansas, was in the lead Humvee of a three-vehicle patrol that was ambushed December 1, 2003, near Habbaniyah, about 65 miles west of Baghdad.

Of the 496 U.S. troops killed in Iraq through last week, Singh was the 44th buried in Arlington, and the first Indian national soldier is gone Suburban Sikh, 21, is killed while fighting for U.S. in Iraq.

Excerpt...
   Legal immigrants now only need to serve in the military before applying for citizenship, he explained.
   "It means becoming a citizen five years quicker if you are wearing the uniform," Kirk said.
   History shows legal immigrants have been an important part of military defenses for more than 200 years.
   "Probably the classic experience is when the Union army met Irish immigrant boats in New York and recruited young Irishmen stepping off the boat into the Union army," Kirk said.

His death has a special resonance for Hardeep Singh, who struggles to make his ethnic identity clear to other Americans even though he's the fourth generation of Sikhs to settle in the United States.

"My dog tags still say 'other,'" he said. "Some people think I'm Muslim. Sometimes I get Spanish. I tell the other soldiers: 'Remember, I'm Indian. I'm brown. Don't shoot me.' "

Sent to me by Pat Donahue
This is a photo taken by my BCT photo journalist who accompanied an airborne rifle company up on top of a mountain to secure and help recover the crash site of a MH47 shot down in June 2005.

On June 28, 2005 in support of Operation RED WINGS, an MH-47 Chinook helicopter, with eight SEALs and eight Army Night Stalkers aboard, was sent is as part of an extraction mission to pull out four SEALs who were in a firefight (3 of the SEALs in the firefight were eventually KIA with one receiving he MOH in that action). The MH 47 was shot down by an RPG as it was attempting to fast rope in the SEAL Team. All aboard were KIA.

This scorched Army Ethos Dog Tag recovered by C/2-504 paratroopers at the crash site belonged to one of the following 8 Army KIA on that the MH47 from 3/160th SOAR and the 160th SOAR:

Maj. Stephen C. Reich, 34, of Washington Depot, Conn.
Chief Warrant Officer 4 Chris J. Scherkenbach, 40, of Jacksonville, Fla.
Chief Warrant Officer 3 Corey J. Goodnature, 35, of Clarks Grove, Minn.
Sgt. 1st Class Marcus V. Muralles, 33, of Shelbyville, Ind.
Sgt. 1st Class Michael L. Russell, 31, of Stafford, Va.
Staff Sgt. Shamus O. Goare, 29, of Danville, Ohio.
Sgt. Kip A. Jacoby, 21, of Pompano Beach, Fla.
An eighth Soldier, Master Sgt. James W. Ponder III, 36, of Franklin, Tn. was also part of the aircrew. Ponder was assigned to the 160th SOAR at Fort Campbell, Ky.

We did not share this photo before because it was too painful and out of respect of the special operators killed that day.

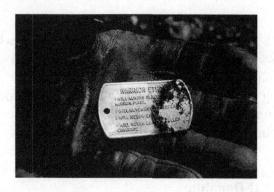

This is a very powerful image especially given the Night Stalkers motto: Night Stalkers Never Quit.

V/R
Pat
"Rock of the Marne"
BG Patrick J. Donahue II
DCG Maneuver, 3ID

Miscellaneous

Timothy L. Francis

When I deployed to Iraq last year, my girlfriend asked me what the dog tag stamp "norelpref" meant. She thought it meant something like "Norel Preferred" and was it some sort of medicine?

I got a laugh out of that.

v/r Dr. Timothy L. Francis
Historian
Naval Historical Center
Naval Warfare Division
Washington Navy Yard, DC 20374-5060

Dog Tag Bracelet

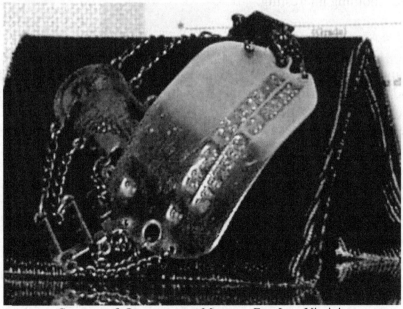

Courtesy of Quartermaster Museum, Fort Lee, Virginia

Major Ricardo (Rick) Turner
Where were you first issued your Dog Tags?
 Fort Monmouth, NJ

Where on your body do you wear your Dog Tags?
 When I'm performing a tactical mission, I loop the chain through one of my belt loops and keep my tags in my back pocket. When performing a tactical mission, I wear them around my neck.

Why do you wear your Dog Tags in this spot?
 I would prefer to always wear them around my neck, but they actually irritate my skin. So, I normally keep them in my pocket to avoid the irritation.

Have you added anything to your chain, if so, how did you come about adding to it?
 One of the things I added was an attempt to prevent skin irritation (unsuccessful). Another was a gift from a chaplain friend of mine before my first deployment. The third is simply a medical identification badge…nothing interesting.

What did you add?
 I've added black, rubber silencers to prevent the tags from making noise when I walk. I also have a Saint Michael medallion that a friend gave me before my first deployment. Lastly, I have a red medical ID tag that identifies me as a G6PD blood deficiency (I'm actually not quite sure what that means).

How do you feel about your Dog Tags?
 Mine are a part of me…they're part of my daily rhythm when I'm preparing for duty in the morning. They are actually the last thing I put on in the morning…and they serve as a sort of mental confirmation that I'm ready for the day.

Do you feel any different about them now, since you were first issued them?
 No, I've always been proud of them and I'm just as proud of them now as I was when I was first issued them.

My dog tags are my original dog tags that I was issued on July 17, 1998…they are a little banged up…and everywhere the Army has sent me, they've gone too.

315th Airlift Wing Public Affairs

"When I deployed, my 15-year-old son gave me a dog tag with his name on it. I carry it everywhere I go," said Captain Cavellos as he rejoined the Charleston team of aerial porters.

Quote:
It's interesting what people hang with those tags and make them more personal.

A crucifix hangs with mine.
Elemanski

Trench Art

Courtesy of the Texas Military Forces Museum, Austin Texas

Kathy McDowell
A collection of e-mails combined from Kathy McDowell

Ginger,

Thanks for the info, I would love to show them to you sometime. What is interesting info, it really never caught my interest until I saw these all together, they belong to my Dad, Father in law, my husband's great uncle and my husband of course but I have them all on a single dog tag chain and noticed the difference. Kind of cool all together like that!

I know that my own dad had really mixed feelings about his service in Vietnam but the pride in his service overall never went away (he is deceased). His dog tags were hanging from the corner of a picture frame in his room. He also had a flag and his black and white photo in his dress uniform(or fancy pants!) I actually have service photos, all black and white of my Dad, Father in-law (deceased) and at least one of my husband's two great uncles who served in the Army AND their tags, when my mother in law passed away about two months ago, we had to go clean out her "packrat" house and fast but I couldn't believe the treasure we found, among other things, LOL. I will gather it up and you let me know what do to with it, I am fascinated by this dog tag thing and my interest was really sparked when I held that handful and the fact that the rest of my husband's family said, oh you have all of that military stuff, I felt really fortunate…

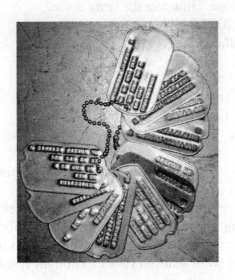

Jimley815

I have too many dog tags-
I try to put as many different religions on them as I can, and then wear those that day…If I feel somewhat serene I wear my buddhist tags- If I feel a little ornery, I wear my Branch davidian dog tags.
Granted- this is only while in country-If I was in Sunny SW Asia I wear my good old Roman Catholic tags
Jimley815

No Name

When I see/seen/saw mother's and wives holding/clutching some dog tags…It reminds me of how folks used to keep a picture in a Locket to remember…and this former Marine has to turn his head, so that no one will see my wet eyes. That's what I think about Dog Tags.

No Name

Dog tags. Some times THAT is all that comes home to the family of a servicemember. Those two small metal tags are the last thing they have left to hold onto. Ive stood there at memorial services and tryed not to shed tears for the lose. However the tears come.

Mon 12 February 2007 04:38

Shared with no name

Bryan Dickerson [mailto:bd1315@xxxxx.xxx]

Sent: Wednesday, January 16, 2008 09:49 AM

Subject: Dog Tags - Navy Guy

Hi Ginger,

Found your post on the Flight Deck over at Neptunus Lex's site. Interesting thing you are doing.

I was a Navy Pilot from 87-07. I always kept a tag in my boot laces. Started doing it in flight school when I heard about a crash of a jet with two guys in it. Seems the guys were pretty torn up and it was hard to tell whose parts were whose (yuck). Thought it might help if ever I was involved in a mid-air.

To this day, I keep a tag in the laces of my running shoes. When I run in the summer, I usually only wear running shorts and a tee shirt. Nowhere to keep ID. If I ever get pummeled by a car (or a plane falling from the sky after a mid-air), I've got some ID with me.

Good luck with your project.

Bryan

Brigadier General Elizabeth P. Hoisington

"BG Hoisington led the Women's Army Corps through a period of dramatic change in the 1960s and '70s and was one of the first two women in the U.S. military promoted to the rank of Brigadier General.

At a Pentagon ceremony on June 11, 1970, Hoisington and Anna Mae Hays of the Army Nurse Corps became the first two women in the United States to have a brigadier general's star pinned on their shoulders. She is also the sister to an older brother, Perry Hoisington, who was a Major General in the Air Force, making them the country's first brother and sister generals.

Hoisington, who came from a military family, enlisted in the old Women's Army Auxiliary Corps in 1942. In 1966, during a period when the role of women was changing as much in the military as in society at large, she was named director of the Women's Army Corps.

Elizabeth Paschel Hoisington was born November 3, 1918, in Newton, Kansas. Her grandfather had helped found the Kansas Army National Guard, and her father was an Army Colonel and a marksman.

When the women's corps was established in 1942, she was eager to enlist. "The minute she heard about the WAC, she wanted to join," said her sister, Nancy Smith of Annandale, Va. "She went in as a private and came out as a general." [98]

99

100

Patriot Guard Riders

Courtesy of Tanna Toney

Michael J. Ulekowski

I currently have the dog tag of my Great Grandfather, who used them during World War I. My father, who served in the Army for 20 years, still uses his as part of his key chain. I use mine to store my USB Stick Drive to keep it from getting lost. Still have mine from my uniform, but now I carry them around because my stick drive is attached to them, and the original P-38.

Michael J. Ulekowski *Date*   5 February 2007

Name of Dog Tag Owner: **SSG Sandra Joy Johnson**

Where were you first issued your Dog Tags? At Basic Training at Fort Jackson, South Carolina

How do you feel about your Dog Tags? I feel that they are an important symbol of the American military. People instantly know that you are a soldier if they see that chain around your neck.

Do you have any special story(ies) about your Dog Tags? I have a separate chain with 3 of my male family member's dog tags on them. One dog is from my maternal grandfather, who served in WWII and Korea with the Marine Reserves, the second one is from my paternal grandfather, who served with the Navy in WWII, and the third one is from my father, who served in the Navy in the 1970's. I took them with me when I deployed to Iraq in June 2009. They are my lucky charms. I would carry the three dog tags in my pocket on a chain in my blouse pocket every mission. Then I would say a little prayer to my deceased grandfather, the Marine, to watch out for my squad and I. I like to think that he is in a section of heaven reserved for warriors, like Valhalla, and that he and his buddies protected us.

Anything else you would like to share: Being that a soldier wears their dog tags on a daily basis, they are a deeply personal item and it is an honor if they give or pass down a set to someone.
SSG Sandra Joy Johnson, MN Army National Guard
Date: 15 January 2013

Name of Dog Tag Owner: Douglas M.F. Womack
Where were you first issued your Dog Tags? In Germany as a Military Dependant. After I enlisted in April of 1969, I was issued Dog Tags while in Basic Combat Training at Fort Polk, Louisiana.

What did you add to it? An antique Mother of Pearl ring that broke when I caught it on a bolt on the top of the vertical stabilizer of a UH-1H helicopter. With the broken band flattened out, the ring formed a cross.

Why did you add to it? To remind me of home and hang on to a keepsake.

Where on your body did you wear your Dog Tags? In Basic Training and Flight School, I wore them on a chain around my neck. Later, while serving in the 23rd Infantry Division (American), I was required to wear them in my boots as well.

Reason for wearing them where you did. Army requirement

How did you feel about your Dog Tags during your service? They were a part of my uniform and equipment.

How did you feel about your Dog Tags after you got out of the service? They reminded me of my life in the military.

Do you have any special story about your Dog Tags? Yes
The Americal Division required its soldiers to wear dog tags in their boots because of the high number of limbs lost to land mines. Shortly after being required to wear dog tags in my boots, it occurred to me that there was no medical technology to reattach limbs. In discussing the matter with my fellow soldiers, and with a nod to the "gallows" humor that helped us survive our tours in Vietnam, like a good Warrant Officer, I had additional dog tags made up for my boots. They read... "SEE OTHER BOOT."

I also lost one of the tags from my neck. I think the addition of the broken ring caused the chain to fail. While exploring the "Tours Of Peace" website, I learned my dog tag had been recovered in Vietnam. After confirming my identity with my Social Security Number, 35 years after it was lost, they mailed my dog tag to me. The return of the tag was published in their 2006 Summer Newsletter on page 2.

Where do you keep your Dog Tags? There is a set hanging from my dresser in my bedroom and another set on a statue, a figure of a pilot in helmet and flight suit, given to me by my brother Terry, a Marine Gunnery Sergeant.
Doug Womack, Grasonville, MD
    29 August 2009

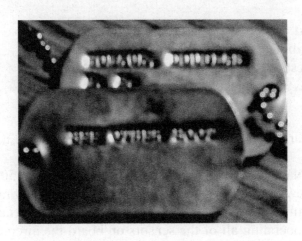

Jason Reid - Questionnaire
June 8, 2007

Whose Dog Tags do you have?   Haywood Reid

Relationship: Grandfather

Under what circumstances did you receive the Dog Tags?
I received them after he passed away

Where do you keep them?
Around my neck

What stories do you remember about your family member wearing them?
No stories unfortunately, he passed when I was very young.
What are your feelings and thoughts concerning the Dog Tags?
They are very special to me, they are the only thing I have of his.
JasonReid
Owner/Artist
Mob Boss Artworks

Tim Kindred
[mailto:vze3zbmv@xxxxxx.xxx]
Sent: Wednesday, January 16, 2008 12:30 AM
Subject:: Navy Dog tags.....

Hello,

I'll just share my own thoughts with you, and you can use what you like.

I was a Navy Aircrewman, and earned a little over 5000 hours of combat aircrew time, mostly in P-3 Orion sub hunters. My rate was AW, which at the time stood for "Aviation Anti-Submarine Warfare Operator" My job was operating all of the sensors on board the aircraft, analyzing the data, and reporting it to the Tacco, or tactical Commander onboard. When I left, it was as a Petty Officer First Class, or AW1.

Anyway, regarding my dog tags, I remember the feeling of first being issued them in boot camp in San Diego in 1976. It was a bonding moment for me, as my father, uncle and cousin had also been Navy men, my father being a Hospital Corpsman attached to the Marines in WWII. It was the point where I had taken my turn in line alongside them, and although I had yet to prove anything ability-wise, it was indeed a shared experience.

When I reached the fleet, and was assigned to a training squadron, I did add to things with my tags. First, I added a P-38 can opener to them. I'd had one for years before, and new the value of that little item as both opener and multi-tool. Second, I removed one of my tags from the chain and attached it to my left flight boot, lachapter fivecing it in above the tongue and under the laces. Many aircrews did this as well. The reason was simple. It was an extra means of identification in case we went down somewhere. We all knew what happened to the human body in a large aircraft accident. Very few bodies remain intact. I don't mean to be so graphic, but it was a simple common sense move to help identify remains.

In a sense, it's like the dark humour we all used to set aside fear. On my flight helmet, I had an arrow made of reflecting tape pointing down, with the words "dig here" on either side. It always got a laugh when someone saw it.

I still have one of my tags. I think that my son when little lost the chain and the one attached to it, but my wife carries the other one in her purse. I don't know why.

Recently, I purchased a replacement set. Since I do a lot of travelling, and have a couple of health issues, I thought it a good idea to start wearing them again in case I couldn't speak for myself, for whatever reason. The tags will also alert the responders to check with the VA, where my medical records are. Who knows if it will help, but it can't hurt.

Trusting that this is of some small assistance, I remain,

Respectfully,
Tim Kindred

Dog Tags from the Collection of Female Commanders,
US Army Women's Museum, Ft. Lee, Virginia that share "Firsts:"

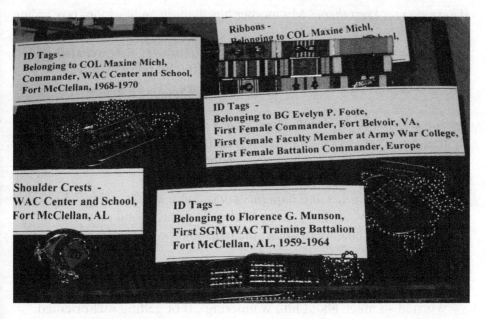

Arnold Welton Sanders

Name of Dog Tag Owner   Jill Sanders Crider
January 21, 2008
Name of Family: Sanders

Whose Dog Tags do you have? Name: Arnold Welton Sanders
Relationship: Father

Under what circumstances did you receive the Dog Tags? Upon his
death in 2003

Where do you keep them? My mother has them in an heirloom box at her
home.
What stories do you remember about your family member wearing them?
My dad wore them all the time, even long after he retired from active
duty and continued as a civil service employee.

Do you know how the family member felt about the Dog Tags?
He treasured them as though they were a badge of honor. I know much
of his identity was tied to his service in the military.

What are your feelings and thoughts concerning the Dog Tags? I
treasure them as well. They always bring back such fond memories of
him every time I take them out of the heirloom box.

Anything else you would like to share:
   When my dad was diagnosed with Alzheimer's disease, my mother
   worried so much about him wandering off or getting mis-oriented.
   He was never one to wear jewelry, so any kind of ID bracelet was
   going to be out of the question. My husband (a Soldier) and my
   sister, a State nursing home ombudsmen, suggested that maybe my
   dad would wear dog tags with his essential information. My husband
   purchased a set and had them engraved, the man never took them
   off! He was buried with them.

Arnold Welton Sanders

Coy Sanders   Paul Sanders   Ova Sanders   Arnold Sanders
Brothers of Arnold Sanders who served in our Armed Forces.

My Heroes Have Always Been...in Uniform

by Jill Sanders Crider (daughter of Arnold Sanders) on Thursday, November 11, 2010 at 12:49pm

As I sit here in my home, having only days ago, welcomed back my husband from Iraq after another combat tour. I am especially thoughtful as we celebrate and remember our Veterans today. Yesterday, I finally got around to scanning and posting photographs of my Dad and his brothers. All combat Soldiers, all enlisted and senior non-commissioned officers, all from a very small town in Kentucky and none of them, that I know of, with more than an 8th grade education. They changed the world.

Between the six of them they gave over 130 years of service beginning in 1936 (one lied about his age and joined the Army when he was 15); all six passed through Ft Knox along the way. One of them earned four Purple Hearts, one was a Korean War POW, held by the Chinese for almost three years; one earned the Silver Star; one had three combat jumps into the Philippines, two earned Combat Infantryman Badges; each received numerous Bronze Stars and Occupation Medals; one taught King Hussein of Jordan how to operate a tank and was a member of the Nuclear Test Platoons of 1953 in the Nevada Desert; one was a reconnaissance scout along the German border for most of WWII; they fought in the jungles of Burma and Viet Nam, the beaches of Anzio and island sands of Corregidor, the deserts of North Africa, the unforgiving mountain passes of Germany and the cold wet valleys of Korea. As a young girl and even into the first years of my marriage, I listened intently to the stories these men rarely told. Those moments were few, and often spoken quietly and I wish more than anything I had asked for more and more ....and more.

When my husband, Jim, was a young Captain attending a school at Fort Benning, he was required to research and write a battle analysis. He spent hours reading and writing and trying to choose which battle to write about. Sensing his query I suggested, "why don't you just ask my Dad? or any of his 5 brothers?" I think for both of us, that moment weighed heavily and we immediately began to see those men in a completely different light more than ever before. For me, in that very moment my father became someone I had never really known before. And my uncles that always played and joked around with us or would say "come here and gimme' some sugar, I haven't seen you in a long time" transformed right before my eyes. My understanding of them changed in my heart too. I had always loved them and looked forward to visits with them. But from that point on, it was different. They were different. From that single moment, whenever I read a book or story about a historical battle in our nation's past, I would think,

"Daddy was right there...Or Uncle Hoover lived through that...." It had changed them and because of it, it had changed me. These men who sat around my mother's kitchen table had saved the world.

Not long ago, we were stationed near Washington, DC. I loved walking the National Mall and taking in the pure meaning and relevance of those few blocks in our nation's capital city. Lincoln, Washington, Roosevelt, the Vietnam Wall, the Korean War Memorial. It is a virtual history book right before your eyes. One Memorial has particular meaning to me. The World War II Memorial is placed near the middle of the Mall and it is... spectacular. And I wish, regrettably, that my father had been able to stand in front of it and see what I see when I have stood before it. He would've been proud and he would've felt like he had something to do with it being there and he would've liked that. No, he would've loved that. I'm so grateful for the people that made sure that it was finally built and for this nation, that he helped keep free, remembered him, his brothers and their friends.

Once while I was visiting the Memorial, I noticed a man standing to the side, alone. We were near each other and as I passed him I quietly said, "Beautiful isn't it?" He replied, "Yes, it is." I spoke again, "Well, thank you." He turned and said, "Don't thank me. Thank my brothers. I was in the Army but I never fought in any battles." I just nodded, smiled and kept walking. I wish I had said, "Thank you for that too....I bet that was just as hard." And I would have meant it just as much. Because as hard as it is to watch my husband continue to deploy, I know that it would be even harder for him to watch his Soldiers, and his friends, go to war without him.

So today, any day really, take a minute to thank a Veteran. Say a prayer of gratitude for them and those still serving today. They wouldn't ask nor expect anything more.

Chapter Four

Modern Day Representations

The Dog Tag has exploded into a representation of everything from their original meaning for dogs to popular icons. The image or representation of this enduring symbol for Military Identification has found its way into the hearts of many who might not even understand the depth of its meaning, except for the basic connotation of identity.

The most well-known icons throughout the ages have been those representing religious objects. All religions have them, and most can be identified by seeing the item that represents their beliefs. It is the connection with identifying objects that the current world lives in; world of getting the message to the consumer and marketing that message the correct way. Religions have always done this without the impersonal definition of marketing.

The age of "netizens" is here to stay. There is a whole world of people who spend hours on their computers, on the *Net*, in a very impersonal way. Our world knows icons as images or applications (apps) representing hundreds of computer graphics. The emoticons and desktop icons are taken for granite and easily passed as meaningless illustration.

A quite popular representation of Dog Tags is used in the movie industry. Famous movies and movie stars have worn them, and our memories remember these images quite easily. Often the reality of the tag is blurred. Heroes, both real and represented as such, wear these tags. They are on movie stars and recording artists. Most have not served in the armed forces, and do not wear them for the same reason.

For the ones that have served, they are too numerous to mention, but I am showing you a few that have a connection to the Dog Tag. Probably the most memorable is the image of John F. Kennedy on a PT boat, shirtless, with his Dog Tags hanging against his chest and a cross hanging with them. His actual Dog Tags are on loan from Sen. And Mrs. Edward Kennedy in the John F. Kennedy Library and Museum

102   103

We have a soldier who became a movie star, Audie Murphy having served with the Third Infantry Division - Rock of the Marne!

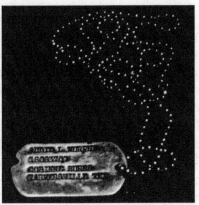

104

His dog tags above are held at the Smithsonian National Museum of American History and were worn by Audie Murphy during combat in Europe. The information on these dog tags includes his name, his serial number, Corrine Burns (a married sister, who he used for his next of kin,) and his home-of-record, Farmersville, Texas. The Audie Murphy / American Cotton Museum, also has a set of Dog Tags from Audie Murphy, but it shows a different serial number on it. It is thought that Audie Murphy received a promotion in the field. He was discharged as an enlisted soldier, and the immediately sworn in as an officer. Thus, he might have been given separate serial numbers for different service terms.

Another well-known man who had a movie made about his life was Alvin York. While there are hundreds of movie stars who have served, this is a soldier who also lived a life worth telling.

105

"For his actions, York was singled out as the greatest individual soldier of the war and when he returned home in 1919 he was wooed by Hollywood, Broadway, and various advertisers who wanted his endorsement of their products. York turned his back on quick and certain fortune in 1919, and went home to Tennessee to resume peacetime life. Largely unknown to most

Americans was the fact that Alvin York returned to America with a single vision. He wanted to provide a practical educational opportunity for the mountain boys and girls of Tennessee. Understanding that to prosper in the modern world an education was necessary, York sought to bring Fentress County into the twentieth century. Thousands of like-minded veterans returned from France with similar sentiments and as a result college enrollments shot up immediately after the war."[106]

There are movies portraying the hanging tags on dozens of actor's chests. John Wayne, Tom Hanks. There are serious War movies, and comedic spoofs. It ranges from The Green Berets to Stripes. There are big budget pictures like Saving Private Ryan and small movies like Saints and Soldiers. The Dog Tags are a common denominator for any rank or service. It stands for the same thing, even though personal thoughts about them may be quite different.

There are numerous movie posters and graphic art designs that show the Dog Tag as part of advertisements and marketing for these and other movies. In the 1950s, school children were taught to "Duck and Cover". This government sponsored program (also discussed in Urban Legend Chapter) bears importance here when discussing the use and connection to Dog Tags. Many schools provided Identification Tags for their students for the same reason soldiers were issued tags – for identification if needed.

Duck and Cover Child Poster

The popular and iconic connection to these tags is worn by many, and used by many. We can see them being worn by such famous people who have never served in the armed services - JLS (a British Boy Band,)

Justin Bieber, Rapper TI, and actor, rapper, and professional wrestler, John Cena. This is not unusual in the music industry, for entertainers of all genres have members who wear Dog Tags with a variety of information imprinted on them. As stated, there are rappers, actors, the famous and the infamous who wear them for whatever reason.

With this said, there are those who have served, are entertainers, and wear their Dog Tags as a remembrance of their previous life. And then there are those who may not have served, but wear Dog Tags to honor and remember those who they represent or sing about to bring awareness to the soldiers situation.

The use of military personnel to tell a story is not new, and it has always been a popular way to reach and entertain all parts of society. The USO is the best known entertainment organization to bring the outside world in to all members deployed. They bring music, laughter, and a touch of home to those deployed in the remotest of places. It is an appreciated service, allowing service members to escape from their own reality even for a moment.

Through the use of humor, cartoons and caricatures have brought the service member a sense of entertainment. Sgt. Rock was a symbol of patriotism during WWII, and he boldly showed his Dog Tags as they hung on his chest. Wolverine of the X-men wears a Canadian Dog Tag that breaks in half like the real ones of many foreign countries. The earlier character of Krypto, Superman's dog, had a Dog Tag with the famous "S" on it in the dog-size version of his master's "S".

The US Army Quartermasters have had a comic strip for years known as, "Gigs and Gags." This strip takes a comical look at life in the field and a soldier's life. The following image is from the August 3, 1945 issue of their magazine. The soldiers are trying to get their buddy to the showers, or the "Sterilization and Bath Co." area, but he's fighting them tooth and nail. You can see that he is wearing his dog tags, as are the gentlemen waiting in line for their turn at taking a shower.

"Quit beefin', you dope. It ain't that kind of sterilization!"

3 AUGUST 1945 108

DC Comics have a character known as Sgt. Rock. When you can see his chest, he has Dog Tags hanging. He is from the WWII era, also.

A more current day comic is one from the Air Force which is called, "Lt. Dahl." In this particular image, Lt. Dahl is standing there with his shirt off, but he still has on his Dog Tags.

109

A spin off of the comic strips has been the world of dolls and figurines. The most well known in the industry are the GI Joe dolls. They have dolls which include Dog Tags as part of their box set. When asked what specific dolls have Dog Tags as part of their set, Hasbro was not able to list their dolls that had this item. However, there are hundreds of collector clubs and personal experts on any of the GI Joes made. All have their own favorites and attachments to their choices.

GI Joe has been called the "Man of the Century" by many for his representation of every War the United States has ever been in. He also represents every service, with multiple variances on specific groups and individuals.

There are the Generals like Patton and Eisenhower,

Presidents

110

Sailors   Soldiers

Marines

and Airmen.

GI Joe has sets representing moments in time that include Dog Tags.

Pearl Harbor

[114] and D Day.

Dog Tags are so recognizable and popular; they have found their way into other dolls and sets. The dolls from the American Girl collection have one, Emily, with an outfit that includes Dog Tags. That wonderful WWI set includes a cardigan sweater from her Aunt Primrose, An English three-pence coin, her scrapbook showing pictures of her family and the English princesses and for safekeeping of her British ration book—with a special message from Mum, and her grandfather's World War I dog tags, which remind Emily to be a brave soldier for England .

Barbie, also quite popular with girls, has not excluded herself from this item. While not representative of the military, Hard Rock Barbie has adapted the Dog Tag as an iconic piece.

[115]

116

The same goes for other less well-known figures. My Scene™ Sutton™, an artist doll who draws comics, and Hikaru Ichijo, an anime collectible includes Dog Tags.

117

On a much smaller scale, but perfect for the young and young at heart, are the familiar small, plastic soldiers. There is a set of 102 soldiers, by the new Helen of Troy, which has a Dog Tag squad and a set of Dog Tags included.

While not specifically a doll or figurine, toy companies, the movie industry, and the video game industry have also taken to popularizing this item in other ways. Battlestar Gallactica has a Dog Tag set of seven that represents characters from the series. Xbox 360 has a game specifically called DogTag. And then, Battlefield 2142, is a computer game where a Dog Tag flash drive is given as part of the set, and you get enemy Dog Tags while playing. By joining the Pure Pwnage Gamer Army, you are sent a set of Dog Tags as part of your membership.

Dog Tags, military or not, could technically be called jewelry since they are to hang on a chain around the neck, and that is the way most people wear them. This is the image we see the most in pictures and movies. It is from this frame of reference that many items have been made. There are so many forms of hanging dog tags, they are too numerous to mention. The very simple design of the tags can have almost anything imprinted on them. Here are only a few of the uses for this kind of jewelry:

Medical Alert [118]

Silver, Gold, Pewter drops with names, initials, diamonds, images, that can be worn as jewelry or hung to anything a person would like to connect them to. You can find,

Patriotic Tags

[119]

Tags for an organization or job

120

Other types of jewelry include:

Bracelets

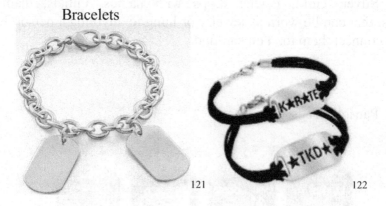

121   122

and Lapel Pins

These tags can come in any color, any material, with anything printed on it. The following tags are samples of those choices:

Color and artwork,
   unlimited choices

Silencer colors,
   unlimited choices

123

124

They are used for fundraisers, spirit tags, team logos, and organizations. They are personal statements, given as gifts, and used for marketing and sales promotions.

   Wine label

125

Luggage Tags

...and Photo Tags.

Zipper pulls

Key Chains

Key Chain Flashlight

129

Thumb Drive

130

Animal Dog Tags in all shapes and sizes

131

Swiss Army Knife

132

In advertisements

 133

 134

Video Games

Dog Tag - XBox 360 game

 135

Military Challenge Coins

136

Movie titles

137

138

139

POW-MIAs have a special place in so many people's hearts and minds, that a strong force of veterans, family members, and citizens supporting the cause, stepped up to the plate and started a petition to ask the United States Postal Service to issue a stamp honoring all POWs and MIAs, from all wars. With over one million signatures, the US Postal Service issued the following stamp:

March 29, 1995 - Stamp News Release Number 95-027 WASHINGTON, D.C. -- The symbolic representation of a pair of military identification tags embossed with the words "POW & MIA -- NEVER FORGOTTEN," displayed in front of the "Stars and Stripes" waving against a blue sky, comprise the unforgettable image on a new U.S. Postal Service stamp honoring American POWs and MIAs. First-day-of-issue ceremonies for the POW & MIA stamp will take place in Washington, D.C., as the stamps go on sale nationwide Memorial Day, May 29. Customers should contact local post offices to find out where stamps will be available in their area Memorial Day. "The ID tag has come to represent many things in the modern military," said Postmaster General Marvin Runyon in announcing the design. "The identification of each person as a unique individual who has the right to hope, to survive, and to ultimately have life after the wounds of combat." "It is a symbol of accounting for and caring for all our men and women in uniform. It is a symbol for commemorating and remembering all our POWs and MIAs -- from the Revolutionary War to Somalia." Many veterans save their ID tags as treasured keepsakes, carrying them around their necks, in their billfolds, on their key chains, and stored with their valuable jewelry.

They pass them down to their children and grandchildren as heirlooms. They reflect on them, and remember the sacrifices they and others made -- and they remember those captured by hostile forces and terrorists, and those who remain missing in action. Carl Herrman designed the stamp after a concept created by Gary Viskupic of Centerport, N.Y. Herrman combined Ivy Bigbee's photo of the ID tags with an image of the American flag taken by prominent photographer Robert Llewellen of Charlottesville, Va. The development of this stamp was coordinated with various veteran and family organizations. This is the second stamp issued by the Postal Service honoring America's POWs and MIAs. The six-cent "U.S. Servicemen" stamp, issued in 1970, read, "Honoring U.S. Servicemen -- Prisoners of War -- Missing and Killed in Action."

140

One of the most interesting uses of the Dog Tag is the Personal Statements people use them for that are for memory sake. It might be shown in shadow boxes, or in US Flag boxes.

Tattoos are some of the most personal and amazing ways to display these tags. They are representative of their own dog tag, a family member's dog tags, or a fallen comrade's dog tags. Becoming much more common, is a tattoo called a "Meat Tag". These tags are mirror images of a personal tag.

It is often a copy of your own Dog Tag and information. It is thought to be a smart thing to do, and represents thinking ahead. If your body were blown apart, hopefully the Dog Tag tattoo would be useful in identifying your body.

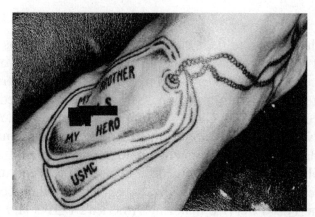

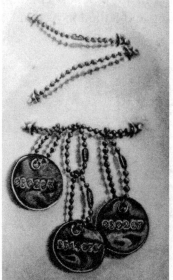
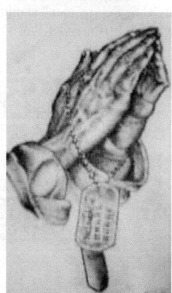

Public Domain Images: foot, side torso, chest

The feeling connected to the Dog Tags is often represented in memorials and statues. In Chapter 2, In Life and Death, we learned about the 14th Quartermaster Memorial in Greensburg, Pennsylvania whose own members served and lost their lives during an Iraqi Scud Missile attack in Operation Desert Storm. And, while we have already touched on the Chicago National Vietnam Vet Museum and their "Above and Beyond Memorial" whose Dog Tags hang for those who lost their lives in the Vietnam War, we go more in depth about this memorial at the end of this Chapter.

In Washington D.C., history is well represented with memorials and Museums, most free and open to the public. At the Vietnam memorial, off to the side, a statue stands that serves to recognize the service of Women in the military during this time. Too often women have served in the military or beside them unofficially and have not been recognized.

This woman standing has her Dog Tags lying against her chest as her eyes and head tilts towards the heavens. She serves with little or no recognition, but that is not why she's there, she is there to do her duty.

This sentiment is represented on t-shirts available for purchase and love beads, popular at the time for those who were against the war are weighed against the Dog Tags that those who volunteered chose to wear.

Not all women wore love beads in the sixties 143

Close to the spot where the Nurse's Statue stands is another statue was designed to help heal those who felt the Vietnam Wall did not give enough respect to those who had died. Three Infantrymen stand portraying those who others felt were not being recognized. The following is a description from the artist himself, Frederick Hart, 1982.

"The portrayal of the figures is consistent with history. They wear the uniform and carry the equipment of war; they are young. The contrast between the innocence of their youth and weapons of war underscores the poignancy of their sacrifice. There is about them the physical contact and sense of unit that bespeaks the bonds of love and sacrifice that is the nature of men at war. And yet they are each alone. Their strength and their vulnerability are both evident dent. Their true heroism lies in these bonds of loyalty in the face of their aloneness and their vulnerability."[144]

145

146

For years the Vietnam Memorial Wall has collected items people have left beside the wall. Gathered in the arms of the Park Rangers that watch over the Wall, these items are collected at dusk each night and taken to be added to a collection of memorabilia that is housed, numbered, and eventually shown to the public in a travelling showcase.

Thousands upon thousands of items are in the collection, and it should be of no surprise that many of these items are dog tags that have been left at the Memorial. This is an image from a part of that collection gathered at the Wall. As can be seen here they are photographed with a similarly personal item, the MIA or KIA bracelets.

With the same sentiment in mind, there is a Memorial in New Jersey that has Dog Tags as part of its sentimentality. "The New Jersey Korean War Veterans Memorial, like the previously completed Vietnam Veterans Memorial, will help to heal the spiritual and psychological wounds suffered by the Korean War veterans, their families and friends. Part of the healing process is to understand America's involvement in that struggle, what it accomplished, and the contribution of our men and women who served. The New Jersey Korean War Veterans Memorial was created to ensure that future generations remember and honor the pride and dedication of those who served, the legacy they continued, and the freedom they preserved." [148]

The Soldier being carried shows Dog Tags hanging

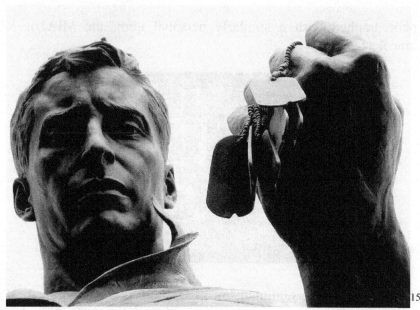

150

The Mourning Soldier Holds the Dog Tags of his Fallen Comrades

At the University of Arizona they have a wonderful building, their Student Union Memorial Building, whose shape represents the Battleship USS Arizona. Surrounding the complex there are many more items in memory of this battleship and those who served and lost their lives on it during Pearl Harbor, December 7, 1941. In particular, there is a sculpture that uses the Dog Tags as a major focus of its parts.

> "Susan Gamble's sculpture, on the north side of the canyon, honors the 1,511 individuals assigned to the U.S.S. Arizona battleship on the day Pearl Harbor was bombed. The sculpture resembles an 18- foot ship's mast and the military dog tags allude to the rigging of the ship. The tags with the names of the 1,177 fallen men are in the diamond shape of an Ojo de Dios (God's eye) and the tags of the 334 survivors are above the tiled portion of the mast. It was the artist's intention to show the vast difference in the number of dead compared to the number of survivors." [151]

152

In Boston, Massachusetts at the famous Old North Church and in the Old North Garden stand rows of Dog Tags hanging above flowers and stones. Memorialized in more ways than one, these Dog Tags are "set aside to commemorate the soldiers lost in the Afghanistan and Iraq Wars. Hundreds of dog tags representing the fallen soldiers from these conflicts hang closely together. When the wind blows one can hear the distinctive metal chimes as they clang together to make their eerie music."[153]

154

Support from the local community, parishioners, and visitors help to keep this memorial updated. "During Harborfest weekend, 2010, 500 dog tags where hung with the help of Roshon Ponnudurei and about 200 visitors. About half of the volunteer visitors were children. Adult volunteers included:

- Three seabees in full white uniforms
- A gentleman who hung a tag in honor of a cousin who died in Viet Nam
- Several parents whose child are either currently deployed, recently deployed or soon will be deployed.
- A husband and wife, she recently returned after deployment with Air National Guard.
- Young lady in urban attire, after she strung a tag said that she had lots of practice with her own tags while serving in navy.
- A chain with about a hundred tags was placed by a National Guard Lieutenant who returned from deployment."[155]

In another very touching and memorable display, you can visit Chicago's National Veterans Art Museum, Above and Beyond Memorial. "On Memorial Day 2001, the National Vietnam Veterans Art Museum added a stirring and spectacular new exhibit to its already highly praised fine art collection. The work of art, an immense 10 x 40 foot sculpture entitled *Above & Beyond*, is comprised of imprinted dog tags, one for each of the more than 58,000 service men and women who died in the Vietnam War. *Above & Beyond* is the first new permanent Vietnam War memorial, other than The Wall in Washington, D.C., to list all those killed in action.

When visitors first enter the museum, they will hear a sound like wind chimes coming from above them and their attention will be drawn upward 24 feet to the ceiling of the two-story high atrium. There they will see tens of thousands of metal dog tags, spaced evenly one inch apart, suspended from fine lines which will allow them to move like a living thing with the shifts in air currents."[156]

157

If there were no story or personal connection to the image or item, then the item *would* just be pieces of metal or a flat drawing of those metal tags. However, it is the internal struggle individuals feel that connect some of us to those ID tags and the emotional eyes we see them through. Thus, whatever representation that takes on, we have a personal connection to that image – good or bad.

In short, what Flusser [?] [?] wants [?] [?] on [?] the [?] [?] of [?] from [?] the [?] [?] would that be [?] of [?] [?] all of these moral boys, however [?] in their struggle into [?] [?] with [?] culture [?] [?] to their [?] [?] [?] appointed eyes we see in our thought [?] [?] representation that [?] on our [?] [?] [?] contradiction to that [?] [?] [?] of that.

Chapter Five

Urban Myths and Legends

Naming Identification Tags - "Dog Tags"

The most easily and acceptable connection to such a name given to Identification Tags has more than one explanation, with no specific proof of historical connection. However, there are three very strong stories that can be connected to the naming of Dog Tags. As simple as they are, it is surprising that the name did not connect to such tags before WWI.

The slave trade might have contributed to the name, had it not had such a negative connotation. As negative as it is, it is the same as any piece of property which the owner wishes to name and keep track of.

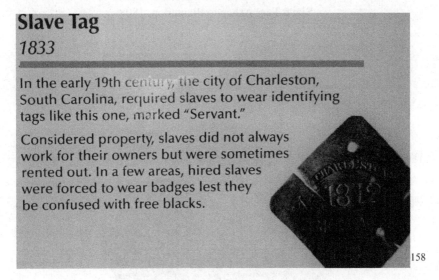

Slave Tag

1833

In the early 19th century, the city of Charleston, South Carolina, required slaves to wear identifying tags like this one, marked "Servant."

Considered property, slaves did not always work for their owners but were sometimes rented out. In a few areas, hired slaves were forced to wear badges lest they be confused with free blacks.

158

Owning a piece of property and naming it, especially your animals became a law in many towns during the mid-1800s. The easiest way to prove ownership was by having a tag or tattoo placed on the animal. It does not take a leap of the imagination to understand why any member of our Armed Services would call their Identification Tags, Dog Tags. What is interesting is why it was not called that when it was first issued, especially since it resembles the tag so closely.

159

Slave Tag, Ashepoo Plantation, 1808

160

Slave Tag, Mansfield Rice Plantation, 1814

Actual Dog Tag, Austin, Texas, 1898

Cotton Bail Tag, Belle Grove Plantation, 1836

Back in 1888, a scrungy little dog with wiry hair crept into the postal office in Albany, New York. None of the postmen noticed him curled up on a bog of mail, sleeping soundly. It was warm inside and this pup had not had such a quiet place to rest in his first few months of life.

He was lucky enough to remain in the building and slept soundly until the next morning when one of the postal clerks finally saw him in the corner, on a bag of mail. A crowd gathered, and rather than kick him out, they decided to take him in and make him their mascot. They didn't know his name or where he was from, but he became a favorite of those who worked in the station.

They named him Owney with no known story behind it. He had no tag to identify him and no one came forward to collect him. While they did not know where he was from or where his home was, Owney made the postal Service his new home and postal bags became his property. He watched over them and slept as if to make sure they would get where they needed to go. In the station or traveling on a train, Owney watched over the bags as they made their way to their destinations.

Originally on a railway car between New York and Albany, his trips began to lengthen until other postal clerks worried about Owney getting lost or stolen. This prompted the Albany office to get him a collar to identify him – "Owney, Post Office, Albany, New York." Much like that of a baggage tag, this identified him and his home, but it did not keep him from becoming the mascot of all railway mail clerks. They fed him and made sure he was safe to travel on to other stations and guard the mail.

An interesting fact for Owney is that as the mascot for all, he needed a tag from each of his stops. Thus, in time, he gathered hundreds of Dog Tags on his collar. So many so that his collar almost weighed more than him, and there was no more room on the collar. The Postmaster General at the time, John Wanamaker, had a dog jacket made for Owney where each of the tags could be sewn on the jacket and spread out the weight of all of his tags collected.

There are keys and tokens, badges and tags. Imprinted on them is everything from a town and its state, to a token for a drink or food. His trinkets and tags that hang from his collar and jacket became thought of as good luck charms. This grew into his being thought of as a good luck charm for the mail clerk's, too.

These tags, with many still attached to his jacket, are on display at the Smithsonian United Sates National Postal Museum where a preserved Owney and his tags can be seen. Not all of the tags are dog tags. There are a variety of tags from places all over the world. Owney did not go to every place the tags represent, but those who loved him and gave him the tags were so fond of him they wanted to give him something to remember them by.

The popularity of Owney and his collection of tags was a well-known fact at the turn of the 19th century. The Postal Service was an important aspect of communication, and identification of him as a mascot was something everyone could connect with. His tags showed the importance of his tags and that identified with everyone and everyplace he went. [163]

164

Owney

Mascot of the Railway Mail Service

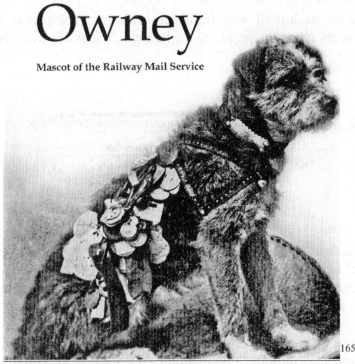

165

Owney, Mascot of the Railway Service, Smithsonian Postal Museum

166

As the late 1920s and 1930s progressed and America slipped into the Great Depression, it is important to note the forming of the Social Security Act. Having its basis as a type of old-age pension plan or social insurance, President Franklin D. Roosevelt hoped to address long range economic issue and establish a Social Security Board. Facing an uphill battle, this Board was eventually abolished. It was replaced with what we now know as the Social Security Administration.[167]

One of the first tasks of the Social Security Administration was to record employers and their workers, and to assign Social Security numbers. This process is called enumeration, and was highly contested. William Randolph Hearst, a staunch opponent to President Roosevelt, used his ownership of and influence with his newspapers to print negative press about the proposed tag that would identify workers.

168

While this tag was never issued by the Administration and was only an idea of many suggested, the proposed tag was used as an example by this negative press. Labeled tag as a "Dog Tag," he suggested all workers would be treated and owned as dogs with private information no longer to be private.

This news was wide spread and easily caught on. It was after this time period that military identification tags were more commonly and regularly called Dog Tags. While they are still labeled as Identification tags in military technical books and regulations, most service members now refer to them as Dog Tags, and the label has stuck.

Identification theories:

Just as Hearst felt a strong opposition to the Social Security card and number, there are others who believe identification by assigned numbers is too much of "big' brother" trying to control the individual.

There are biblical beliefs that Satan wished to number the people, and such things as the Sins of David would be recorded. This is only one list of many where conspiracy theorists fear mass identification will only being about loss of personal privacy. The argument is repeatedly brought up when a National ID is addressed, or even Driver's licenses or medical cards. Actually, any card where you are assigned a number with your name.

The theorists use the past as examples of such inappropriate means to identify. History, they remind us, shows that Nazi Germany, the Soviet Union, South Africa, and more have misused the identification system. The newer bar coded ID tags for everything from gasoline card to medical cards are doubly worrisome for many of the individuals and organizations that wish to defy any type of Identification system. Fearing that any such identification system will misuse the info, these organizations and the individuals, who support the theories discussed here, will always have a large following of those who disagree with whatever type of identification system is assigned.

Notch in the Dog Tag

Fictional Story with Identification

"Go ahead, Joe, kick it in!" Traphi demanded. "We gotta go."

Joe looked down at the piece of metal placed between Ohara's two front teeth, then looked up at the guys staring at him and waiting for him to kick it up into the teeth.

"Geeze! It's awful. Can't we just leave it here and tape it or something?" Joe asked.

"The notch is in place, all you have to do is kick straight." Traphi told him.

Joe closed his eyes, pulled his leg back and....

Back to History

A typical tale and scenario imagined for the notch on a rectangular Dog Tag. Repeated many times in movies and told from one soldier to another, this is an urban legend spread from a very innocent theory of the notch. However legitimate it might seem, it is not the reason for the notch. Tom Bourlier, of Mortuary Affairs Center, Ft. Lee, Va, debunks the legend. "The notch was there because the embossing machine used in those days required it to hold the tag steady while being printed. The notch is not there today because a different machine is used to imprint the tag."

One of his best reasons for not using the Tag as told by this urban legend makes the most sense. As important as dental identification is to identifying remains, just imagine what forcing the tags through the front teeth would do to the teeth and the jaw. Doing so would change the formation of its alignment and thus destroy a chance for proper forensic analysis.

Dog Tags Tied to a Boot

As sent to me:

> In Nam we had one dog tag around our neck and one in our boot laces. This was because we suffered so many casualties from booby traps in Quang Nam province, where I mostly operated in "I" Corps. We had a lot of loss of limb injuries, many feet and legs. We figured it was easier to identify us if the worst happened. A good friend of mine tripped a 105 artillery shell and proved that it was a good policy. To this day, I still carry my two dog tags, and I carry them separately. One is on my key chain and one is on my wife's key chain. Before I retired from the Fire Department, I carried one in my helmet and one on my bunker coat, along with my accountability tag. In Nam, I carried my P-38 on my dog tag chain and I still have it and carry it on my key chain. My most prized possession is my zippo lighter that has accompanied me since my arrival in Nam and still resides in my pocket. It still works, although I no longer smoke, and I still remember when we would refuse to light it up three times, only two. The third light was considered a sniper check and you were asking for it. Yes, we were a superstitious lot and I have to admit, I still am.
>
> Semper Fi

During the Vietnam era, it was quite common to place one tag in your boot laces and one around your neck. As stated by this response above, many people believe the boots will make it through anything so if you tie one of your tags in the strings of the boot, you will be identified. Basic training instructors required many recruits to wear them just this way, and many swear by the concept.

What one must remember is the basic reason for wearing the Tags. They are to be used for identification in case of death. During war, it is understandable if more than one person were to be blown up, their body parts could get mixed together. The tags hanging around the neck are the proper place to wear both tags. You might lose a body part, even your head, but your torso is a large area with many layers covering your skin. Those two tags lying next to your chest are made and protected by those layers, and most easily accessible for medical treatment and immediate burial. One tag stays with the body, and one goes on a marker for temporary burial if necessary. If someone has to take the time to find a body part, time is lost, and it might not be yours.

Religion on Dog Tags:

Through the many changes the information imprinted on the Dog Tags has gone through, the most questioned seems to be the acceptance and choices of religion as allowed on the Tag. While there were only a few choices when the Dog Tag was first implemented, there are now dozens of choices of religion to choose from. And, one may still choose no religion or no preference.

Different material or Colors for Tags:

Myth 1: The colors of red and green were chosen to make it easier for soldiers to remember how to use them.

> Red – For the color of blood, and to be taken away since the soldier was dead.

> Green – For the color of grass, and to remain with the body.

Myth 2: The two are made out of different material to withstand different elements.

> Red – For the color of fire and to withstand heat. It would dissolve in water.

Green – For the color of seaweed or moss. It would withstand water, but not fire.

In Evelyn Waugh's "Sword of Honour" Trilogy the protagonist is reminded to remove the Red Disc, leaving the Green with the body for future identification. The grissly mnemonic being "remember, green is the colour associated with putrefaction". Presumably the colour-coding existed to stop two discs from the same body being handed in and thus stop poor Mrs Bloggs receiving two "Regret to inform you..." Telegrams and thus assuming both her sons are dead.

While similar to the myth which seemed most helpful to those who wore them, the tags were not made with color coordination for soldiers. The red tag was to be taken from the two and offered with the personal effects upon death of the individual. The green tag was to remain with the body for ease of future identification.

Lost and Found - Dog Tags found in another country and returned to long lost service members or their families.

There are many heartwarming stories of dog tags being found in another country, sold to sincere people who would like to return them to their rightful owners. It is hard to believe that such a thing could be incorrect and a trick, but researchers are saying just that. The internet makes it too easy to find and gather personal information and use it for questionable activity. Preying on those that wish to do well. While not all finds are dishonest, it takes a keen eye and a lot of research to distinguish between the real Dog Tags that were lost and ones that have been made to look quite real.

I read a very interesting book on the lives of deep see scuba divers who search for underwater treasure. The book, Shadow Divers, details the dive and search of a World War II German U-boat and the lives that were affected by the journey. It was not just the thrill of the story, but the ultimate connection the divers felt towards the families and remains of those who died in this sunken U-boat. Many divers are considered to be scavengers of such finds, and it is the scavengers who make a bad name for others who dive for history and are willing to set aside such glories of treasures to do the right thing with remains.

Not to be confused with trash divers, both battlefield and scuba diving scavengers have a place. There are pros and cons to the field of scavenging, and lots of money to be made or emotional satisfaction with the "loot" in the findings. For the sake of the items as Dog Tags, calling the bounty found to be "loot" is sacrilegious. Some people feel the taking of items is a plunder that is too scandalous to justify. Maybe the argument is they might never have been found if it was not for the searchers, but removing the personal items from the remains eradicates the ability to begin the identification. Especially if there is no way to connect the remains with positive DNA.

"Many a soldier's memory lives on in the minds of his kin (or with some caring soul), in homes throughout the world, only through the preservation of his few worldly remains, be they Dog-Tags, badges, personal effects, photographs or medals."168 Maybe there are no more relatives of those whose remains are found, but it is the thought of disturbing remains that is disconcerting to many people. There is no answer to those unprotected fields and oceans. They hold a mystery that teases us in wanting to know and find out, and yet knowing we should not without purpose and meaning to those whose remains we search.

"The Moron Corps"

Unkind and definitely not politically correct, this name "moron Corps" was given to a selected list of enlisted personnel. This group was given the derogatory nickname by other soldiers, but it was billed as a Great Society Program. These enlisted draftees were called, McNamara's Project 100,000. These members were a group of draftees who failed the minimum Armed Forces IQ test, but were enlisted anyway. It was widely thought to rehabilitate some and be a way out of poverty for others. There was a shortage of personnel, so this group filled the void. The Dog Tags of this group have their own distinctive markings added to the everyday issued Dog Tags. This lent itself to belittling and disparaging remarks from others, thus ostracizing them within an organization that they were fighting to sustain.167

Whether they were dying in larger numbers, or just enlisted in units that were sent to infantry positions where dying occurred more often, a large percentage of these service members died while serving their country.

Cadbury Chocolate Tin

A very interesting side note to the chocolate tin given to British soldiers by Queen Victoria is the history of the manufacturer of the chocolate tin. Cadbury was the Queen's choice of chocolate at the time and wanted her troops to have the finest chocolate as a gift. The issue was not that they happily supplied her with Chocolate, but the issue of a gift to the soldiers who were at war. The Cadbury families were Quakers, and as members of the Society of Friends as they were called, were pacifists and did not believe in military actions. Many of the top chocolate manufacturers of the time were also members and to help justify their actions, the Cadbury Company involved other companies in the making of the tin and chocolates that went to the soldiers. The tins themselves did not have the name of the Cadbury Company on them, but the paper on the inside did. This was important for the Queen who wanted her troops to know she had spared no expense for them and purchased the best chocolate of the time.

Because the tins were made of metal, soldiers began using the tins as a place to hold their personal items for protection. Many kept their Dog Tags in the tin, and I hear they still do.

169

Items Connected to Dog Tags

The P-38 –

While not part of the Dog Tag or required to hang with it, the P-38 is as common to the service member as every other part of the set. It is commonly called "John Wayne" or a church key. "John Wayne" because he was shown in a training film opening a can of K-Rations. However, it seems that some people also called their toilet paper which was issued "John Wayne" because he took no $*/t from anyone in his movies. This item was originally issued with the K and C rations to open items that required a can opener. The "church key" is most likely an indirect hit the religious sector as the opener was obviously not designed to access churches. One rationalization might be from monks. As they often brewed in their cellars, it would be locked, and the monks carried those keys to the cellar. Or maybe as current as prohibition where locking the liquor away from others, they sarcastically called it such. Whatever the reason, it has forever been connected to this item and often called such. The P-38 and 51 was placed on the Dog Tag chain for ease and quickness of use.

170

From: ANDREW BAYLEY [x-xxx@msn.com]
Sent: Thursday, July 26, 2007 10:10 AM
To: INFO@DOGTAGHISTORY.COM,
QUESTIONNAIRE@DOGTAGHISTORY.COM
Cc: 'a-bay_1'
Subject: DOG TAGS

My dog tags was not only means of id, but were also used by me as a utensil.. in order to open a c-ration can it was necessary to use the g.i. church key (can opener) which was on my dog tag chain. As the tags were already out of my shirt, I used a tag as a spoon to scoop out the cold beans, pork patties, etc, etc. Today my tags & key hang alongside my medals and they still contain the dirt, grime and food particles and when asked why haven I cleaned them. I just answer "it's a reminder, that's how an infantryman lived on the line"

Proud Korean War Veteran

Andrew E. Bayley

Deer Park , N.Y.

Clickers, or Crickets for the Airborne – Another "style" of Identification

While researching Dog Tags, it was brought to my attention that the Clicker was a most personal item to many veterans and shared a similar but different aspect of identification. Mac Purifoy, of Temple, Texas, told me his father talked about the clicker, and he shared with me a copy of an article written about his father by Jonathan Graham.

171

Typical of this "make do" spirit was Al's own experience soon after the drop. The paratroopers had all been given small signaling devices to aid them in linking up with other paratroopers in the dark of night— the device when clicked sounded like a cricket. Soon after he landed, Al heard a "click" and responded with a double click— a voice called out, "This is 'Killer.'" Al had been taught all of the commanders and units code names, but beyond his company and battalion name, he suddenly couldn't recall who was who, so he asked, "Killer who?" Back came a voice, "Killer Taylor." Al had a little guy in his unit named Taylor, so Al asked, "Shorty? Where did you get this Killer stuff?" Back came a very commanding voice, "No. No. This is Killer Taylor and Killer Minor is in a tree down there. We need to get him out." Suddenly Al realized to whom he was speaking. Minor was part of the code name for the assistant commander in every unit, and Killer Taylor was Brigadier General Maxwell Taylor, who'd taken over command while the unit was training in England. So on this most memorable of mornings, a Private and a General set out to get another General, Anthony McAuliffe, out of a tree. During the early morning hours, the small band grew as they came across isolated paratroopers.

Made by a British manufacturer, this roughly 3 x 1 inch small toy was used by paratroopers during the invasion of Normandy in WWII. The action of clicking allowed paratroopers to acknowledge one another with having to speak. If you heard something and wondered if it was friend or foe, you would click once. A "friend" would click twice to acknowledge. As long as it lasted, this was an ingenious way for "friends" to acknowledge each other.

This toy and its use have been illustrated in movies. In "The Longest Day", John Wayne introduces the clicker to his soldiers and explains how to use it. In this movie, the clicker is shown as causing confusion to an American soldier when a German soldier loads a bullet into his rifle. They do not actually sound alike and should not have caused confusion. However, once American soldiers were captured, there are stories of Germans using the clickers against other American soldiers as trickery.

172

Housewife

Not the kind that is married and stays at home, but the kind that is carried with a soldier and carries sewing implements. Most were made of fabric and rolled up to be carried easily without loss of items.

This kit, from the Civil War, belonged to Augustus Jones, Co. I, 20th Maine Volunteer Infantry.
Image courtesy of the Gettysburg National Military Park, GETT 31096

Changes in the Necklace

The reason for abandoning the old nylon string that they use to use for dog tags was the injuries it caused if you were burned and the string melted...*common theory*.

As long as we have had the Dog Tag and its changes throughout the years, there have been as many changes to the necklace or ways service members "wear" their Dog Tags. While there are many stories of why the necklace has changed it comes down to a very basic reason for the metal chains. The metal can withstand many different elements and environments. Very plain and simple.

The Rupture Duck or Honorable Discharge pin and its many myths...

173

The following information from the American War Library:

1. The "Ruptured Duck" applies only to the WWII era.
Not true. Actually, the plan for a multi-service branch, universal Honorable Discharge Lapel patch originated in 1919 at the close of WWI. The purpose of the patch, and later pin, was to permit Honorably Discharged military personnel to wear their uniform for a period of time after they left military service due to their inability to afford civilian clothes, while at the same time identify themselves as no longer active duty personnel. The pin version of

the patch was intended to permit civilian dressed, Honorable Discharged personnel to identify their former military status easily when applying for work or veteran's benefits. The patch and pin were also intended to replace and supersede all previous Honorable Discharge devices. Neither the patch nor pin were put into production until years later.

2. The "Ruptured Duck" ended with WWII.
Not true. The Ruptured Duck is a permanent 'hardware' device with no expiration date. It has replaced all previously issued Honorable Discharge lapel pins.

3. The "Ruptured Duck" is not the only Honorable Discharge lapel pin. The Navy, Coast Guard and Army have their own Honorable Discharge pins today.
Not true. The Ruptured Duck is the only official all-branch "Honorable Discharge" lapel pin. The current Army, Coast Guard and Navy pins sometimes issued to Retirees are "Honorable Service" pins that are authorized principally to age and medical retirees. The military definitions of "Discharge" and "Service" are not to be confused as meaning the same.

1. The "Ruptured Duck" is no longer distributed by the military. True and Not true. Although there is no regulation that requires any branch of the US military to issue any military award 'hardware' item, just as all military medals, badges and other 'hardware' items, the Ruptured Duck is still purchasable in US military Post and Base Exchanges and continues to be manufactured by official US military medal suppliers.

2. The design of the Ruptured Duck is not the original design
True. The original design conceived in 1919 bore the flat image of an eagle as depicted in the Presidential Seal. The image was changed in May, 1943 after the Washington Conference (code named The Trident Conference) between Roosevelt and Churchill to depict an eagle appearing to initiate flight (The Eagle Has Flown). This image was intended to coincide with the timing of the first major Allied Offensives against the Axis Powers in the P
Pacific and Atlantic.

3. To this day it still remains commonly stated by many since 1944 that *"No one knows how the Ruptured Duck got its name but for many decades it was said that the Duck got its (nick) name from the unknown wife of an unknown Army Air Corps airman who mockingly told her husband that the spread-eagled figured looked more like a "ruptured duck" than an eagle taking flight or fanning its wings."*

Not true. This myth was intentionally created by Louis B. Mayer of Hollywood fame. Mr. Mayer spent hundreds of thousands of dollars spreading this myth to save the movie career of one of his most famous actresses, Hedy Lamarr, who had recently escaped from Nazi Germany. Ms. Lamarr had been married to Friedrich Mandl who owned a network of arms factories controlled by the Krupp Family. Ms. Lamarr gained infamy in Germany not because of her nude acting, which her husband opposed, but because it was confirmed that it was she and not her husband who came up with revolutionary ideas to improve weapons design and production in the Mandl section of the Krupp Arms works. It is believed that her husband conspired to kill his wife after having been humiliatingly confronted by others in his elite circle of Nazi megalomaniacs that his wife was fully known by all to be the originator and owner of his military enhancements. But learning about his murder plans Ms. Lamarr, along with her maid who were both inspired by their mutually adored Jewish heroine, Judith, drugged her husband and fled

Germany. Upon eventually arriving in the US from her long escape route from Europe with the aid of a Jewish "Underground Railroad" stretching from Germany to the US, Ms. Lamarr was quoted as saying that her terrible and hazardous flight originated -- in the actresses words -- on a 'broken bird'... (*"segeltuch gebrochen"*). In English, the German "segeltuch gebrochen" spoken by Ms. Hedy Lamarr translates to "Ruptured Duck". The term was picked up immediately by the movie-star crazed female employees of the manufacturing plant that produced the "Duck" and labeled their shipping boxes "Ruptured Ducks", partly in commemoration of Ms. Lamarr's heroic flight, but mostly because it was common practice -- if not required policy -- during WWII to label shipments destined for the war theater differently than their true contents so as to not inform enemy agents about the actual contents. The term "Ruptured Duck" had forever caught on as the Honorable Discharge Lapel pins nickname... thanks to Hedy Lamarr.

However, in 1944 Army Chief of Staff George C. Marshall issued classified Special Order #131 directing that all historical information contained in any medium, *"... paper, microfilm, acetate, film, etc..."* on the Honorable Discharge Lapel Pin, *"...commonly referred to as 'The Ruptured Duck'...* currently residing in any command will be immediately destroyed. General Marshall's order was intended to prevent *"...possible serious and severe reduction in troop morale"...* should the continued use of what he considered a *...disparaging term..."*, "Ruptured", be applied to the Honorable Discharge lapel pin. Within a month virtually every military document providing the history of the Ruptured Duck virtually disappeared. Within a year the common statement as to the origin of the Ruptured Duck was replied with "nobody knows".

It would be another fifty-one years (during the massive declassification of wartime records ordered by President Bill Clinton for POW research) before declassified reports revealed the reason for General Marshall's well-founded reason for killing off the history of the Ruptured Duck since he realized it was impossible to eradicate its name, for fear that *"...possible serious and severe reduction in troop morale"...* could result if it were disclosed that the top Secret code name of one the highest United States military officers was "Duckpin". The codename "Duckpin" was assigned to the four star, soon five star, general whose singular being required the highest level of confidence of all those he commanded. The General codenamed "Duckpin" (in 1942) was Dwight David Eisenhower.

NOTE: Codenames for others were: Chiang kai-Chek, "Peanut"; Josef Stalin, "Glyptic"; FD Roosevelt, "Victor"; Winston Churchill, "Former Naval Person".

7. Only Honorable Discharge personnel can own the RD.

Not true. Individuals who received an Honorable Discharge during a previous enlistment cycle, but later received a less than Honorable Discharge after a subsequent cycle are still permitted to possess their original Ruptured Duck eligibility for that previous cycle only, and are prohibited by law from disguising, misrepresenting or assert Honorable Discharge as their final discharge status.

8. A serviceperson may acquire and wear or display as many RD's as the number of Honorable Discharge's he received for each re-enlistment period.

Not true. A recipient is eligible for only one Ruptured Duck regardless of the number of times he received an Honorable Discharge upon re-enlistment.[174]

[175]

By Regulation,

The Honorable Discharge Lapel Pin ("The Ruptured Duck") is the official emblem of Honorable Discharge for all service branches of all eras. It replaces all previously issued Honorable Discharge lapel pins or buttons and is retroactive to the Revolutionary War. Honorably Discharged personnel of all four military service branches (*and Coast Guard personnel during wartime assignment to the War Department, Navy Department or Department of Defense*) are eligible. The Pin may be worn on civilian clothing. The Pin should be displayed among military medals in shadow boxes.

Miscellaneous:

The Fly Paper Report – Harold Jones

I was a young kid (10 years old) when Pearl Harbor was attacked on Dec. 7th, 1941. But, I recall many of the incidents, etc. that occurred during WWII. I was quite involved in all this, as we ran the local "Arcadia City Dump" in Southern Calif. (called "Land Fills" nowadays!), and my Dad picked up the food scraps to feed our hogs (was called "garbage" back then) each day at several of the smaller Army camps near where we lived (including the MP's camp located at the Santa Anita Race Track in Arcadia, Calif., which was used as a "Relocation Center" for the local Japanese residents who had "Truck Farms" in the area [they raised and sold vegetables, fruits, berries, etc.]).

Soon after the Pearl Harbor attack, President Roosevelt ordered these Japanese people be sent to "Relocation Centers" for security reasons (and as I recall, later on they were moved again to various camps for the duration of the war -- some went to "Manzanar" near Lone Pine, Calif., and some went to "Tule Lake" at Newell, Calif. [in Modoc County, Calif. near the Calif./Oregon border], and locations in other States as well). Santa Anita Race Track was a horse racing track, but was closed due to the war (no large gatherings of people in case of an attack, we were told), so "Uncle Sam" took it over. Once the Japanese were moved out to other locations, it became an Army Ordnance camp (known as "Camp Santa Anita", as I recall) until the war ended, then was once again (and still is) a horse racing track.

The "Fly Paper Report" surfaced when some "Enterprising G.I.s" thought they'd play a little game with the Mess Sgts., I guess. They made up an "Official" looking form and called it the "Monthly Fly Paper Report". The Mess Halls had sticky fly paper sheets (called "Tangle Foot", as I recall) placed around inside the building, and sticky "Fly Ribbons" that were attached to the ceiling and pulled downward to catch flies that landed on the sticky surfaces, and then got "stuck" (would now be called "Cruel and Unusual Punishment", probably!!). The "Fly Paper Report" form instructed the Mess Sgts. to count the number of dead flies stuck to the paper and send this info in (to some bogus location, I'm sure) on a monthly basis. Being it was an "Official" looking form, the Mess Sgts. complied for a while, but didn't bother to send in their reports after a while ("just another damn stupid form to fill out", they no doubt thought).

This went on for a while, and when the "Enterprising G.I.s" weren't getting the report forms anymore, what did they do -- you guessed it --

they made up another "Official" looking form letter to send the Mess Sgts. asking "why no Fly Paper Report had been sent in for XXXX month, and to send this overdue report in immediately!!" Leave it to the "G.I.s, huh? What the outcome was, I don't know!!

Harold Jones
Gardnerville
Wed February 27, 2008

Historical Fiction

Fictional story with Identification

The Hunley - Charleston Harbor February 17, 1864

Lt. George Dixon surveyed the scene one last time as his crew began to descend into their submersible. He held some personal items from his pocket, and he unknowingly rolled them between his fingers as he gazed across the water.

J. F. Carlson called out to him as he stood at the hatch. Two of the other men waited behind him.

"What you got there, Lt.?"

Dixon gathered his thoughts as he looked down at his hand. He smiled and looked back at the remaining crew.

"My life preserver." He told them.

They laughed. Arnold Becker slapped Carlson on the back of the shoulder, and said, "I don't think that will do it. Doesn't look like any life preserver I've seen."

They all laughed again.

"I'll keep to my own, if you don't mind, Lt." Carlson said as he and Becker climbed down and disappeared into the hull.

"Don't mind them, George. Having been sunk twice, you can carry any life preserver you feel is worthy on board her." 2d in command Joseph Ridgeway told him and stepped down into the Hull.

Lt. Dixon smiled at Ridgway and nodded as he opened his hand and looked down at the item he called his life preserver. It didn't bother him that the men joked about it. He knew better. He flipped the one piece he specifically called his preserver over and rubbed his thumb across it. He thought back to the Battle of Shiloh and his amazing luck. Others were not so lucky and he knew that he might just as easily have lost his leg that day if it were not for this coin that he held and called his life preserver.

Having left his sweetheart in Mobile, Alabama, he was grateful she had given him this twenty dollar gold piece. He always kept it in his pocket and during the battle a bullet hit him in the leg. Feeling the sharp pain of the impact, he reached down assuming the bullet had breached his skin. To his astonishment, the coin had obstructed the bullet and taken the brunt of the impact. There was no penetration.

Dixon looked back down at the coin and read the inscription he had engraved on it after this incident. "Shiloh. April 6, 1862. My Life Preserver. G.E.D."

Queenie, his sweetheart, had reminded him to always keep it with him, and he had no issue complying with her request. He agreed with her – this was his life preserver – and no bit of teasing from his crew members would change his mind.

He rolled the coin back into the other items and thought of Queenie. She was so supportive and loving. He held her engagement ring in his hand, knowing when next he saw her, he would ask for her hand in marriage.

In his letters home to her, he had only told her basic things about the Hunley because he did not want her to worry. He had especially not told her of its two previous mishaps and sinkings. Even the crew hated talking about it. He would rather look ahead and think about her as his wife, and continue to hold on to the gold coin she had given him. He would make it through.

Ridgway poked his head out of the hatch. "No sign of Walker, Lt. Do you want to wait?"

"No," he answered, "we've waited long enough. The eight of us can maneuver this beast just fine. Let's get cranking."

Ridgway disappeared back down and Dixon stepped up, ready to descend into the Hunley. He looked at the few remaining family, friends, and onlookers who had come to watch this submersible go out on its voyage. Queenie was not there, but his hand wafted past his pocket and he felt her just as close as if she were there with him. He was ready. He saluted and slowly pulled the hatch over him and closed it.

Inside, the eight men were cramped and conditions were rudimentary. There was no fresh air and the men had to hand crank her to move her in the water. Very brave, or just plain adventurous, didn't matter now. These men were on a mission and it would take their professionalism and a strong constitution to endure this voyage. They were after a Union blockade ship called the Housatonic, and each of them understood the importance of sinking her.

Lt. Dixon called for the candles to be blown out. The sailors had to do their jobs and sit in this pitch black vessel. When no one spoke, the creaking and rocking of the Hunley and the reality of what they were doing might make anyone's imaginations go wild, but not this crew. They were ready and willing to make this mission a success.

In the darkness, Corporal Carson spoke out again. He always made light of things and this was no exception. "Lt., did I ever tell you what I keep in my pocket?"

"No, Carson, you haven't."

"It's a medallion off a dead Yank. His name was Chamberlain, and I found it on the ground at Morris Island. It's my own special souvenir. Yep, that's what I keep in my pocket. That's my life preserver." Carson laughed, but no one else did. The reality of the situation did not have many of them in joking moods.

The Hunley continued to creak, and as time went on, the presence of their breathing and body warmth caused the inside of the ship to sweat. It dripped on the men as they felt their bodies cramping and each breath sucked more oxygen from the cabin. No one spoke, for that deprived them of more oxygen. They had to stay focused and strong. They needed to make history today.

Back to History

The Historical Record of the Hunley

While not the first submarine, the Hunley is the first recorded submarine to sink another ship. During the Civil War, the Hunley was a Confederate submersible that had a rough start. It had three different names, and the first two models sunk, killing its crew. Its final name was taken from the man who donated the money to have it built. He was a wealthy slave owner who used many of his slaves to do the unpleasant task connected with the Hunley.

The vessel was made to hold 9 seamen, however, to think about 9 grown men having to work and sail within her hull is a frightening scenario. The first two vessels were sealed with sailors inside and the remains were only retrievable by sawing off the sealed hatch. She had no fresh air, was lit only by candlelight, and was moved in the water by men hand-cranking her. It was cramped quarters requiring most to be hunched over or legs bent at all times. The warmth from the bodies would cause the inside to sweat. [176]

Photo # NH 53545 Midships section of H.L. Hunley

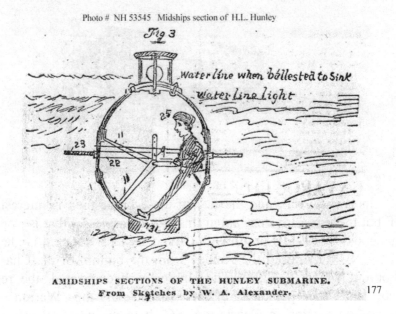

Fig 3

Water line when ballested to Sink

water line light

AMIDSHIPS SECTIONS OF THE HUNLEY SUBMARINE.
From Sketches by W. A. Alexander.   177

Photo # NH 53544 Inboard profile & interior plan of H.L. Hunley

LONGITUDINAL ELEVATION IN SECTION AND PLAN VIEW OF THE CONFEDERATE SUBMARINE BOAT HUNLEY.
From Sketches by W. A. Alexander.

No. 1. The Bow and Stern Castings. No. 2. Water ballast tanks. No. 3. Tank bulkheads. No. 4. Compass. No. 5. Sea cocks. No. 6. Pumps. No. 7. Mercury gauge. No. 8. Keel ballast stuffing boxes. No. 9. Propeller shaft and cranks. No. 10. Stern bearing and gland. No. 11. Shaft braces. No. 12. Propeller. No. 13. Wrought ring around propeller. No. 14. Rudder. No. 15. Steering wheel. No. 16. Steering lever. No. 17. Steering rods. No. 18. Rod braces. No. 19. Air box. No. 20. Hatchways. No. 21. Hatch covers. No. 22. Shaft of side fins. No. 26. Cast-iron keel ballast. No. 27. Bolts. No. 28. Butt end of torpedo boom. No. 23. Side fins. No. 24. Shaft lever. No. 25. One of the crew turning propeller shaft. No. 31. Keel ballast.   178

This particular submersible was built to ram other ships depositing explosives and cause a hole in their hull to sink it.

179

Its own history and the fate of these brave men is interesting in itself, but there is a mystery about this particular vessel that is important to this book. In 1995, a group with Clive Cussler's National Underwater Agency (NUMA) raised the Hunley from the bottom of the Charleston Harbor on August 8, 2000. The Hunley was excavated, the remains buried, and the personal effects placed in the Warren Lasch Conservation Center in Charleston, SC. It is the personal effects that draw us in.

As told in the fictional story of the Hunley, above, the ring and gold coin held by Lt. George Dixon is true. Whether or not his sweetheart gave it to him, or that the ring was for her, the family of Queenie Bennett says that it is a story passed down through their descendants and they believe it to be so. A romantic story to believe and hope for as one thinks of Lt. Dixon and his men dying in such a horrible way. To think he was comforted by an item from a loved one helps us to comprehend such a terrible fate.

What has been recorded is the story of the gold coin, and Lt. Dixon's luck of a bullet hitting the coin instead of piercing his leg at the Battle of Shiloh, 1862. He was a soldier who fought in that battle and then volunteered to be the commander of the Hunley. It was through the careful sifting of his remains that the ring and the coin were found. The coin still having an indentation where the bullet hit it, and also the engraving of his words: "Shiloh. April 6, 1862. My Life Preserver. G.E.D."

The other mystery to the Hunley is the finding of a Union soldier identification disk. Since it was a Confederate submersible, it held many a story of why such a disk would be on it. The man whose name is inscribed was on the list of deceased from the fight at Morris Island. His remains were never identified, but fellow comrades spoke of him and how brave he was in the last minutes of his life. Of all the stories and theories read, the most probable is the story shared in the fictional Hunley story.

Ezra Chamberlain enlisted in the Union Army in September, 1861 and was assigned to the 7th Connecticut Volunteer Infantry Regiment, Company K. He served at several garrisons before his Regiment moved south to Port Royal.

Corporal J.F. Carlson was a privateer by trade, collecting and taking personal property for sale or trade. Once he was in the service of the Confederate Army, it is easily believable that he would have no qualms about taking something from the battlefield as a souvenir. It is recorded that he was at Ft. Wagner, Morris Island near Charleston a few days after the battle where Ezra Chamberlain died in1863, so it is likely he could have picked up his Identification Disk and kept it with him.

The sailors who died on the Hunley, February 17, 1864, were not identified by their own identification disks or coins, but they have been identified through records and forensic science. There is an organization that keeps their memories alive, and has recorded the history of this vessel. It is the Friends of the Hunley, Inc. The Hunley is managed by the United States Department of the Navy, the United States General Services Administration (GSA), the Advisory Council of Historic Preservation (Council), South Carolina Historic Preservation Officer (SHPO), and the South Carolina Hunley Commission.

Chapter Six

Military Use of Dog Tags – Today and in the Future

To become a member of the Armed Forces, enlisted personnel must go through a Military Entrance Processing (MEPPS) station. "The Military Entrance Processing Station (MEPS) plays a vital role in maintaining the nation's military might by ensuring that each new member of the Armed Forces: The Army, Marines, Navy, Air Force and Coast Guard; meets the high mental, moral and medical standards required by the Department of Defense and the military services. Featuring modern facilities and equipment, today's modern MEPS bear little resemblance to the traditional image of the drab "Induction Station" known by previous generations of American soldiers, Marines, Sailors, Airmen and Coast Guardsmen."[180]

However, it is not until they reach their own services basic training or similar training that they are issued their Dog Tags. Being one of the first items they are given, they are to always have this on them. It is considered their individual responsibility to have this item on hand and to realize the significance of it.

In reference to AFI 36-3026[181], all services share this directive. It is by order of all Secretaries' of the Army, the Navy, the Marine Corps[182], the Air Force, Transportation, Commerce, and Health and Human Services. While those on active duty are the most known to have and wear the Dog Tags, this directive also states that civilians overseas, dependents, and US nationals should also be issued and wear these tags.

It is the handling of deceased personnel that drives the importance of issuing and wearing these tags. In a book by Allen Clark, a Veteran of Vietnam, called, Oh, God I'm Dead, he makes the point of being unknown all too real. While in the Green Berets, he is on patrol from their camp in Dak To, looking across the Dak Poko River and hearing mortar rounds coming closer and closer to their position.

As they were being fired upon, he was calling for fire to this certain spot, "Get 'Puf the Magic Dragon' here right away!"[183] (Puff the Magic Dragon' that he called for was a gunship aircraft whose mission was for life-saving close air support.[184]) He felt a thud and was knocked forward. He states, "Oh my God, my legs, my legs, help me. Oh, God, I'm dead." Two Sergeants put him on a stretcher and get him to a bunker. He tells another Sgt., "I'm here under an assumed name. Please make sure my wife knows if I die."[185]

Captain Clark lost both legs because of this incident. He was fortunate not to lose his life, but his story resonates with the ultimate reasoning for the Dog Tags and having identification on you. While he was part of the Green Berets, their missions were often classified and dependent on their ability to be unknown. However, the reality of his condition made him realize the situation he faced, and he wanted his wife to know what had happened to him.

Today's Armed Forces take seriously the state of total readiness. There are specific initiatives to enhance the personal readiness within the organizations. While the Army addresses ten factors, one is the Uniform Policy Mission, and as stated in AR 670-1, the Id Tags are part of that uniform readiness. The other services share in this like-minded readiness belief, whether specifically stated in their regulations or not, realizing that to go back to our pre-1917 beliefs would be detrimental to the process of individual readiness for all.

Dog Tag Printing Machine

The Dog Tag is placed in a machine that stamps the information required onto it. The current contract for this machine is the GSA Contract #GS-25F-0043L. There are manual and electric machines which emboss or deboss the information on the metal tag. Throughout the years, the machines have either been Graphotypes or Addressographs.

TOUR BY GENERAL

Maj. Gen. George Grunert, administration chief of the army services of supply, inspects a "dog tag" (identification tag) machine operated by WAAC Auxiliary M. B. Gaines at Fort Des Moines army post. The general swept through the post in a one-day inspection of its work and facilities.

186

While several methods and options were explored, the Addressograph used the Graphotype with minimal modifications which could immediately be pressed into service without the need to manufacture a totally new and dedicated machine. The only qualification the Addressograph Graphotype could not meet was that of the 18 character per line spacing. The military made the decision that the 15/16 character per line spacing would be sufficient for a majority of the military applications and issued an approval for a deviation request allowing for the 15/16 character spacing.[187]

Upon approval of the deviation request, the Addressograph Graphotype became the primary imprinting machine for military identification tags and has still remains in military inventory to this day. Since the time of WWII the Addressograph Graphotype machine has been the primary machine used to imprint military identification tags or dog tags.

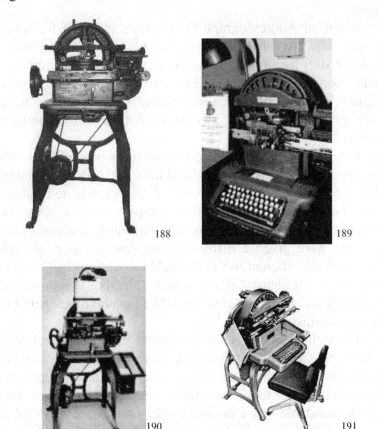

188

189

190

191

6200 Series Manual-Electric   6300 Series Keyboard-Electric

Not until the mid-1980s did the Government begin to replace the Addressograph Graphotype machines with newer more modern "computerized" machines.

192

Though the Addressograph Graphotype machine is no longer manufactured these machines can still be found within elements United States military worldwide. Only when a Graphotype needs replacement for mechanical reasons does the military "retire" or dispose of these machines.

When an Addressograph Graphotype is slated for retirement it finds its way to the Defense Reutilization Marketing Service (DRMS/DRMO) facility and is either auctioned off as "military surplus" or sold for scrap metal. The current lines of computerized embossing/debossing machines are smaller, faster and have the ability to run high production runs of identification tags with minimal operator interaction.[193]

The first use of Federal Stock Numbers was in 1949. FSN's did not become managed and standardized until 1952. Prior to Federal Stock Numbers military services (i.e. Army & Navy) operated independently and maintained their own separate supply systems with their own respective procedures for cataloging items and material. As a result, many items were given a different name and number by each of the services, making efficient use of available stock impossible. Evaluation of logistical problems after WWII clearly demonstrated these inefficiencies and led to the creation of the Federal Stock Number and an agency to administer the FSN.[194]

The military purchases replacement imprinting equipment based upon bid and Government Services Administration (GSA) contracts. What this means is, there are a host of companies currently providing imprinting machines to replace the Graphotype machines. While it is fully understandable that equipment over time becomes dated and may need replacement for a variety of reasons, no imprinting machine or current replacement will ever have the long lasting impact the Graphotype has had on the United States Government or the military.

The current crop of replacement "computerized" imprinting machines has no character. They are fabricated from plastic and resemble table top laser printers. While there is no argument that these machines are technically superior to the Graphotype, these machines have become just another piece of "computer" equipment. The newer imprinters have no personality. Here are a select few:

[195] CIM Metal 3000 - Side Eject Automatic

[196]

CIM M10 - Manual Metal Plate Embosser

[197]

CIM ME1000 - Manual Feed Metal Plate

Current imprinting machines generally have more features such as:

Hopper Feeding - so that 100's of dog tags can be made per hour.

Computer Interface - so that dog tags can be made from spread sheets and data bases full of information.

High Speed Printing capabilities - that allow the machines to crank out 1000's of dog tags per day. Some of these machines boost that they can complete one tag every 18 seconds complete with five lines of information.

LCD Displays - for manual entry verification of data being imprinted or visual diagnostics.

The current GSA catalog indicates that the machine recommended for dog tags or military identification tags is a debossing machine, but both types of imprinting are acceptable today. The notched dog tags of WWII, Korea and Vietnam were also debossed."[198]

Emboss – Embossing is to press an image into paper, metal or plastic so it lies above the surface. The creation of a raised (embossed) image by pressing a shape into a sheet of paper with a metal or plastic die, so it lies above the surface. This would be very similar to a coin or a credit card.

199

Embossed Tag, Letters raised

Deboss - a machine presses a die into the surface of the material, resulting in a depressed imprint. To press an image into material so it lies below the surface.

Debossed Tag. Letters indented

Dog Tag Necklace   **Necklace, Personnel, Identification Tag**

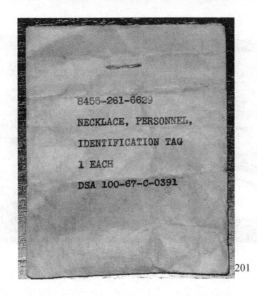

The actually necklace has had many variations for individuals through the years. Whether through changes in regulations or personal preferences, the material and style has had its differences. You can see this in many of the images or in writings when being described.

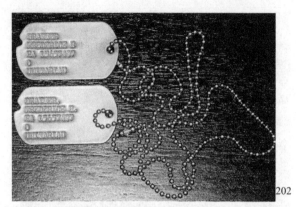

202

A typical metal chain. This one's owner was a Unitarian, and from the collection of Richard Clayton

Materials used have been made of cloth, string, leather, nylon, metal link, metal beads, rayon, etc. The original tags issued, did not have a necklace issued with them, and many people used what they had. To secure the tags on the necklaces, rings, snaps, ties, and pins have been used.

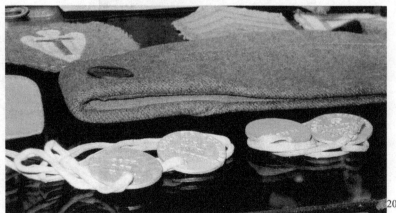

203

WWI Tags on cord chains

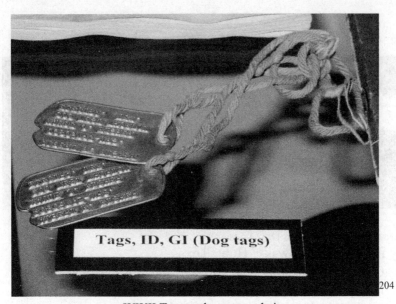

WWII Tags and a cotton chain

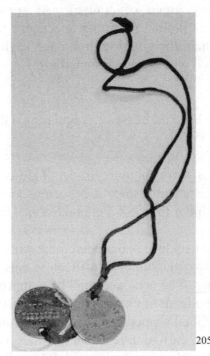

Between the Wars, Dog Tags on a leather chain

The wearer of the necklace and their personal preference has worn them as is, they have added plastic covers or fabric socks to protect them from pulling hairs, from heat or the cold, and from any noise they might make as they hang.

Women often crocheted small bags to hold their identification tags.

206

Crocheted Pouch to hold the Dog Tags
Story from Liz Barkowsky, Hunt, Texas

> Ok, here is a story for you.....when my dad was in the European theater .... France ... he complained to my mother that his dog tags were cold on his skin .... so she crocheted him a little draw string pouch to tuck them away in (army green of course). At some point he crossed a check point....fumbling to retrieve his dog tags from their pouch, the guard let him pass, saying that only an American GI would have such a thing....

Even the covers have been addressed in regulation, GSA Federal Service Supply, A-A-55182.

Today there is a much more in-depth description of what the necklace should be. Especially since it is seen as Government property, it is to be regulated. Under the GSA Federal Service Supply, A-A 55245:

Abstract. The necklace is intended to be worn by military personnel to support two personnel identification tags.
Salient characteristics. The necklace shall be comprised of a main loop and extension loop, made up of chain. The chain shall be comprised of bead shaped and dumbbell shaped elements. The chain and splicing links shall be fabricated from corrosion resistant (stainless) steel. Each bead shaped element shall be Number 3 size, with 97 beads per foot and a tolerance of plus 3 beads, minus none. The overall length of the main loop chain including the splicing link shall be 27 inches, plus 1/4 inch, minus 0 inch. The overall length of the extension loop chain including the splicing link shall be 5-1/2 inches, plus 1/4 inch, minus 0 inch. One splicing link shall be used to join the ends of the main loop chain and

one splicing link shall be used to join the ends of the extension loop chain. All parts of the necklace shall be freely rotatable and longitudinally movable relative to each other. The necklace shall be given a bright polished finish.

2.1.2 Other Government documents, drawings, and publications.

Drawings

3.2 Materials and components.

3.2.1 Steel, corrosion-resistant. The steel shall conform to types 304, 305 or 316, condition annealed, hot-rolled or cold-rolled of ASTM-A 240.

3.3.1 Loop and extension. The main loop and extension loop shall be made of chain. The chain shall be composed of bead shaped and dumbbell shaped elements fabricated from steel specified in 3.2.1. There shall be not less than 7 nor more than 10 bead shaped elements in each inch of necklace length. All parts of the necklace shall be freely rotatable and longitudinally movable relative to each other.

3.3.1.1 Dimensions. The overall length of the main loop including the splicing link shall be 27 inches, plus 1/4 inch, minus 0 inch. The overall length of the extension loop including the splicing link shall be 5-1/2 inches, plus 1/4 inch, minus 0 inch.

3.3.2 Splicing links. The splicing links shall be fabricated from steel specified in 3.2.1 and shall conform to the details and dimensions of Drawing 4-1-486. One splicing link shall be used to join the ends of the main loop and one splicing link shall be used to join the ends of the extension loop.

3.4 Breaking strength. When tested as specified in 4.5.1. The main loop and the extension loop shall have a breaking strength of not less than 15 pounds and not greater than 32 pounds. The section of the loop tested shall include the splicing link.

3.5 Finish. The necklace shall be given a bright polished finish.

3.6 Marking. The contractor may place his identification on the splicing link provided there are no rough edges and the splicing link is not damaged or impaired.

4.5 Methods of inspection.

4.5.1 Breaking strength test. Two breaking strength determinations shall be made on each sample unit (one on the main loop and one on the extension loop). The testing machine shall consist of a means of supporting the chain; and a means for slowly and uniformly applying the load to the chain, and a means for determining the applied load. The chain material shall be inserted in the machine in such a manner that there are no kinks in the chain, that the supporting means and the load applying means do not damage or distort the beads, and that the chain section tested includes the splicing link. A load of 0 to 15 pounds shall be applied uniformly over a period of 1 minute. The load shall then be uniformly increased to determine the maximum breaking strength. If the chain breaks within three beads of the clamping device the test shall be disregarded and repeated. The results shall be reported for each loop to the nearest 0.1 pound. Any result not falling within the limits specified in 3.4 shall be considered a test failure.

6.1 Intended use. The necklace is intended to be worn by military personnel to support, in a regulation manner, two personnel identification tags.

Miscellaneous Items and Information Connected to Dog Tags

Silencers –

Above was shown a very homemade type of silencer. This was not, and is not unusual. Remaining as quiet as possible can be a life or death situation, so silencing the clanging of the Dog Tags and the chain was a very realistic concern. Military service members have been very creative in fulfilling this need. They have removed pieces of rubber from the gas masks, taped them, stripped pieces of fabric, and.......... While choices are out there, the Army actually details its specifications for the wearer.

4-1-481 Cover, Personnel Identification Tag

3.2.1 Plasticized polyvinyl chloride. The Plasticized polyvinyl chloride composition shall be non-toxic (see 3.4) and self-extinguishing, when tested as specified in 4.4.1.2. The material (after curing) shall be soft flexible electrometric plastic conforming to the requirements specified in table I when tested as specified in 4.4.1.2.

3.2.1.1 <u>Color.</u> After curing, the polyvinyl chloride shall match color 33613 of FED-STD-595.

3.3 <u>Construction.</u> Tag covers shall be molded in accordance with the details and dimensions of Drawing 4-1-481. All lettering on the face of the cover shall be raised, shall be legible in the end product, and shall be as shown on Drawing 4-1-481 (see 6.4). All excess material shall be removed in final processing. The finished cover shall be capable of being irreversibly marked with a standard Government ball point pen using heavy pressure. Marking shall remain legible after washing when tested as specified in 4.4.4. At the option of the contractor, core pins may be used to support the spacer plates in the mold, provided the core pin holes do not interfere with the prescription marking areas on the covers.

Dog Tag – Identification Tag Composition

Dog Tags, chains, silencers, and the P-38 can be purchased in military stores, surplus stores, and online. There are hundreds of websites that allow you to purchase them in any color, with whatever information you would like on them. The Chapter on Icons shows images of these choices and lists them in more detail.

"MONEL alloy 400 was patented a century ago in 1906 by the International Nickel Co. It was originally simply referred to as "Monel Metal". It was named after the president of the company, Ambrose Monell. Monel was used for GI dog tags because of it resistance to corrosion (seawater, body fluids, etc.) and the fact that it was readily formed (stamped). Keep in mind, that Monel was developed prior to the advent of stainless steel so it was used for many applications for which we now use lower-priced, iron-base stainless steel products. Interestingly enough, Mr. Monell served in the Canadian army ... unfortunately; we don't know whether he wore "Monel" dog tags." Lew Shoemaker, Technology, Special Metals Corp, e-mail answer, March 19, 2007

207

Ambrose Monell

Current Regulations for the following United States Services –

Army, Air Force, Navy, Marines, and the Coast Guard require the identification tag, but each of the services handles how they require it quite differently. As can be read, the Army and the Air Force list the item in a regulation as required by all members. They list specific details and go in depth, considering the Tag to be an important part of the uniform. The Navy and the Coast Guard do not have anything specifically written for the item beyond acknowledgement of it. The Marines consider it an item used for administration purposes more so than a uniform requirement. All of the services follow suit for their corresponding agencies such as the Reserves or the National Guard. The listings below show only the part of the regulation, if at all, which has to do with discussion of Identification Tags.

Headquarters, Department of the Army
Washington, DC
3 February 2005
Army Regulation 670-1
1–16. Wear of identification tags and security badges

Excerpt:
a. Identification (ID) tags. The wear of ID tags is governed by AR 600–8–14.
(1) Soldiers will wear ID tags at all times when in a field environment, while traveling in aircraft, and when outside the continental United States.
(2) Personnel will wear ID tags around the neck, except when safety considerations apply (such as during physical training).
b. Security identification badges. In restricted areas, commanders may prescribe the wear of security identification badges, in accordance with AR 600–8–14 and other applicable regulations. Personnel will not wear security identification badges outside the area for which they are required. Personnel will not hang other items from the security badge(s). The manner of wear will be determined by the organization that requires wear of the badges.

DEPARTMENT OF THE NAVY
HEADQUARTERS UNITED STATES MARINE
WASHINGTON, DC 20380-1775

MCO P1070.12K
14 Jul 2000
MARINE CORPS ORDER P1070.12K W/CH 1
Subj: MARINE CORPS INDIVIDUAL
Listed in The Marine Corps Individual Records Administration Manual (IRAM)
7005. NOMENCLATURE AND STOCK NUMBERS. Listed below correct nomenclatures and NSNs to requisition ID accessories:
1. Necklace, Personnel, Identification Tag - 8465-
2. Tag, Identification, Personnel - 8465-00-242-
3. Tags, Medical, Warning - 6530-00-142-8775.

NAVY PERSONNEL COMMAND, NAVPERSCOM
Millington TN 38055-0000

1000-1009 Navy Military Personnel, PERS-352

(a) Executive Order 9397 (requires federal agencies to use social security number (SSN) as numerical identifier directive)

(b) 10 U.S.C. 5013 (authorizes SECNAV to collect SSN)

(c) Directive-Type Memorandum (DTM) 07-015-USD (P&R)- "DoD Social Security (SSN) Reduction Plan" of 28 Mar 2008

(d) Privacy Act of 1974

BY ORDER OF THE SECRETARY OF THE AIR FORCE
AIR FORCE INSTRUCTION 36-3103
1 May 1997

Supersedes AFI 36-3103, 2 May 1994. Pages: 3

Distribution: F

This instruction outlines when and how identification (ID) tags are issued to Air Force members and when they are to be worn (or in the member's possession). It applies to all active duty Air Force and Air Reserve Component (ARC) personnel to include Individual Mobilization Augmentees (IMA) of the Air Force Reserve. It specifies commander, Military Personnel Flight (MPF), Unit Deployment Manager (UDM), and member's responsibilities for ensuring tags are prepared, issued, and worn (or in the member's possession). It carries out Air Force Policy Directive (AFPD) 36-31, *Personal Affairs.* Process supplements affecting any military personnel functions as shown in Air Force Instruction (AFI) 37-160, volume 1, table 3.2, *The Air Force Publications and Forms Management Programs--Developing and Processing Publications,* with HQ AFPC/DPWRC, 550 C Street West Suite 15, Randolph AFB, TX 78150-4717.

SUMMARY OF REVISIONS

This revision outlines Unit Commander, MPF Commander, and UDM responsibilities to comply with the Identification Tag Program. It expands guidance on issuance of ID tags and provides clear guidance on wear of ID tags.

1. Responsibilities:

1.1. Unit Commander will:

1.1.1. Ensure one set of ID tags are issued to each member.

1.1.2. Ensure each member understands when and how ID tags are worn.

1.1.3. Inspect the accuracy of ID tags annually to ensure information contained on them is accurate and complete.

COMPLIANCE WITH THIS PUBLICATION IS MANDATORY

2 AFI36-3103 1 May 1997

1.2. MPF Commander will:

1.2.1. Ensure procedures are in place for preparation and issuance of ID tags as required by this instruction.

1.2.2. Ensure procedures are established to dispose of improperly prepared or surrendered ID tags in the most economical method locally available according to AFI 37-132, *Air Force Privacy Act Program.*

1.3. Unit Deployment Manager:

1.3.1. May retain ID tags for members assigned to deployment positions as required by local policy.

1.3.2. Can keep ID tags in a central location within the assigned unit when not in use by member.

1.3.3. Ensures procedures are in place to check out ID tags when needed by member.

1.4. Member will:

1.4.1. Wear or have ID tags in possession while performing duty as an aircrew member.

1.4.2. Wear ID tags while engaging in actual or simulated combat.

1.4.2.1. Actual combat is defined as any duty in a declared war, hostile fire or imminent danger zones, a peacekeeping or humanitarian operation, or a contingency operation to include rotational Temporary Duty (TDY) operations.

1.4.2.2. Simulated combat is defined as duty to support any local, major command, or Joint exercises.

2. Issuance of ID Tags:

2.1. Issue ID tags:

2.1.1. Upon entrance into active duty or Air Reserve Component.

2.1.2. When information contained on ID tag is invalid or ID tags are missing.

2.2. ID tags machine must be equipped to emboss 18 characters on each line, 5 lines on each tag.

2.3. An ID tag set is defined as two tags, one long-length neck chain, and one short-length neck chain.

2.4. ID tags and chains can be ordered through Base Supply using the following National Stock

Numbers (NSN):

2.4.1. ID tag - NSN 8465-00-242-4804. 100 tags per box.

2.4.2. Chain necklace - NSN 8465-00-261-6629. 100 sets per box. Each set contains one long and one short neck chain.

2.5. ID tag preparation:

2.5.1. First line - Name (last name, first name, and middle initial). If entire name does not fit on first line, emboss the last name only on the first line. The first name and middle initial will then fall on the second line, and the information prescribed for each of the remaining lines will advance to the succeeding line.

AFI36-3103 1 May 1997 3

2.5.2. Second line - Social Security Number (SSN) beginning with the first space. *EXAMPLE:*

123-45-6789. Leave two blank spaces and put the letters AF.

2.5.3. Third line - Blood type. Abbreviate Rhesus (RH) factor (either POS for positive or NEG for negative).

2.5.4. Fourth line - Leave blank unless lines two and three carry over.

2.5.5. Fifth line - Designation of religious preference. Show religion or sect designated. If possible, spell out the preference. If member does not wish to designate a preference or make a statement, emboss NO RELIGIOUS PREF.

3. Reissuing Limitations:

3.1. Reissue ID tags only to replace lost tags or to correct changed or erroneous data.

3.2. Do not reissue ID tags to correct administrative errors. Examples are:

3.2.1. Name is correct but does not contain punctuation.

3.2.2. SSN is correct but does not contain hyphens.

3.2.3. Religious preference is embossed on the fourth line versus the fifth line.

4. Wear of ID Tags:

4.1. Wear ID tags around the neck unless such wear creates a valid safety problem. *EXAMPLE:* Precluding injuries to aircrew members during ejection or bailout.

4.1.1. When around the neck, tags will be worn underneath the appropriate garment. *EXAMPLE:* Shirt or blouse.

4.1.2. One tag will be placed on the longer length necklace and one tag on the shorter necklace. The shorter length necklace with tag will be suspended from the longer length necklace with tag.

4.1.3. ID tags may be carried in the pocket when safety factors preclude wear around the neck.

4.1.4. ID tags will not be worn or on the person when working on electrical equipment or systems.

4.1.5. Items such as bottle openers, knives, and so on, will not be worn on the ID tag chain. *EXCEPTION:* Medical alert tags issued by competent medical authority may be worn.

MICHAEL D. McGINTY, Lt General, USAF

DCS/Personnel

United States Coast Guard
U.S. Coast Guard Navigation Center - NAVCEN MS 7310,
Alexandria, VA 20598

COMDTINST M1020.6F -

PURPOSE. This Notice publishes a change to the Uniform Regulations Manual. This Notice is applicable to all active and reserve Coast Guard members and other Service members assigned to duty within the Coast Guard.

2.A.1: Identification Tags: Optional with any uniform, but must be concealed at all times.

4.D.9: Identification will consist of the name and grade of the judge to who issued and the words "Military Judge, USCG" placed on the identification tag provided within the robe.

The Future of Identification Tags

The importance of identification in today's battlefield runs simultaneously with the accessibility of an individual's medical records. The majority of deaths in our earliest wars can be attributed to lack of immediate care and disease. The availability of transport to medical treatment, cleanliness of medical facilities, wound care; clean water, sanitation, and healthy food all play a role in the lower mortality rate in today's wartime conditions.

Looking at identification in this perspective, it is easy to understand why the information we have seen imprinted on the Dog Tags in the past are not in-depth enough. Things happen quickly as was told in the fictional story about Iraq in the first chapter. Thus more information that can be put on a Dog Tag is needed for the first responders and the entire medical process.

In 1997, President Bill Clinton directed "the Department of Defense and Veterans Affairs to create a new Force Health Protection Program. Every Soldier, Sailor, Airman and Marine will have a comprehensive, life-long medical record of all illnesses and injuries they suffer, the care and inoculations they receive and their exposure to different hazards. The records will help us prevent illness and identify and cure those that occur." The Personal Information Carrier (PIC) was developed to hold twenty years of medical records and images taken during this time. Slightly smaller than the size of a Dog Tag, this PIC offered the benefit of a person's medical records without the bulk. Easily accessible to anyone in their medical community.

208

This PIC has the look and feel of a memory card that you use in your digital camera. The downside of this type of tag became known as it was being tested in the US, UK, and Norway. Researchers found that soldiers did not always keep the PIC with their Dog Tags, and finding the PIC on the body became an issue. Medical personnel had to search pockets, back packs, or go through several layers of clothing trying to find the PIC. This was not conducive to helping an individual who needed medical assistance right away. If any part of the body or equipment were separated from the body, medical personnel were back to square one.[209]

They also found the PIC failed under certain environments and conditions. Temperature, sweat, rough handling, and the passage of time played an integral part in the failure of the PIC. Another type of Digital Dog Tag needed to be made to withstand the common conditions soldiers lived and worked under.

Solving this issue was a priority for the US Congress and in April, 2004, President George W. Bush stated, "Within ten years, every American must have a personal electronic medical record...The federal government has got to take the lead in order to make this happen by developing what's called technical standards." Knowing how important individual information is to first responders, the Medical Research and Materiel Command (MRMC) and Telemedicine & Advanced Technology Research Center played a key role in developing the Joint Electronic Information Carrier (EIC). The EIC has been fielded with service members numerous times to continue its development and improve its capabilities.

Frequency of Operation	3-10 GHz
Modulation	MB-OFDM
Data Rate	>100Mbps
Range	30 Meters, Extended Range option ~1Km
Memory	512 Mb-16GB, options
Encryption	128 bit AES, FIPS 140-2 evaluated encryption, Malware installed
Physical Specifications	Dimensions (lxwxh) 64x24x12mm 17.0 grams
Environmental Specifications	Operating Temperature -20°C to 80°C Operating humidity 100%, Ruggedized IP68
FCC	FCC Part 15 compliance
Battery Life, between recharges	1 year, 24x power cycles with 20 MB data transfers each cycle
TRL	Level 6, ready for TRL7 applications
Expected Field Life	3-years

From Medical Research and Materiel Command (MRMC) and Telemedicine & Advanced Technology Research Center. Joint Electronic Information Carrier (EIC).

210

The EIC is once again worn like the traditional Dog Tags, and is close to their size and often carried alongside the Dog Tags. The current generation of EICs or Digital Dog Tags can be tracked wirelessly and found within a 2-10 meter range. The benefit of having this is immeasurable. If a soldier is separated from his EIC, a small device scans for the tags within range and transmits the information. The information is encrypted.[211]

From a physical form factor standpoint, this device is ruggedized to withstand excessive shock and reliability in austere environments. The EIC contains a Universal Serial Bus (USB) physical interface. This will facilitate anywhere, anytime communications with all standard personal computers and future electronic devices. The USB interface was identified as the standard physical interface for the next Electronic Information Carrier by the Services and Joint Staff. The physical size of the device is comparable with the current military issued "Dog Tag" and the commercially available USB thumb drives.

212

"The storage capacity of the device is currently set at one gigabyte due to cost effective technology capabilities; however, capacities as high as 16GB are currently available. This storage allows for saving and transporting demographics, allergies, medications, and a complete medical history for a single soldier as well as digital medical images and even video and audio. During the past 5 years, this cost break line has increased 100 times. Future EICs will leverage the most recent cost effective standard. The EIC is recognized by the PC as a standard removable drive. This standard drive is accessible in the same way for direct connection and wireless connectivity. An internal battery is required for wireless communication. This battery has been demonstrated to provide up to four months of power without recharging. Charging occurs automatically while inserted directly to the PC. Some advanced battery saving algorithms are included that provide sleep operation for the EIC. A life of more than one year with routine use in the field is expected.

The addition of wireless capability offers the greatest advancement to what is currently available in a commercial off-the-shelf solution. This capability provides several key functions that make the EIC a revolutionary prototype for future military medicine. A prototype delivered to the U.S. Army Medical Research and Materiel Command in November 2008 provided a functional wireless communication storage device that effectively transmitted data up to 10 meters within FCC guidelines. Read/write ranges of 1 kilometer can be realized in a deployed setting by increasing the power output. Although, currently there is no defined standard for wireless communication among mobile devices that is approved for theatre, the EIC leverages encrypted secure communication the meets or exceeds the DoD security requirements. The wireless interface is managed by a wireless USB transceiver and behaves in the same way as if the EIC is directly plugged in.

A secondary wireless signal within the EIC provides authentication, patient tracking and proximity for anyone who carries the device. This patient tracking capability allows the EIC to integrate with TMDS, JTTR and any other adopted military storage and tracking system. Proximity features can provide single sign on and authentication capability. Using a special low-rate, long-range mode, the EIC can transmit an emergency beacon that is virtually undetectable by the enemy, that includes critical local data (health, GPS, etc.).

A complementary demonstration of synchronization functionality took place the first week of December 2008. This demonstrated automatic data synchronization between EIC and a health information system (HIS) such as AHLTA, to include any civilian health information systems that are "interface enabled". There are additional Digital Rights Management (DRM) benefits that support tailored permissions on the EIC or HIS. This capability supports seamless bi-directional synchronization of encounter data between patient's EIC and AHLTA-T application. This also provides a controlled and secured method to non-military facilities for viewing and adding their encounter information to the soldier's "personally-held" EIC. This makes Patient's '911' information available in case of medical emergencies without requiring any installation."[213]

It is hard to believe that technology could get any better, but research and development for the EIC program continue to work on doing just that. Knowing someone in the platoon can help immediately with a hand held device has far surpassed the original disk offered the Union Army by John Kennedy. Technology has advanced, but the EIC must still be carried by the individual in the field, and the Dog Tag still remains an important part of identification.

"Wearing your ID tags is one of the easiest actions you can make towards achieving total readiness, so take those tags out of your dresser and put them around your neck. Remember -the simple information contained on that small aluminum tag can speak for you if you can't speak for yourself; it could mean the difference between a positive identification and an uncertain future for those who survive you, should your identity be "...known only to God."[214]

Chapter Seven

Foreign Dog Tags

*"Show me the manner in which a nation or community cares for its dead
and I will measure exactly the sympathies of its people, their respect for
the laws of land, and their loyalty to high ideals."*
Attributed to William E. Gladstone
former Prime Minister of Great Britain [215]

While the nickname "Dog Tag" is American, the use of
identification tags is not solely an American idea. Many countries have
used some sort of identification throughout the years, and have their own
history to be told. They have unique shapes, materials, and information
imprinted on them, but all are basically for the same reasons. To their
government, they are for identification and collection. For the person and
their family, they are for identification and memory.

"Back in the days of sailing ships, sailors would often have a
gold ear-ring in their left ear, so that when they died and burial at sea
took place it served as payment for someone to give him a Christian
service before casting off into the sea, hence he was being remembered.
During the Napoleon Wars (1799-1815) many of the French-English
soldiers began doing the same, for on the battle field the dead were
placed into mass graves with little too nothing said. So by having the ear
ring payment was made for a proper service." [216]

The following countries have record of personal military
identification in some sort, there might very well be more, but these are
what I have found through my research:

Great Britain	France
Poland	Russia
Finland	New Zealand
Canada	Japan
China	Australia
Belgium	Italy
Hungary	Austria

As in the United States, paper records have been found listing
personal information and have been kept with records. Most paper

records are kept within something, often a small metal clip or locket much like the American one shown.

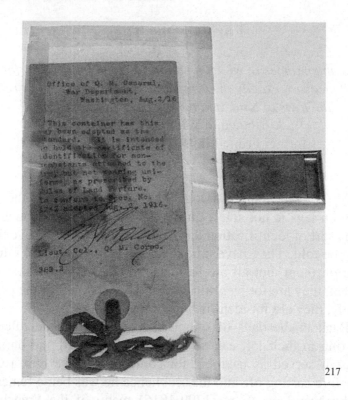

217

This kept the paper relatively safe from dirt, fire, sweat, and normal wear and tear. If not folded and secured in such a clip, the information might be kept in a booklet or pamphlet like a passport is today, or as an identity card or leaflet. The information, most times, was the same – name, address, unit.

The first time Great Britain documented having an identification disk by their Government was during the second Boer War in South Africa. Troop morale was low. Most of the country believed this war was supposed to be over quickly, especially the soldiers. Queen Victoria worried about this and decided she wanted to give a gift to her soldiers and sailors for Christmas, 1899.

Royal commemoratives date back to the 15th century for Britain.[218] Queen Victoria wanted to send her units something from home and a small tin to be filled with chocolates was made. Filled with this luxury and made by a company called Cadbury, this tin was red and showed the Queen's profile on the top of the tin. Over forty thousand tins were sent to soldiers and sailors of British and Australian service in South Africa.

208

A perfect size for chocolates, but the tin was not much use for anything else. It found its way into the history books as a possession which held the items of a fallen soldier or sailor and it was shipped home to their families with their identification items inside. The identification means was often a strip of fabric or personally engraved items. Thus, the same as during our Civil War, this was to be kept in their pockets. The tin is now a cherished collectable to those families which kept them, and to the collectors who scavenge websites, flea markets or "Boot Fairs," and estate sales looking for the tins and the items they held.

For Britain and Australia, regulations addressed the importance of identification around the same time as America, in 1906, and then followed suit in the same around World War I to require two disks to be carried around their necks with one disk being made of a fiber board and the other one in metal. The two identification tags were different shapes, and as in many countries, different colors at times. The colors most used are natural, red, green, and the metallic silver. One was to be buried with the soldier for future identification, and the other was to be shipped home with the remains and effects.

E-mail from **Peter Harrington**, March 13, 2007
Peter Harrington
Curator
Anne S. K. Brown Military Collection
Box A, Brown University Library

Dear Ginger:
I am afraid that we don't have any dog tags in the Military Collection here at Brown, but I am attaching a scan of a WWI British dog-tag (actually my grandfather's), that might be of interest for comparative purposes. [49715 Pte. Whitehurst, J, 1/7 M/C (Manchester Regiment) C.E. (Church of England)].

My grandfather, James Whitehurst, died in 1968, and never really shared his experiences with me. I do recall that he still had shrapnel in his hand and legs (my grandmother had several pieces of shrapnel that she had 'worked' out of his body over the years), a small hole in his temple, and was missing three fingers. He was crippled in one arm. I was told that he was very badly wounded (on the 'Somme' although I have not confirmed where he was wounded) and that a friend had crawled out at night to bring him back. He spent months recuperating in a military hospital in Manchester, England, where he met my grandmother who was a nurse there. She, herself, had wanted to go to France to nurse but her brother did not encourage it. It turned out that the hospital eventually became a school which I attended for 3 years!

My grandmother's brother, Edward George Godfrey, was in a reserved occupation in the summer of 1914, but apparently a girl gave him a white feather, and moved by it he joined a cavalry regiment, but realizing the unlikelihood of seeing much action, transferred to the King's Own Yorkshire Light Infantry, and was in the trenches by October 1914. He went right through to 1918 only to be killed near Ypres in the April. I don't have his dog tag but I do have a diary dating from 1914 until late 1915 when he was heading for Salonika.
Peter

Most countries that had identification disks of some kind were made of metal. The information imprinted on it was normally individually done by hammering or scratching the info onto the metal surface. The fiber board tags were hand stamped leaving an impression on the board of the information. This type of tag was found not to be as tough as the metal version. While there are still countries using the fiber board as a tag, it is used as a secondary tag.

From: **Lyne-Gordon David**

  Hi Ginger,

     At last, I've found my Dad's RAF tag (1.5" x 1.25") and punched 'D C GORDON, CE (Church of England), 133765 on the obverse and "13" on the reverse. It's a sort of dark green fibrous material.

David

D C Gordon

From: Lyne-Gordon David   [mailto:d.lynegordon@xxxxxxx.com]
     Sent: Thursday, February 7, 2008 10:01 AM
     To: images@dogtaghistory.com
     Cc: ian.brown47@xxxxxx.com
     Subject: RE: Stalag XIII

Hi Ginger,

The tag was found (by me) in the grounds of my parents hotel in Folkestone, Kent (UK). The hotel had been set up by my grandparents in 1923 and during WWII it had been briefly occupied by the Royal Canadian Army Service Corps until they went to France post-D Day. At the end of the war it was used temporarily to house armed services' personnel returning from the Continent. My family gave it up in 1977 and it was demolished in 2003.

Number 9211 was probably J.H. McKenzie, 26249, Pte, 2NZEF, from New Zealand. I say probably because there was some duplication of POW numbers, but very little in the 9000's. I must thank Ian Brown for this as yet unsubstantiated information.

David

Lyne-Gordon David <d.lynegordon@xxxxxxxxx.com>
Monday, February 18, 2008 07:39 am
Hi Ginger,
Here are a couple more treasures for your research and site. Cyril
Newall was with BEF (British Expeditionary Force) serving in The
Buffs. He was picked up at Dunkirk, he and his comrades had somehow
been overtaken by German troops and thus captured. He was taken to
Stalag XXA (see tag and hanger) and Buffs ID(?). His son John Newall
kindly loaned me these pieces. They are now in the "safe" keeping of his
grandson, Josh Newall.
 Best regards,
David

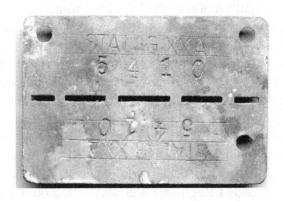

The Identification of a German Soldier found in the Heidenkopf at Serre, by Alastair H Fraser

"Since 1997 a group of archaeologists, historians and enthusiasts have been carrying out a series of digs, mainly in the village of Auchonvillers (France), in conjunction with a project to collect information on the immediate front line area. As project historian I have been working on this for about seven years and with help from contributors all over the world I have amassed an impressive amount of material on one small section of the Western Front.

In October 2003 we were invited to participate in an archaeological investigation to be conducted in a field east of the Serre to Mailly-Maillet road on the old Somme battlefield. Following the discovery of the three sets of remains the team began work on the process of attempting to identify the men. The investigation was started by myself in Britain and Volker Hartmann in Germany. One German soldier, the subject of this study, has been identified and we are hopeful that documents found on the second German may result in his identification as well. The British soldier was a member of 1st King's Own (Royal Lancaster) Regiment and was killed on 1st July 1916 but efforts by CWGC and ourselves to identify him have been unsuccessful.

He was buried this summer in Serre Road No.2 cemetery, very close to where he fell.

German no.1, as he was then known, was found lying on his back in a small depression east of a German trench near Serre Road No.2 cemetery. His head was missing, probably removed by subsequent ploughing, and he had no headgear or personal weapon although the remains of his uniform, ammunition pouches and bread bag were still in situ. These presented some interesting features from which it was possible to make a reasonable deduction on his unit and date of death.

There are considerable difficulties inherent in an investigation of this nature. Despite battlefield clearance and burial in July 1916, the spring of 1917 and after the war the Heidenkopf or Quadilateral position is likely to contain large quantities of human remains from the British, French and German armies. The history of the German 121 Reserve Infanterie Regiment for 1st July 1916 sets out the scale of the problem. "There were about 150 German dead in the Heidenkopf in a relatively small area and about three times that number of English." This area was fought over in October 1914, June 1915, July and November 1916 and March and April 1918. Added to that it saw routine trench warfare during much of the period, with mortaring, shelling and sniping likely to cause fatal casualties.

It is also worth bearing in mind that although the German Army had a precise, highly detailed and well documented system of regimental identification this did not long survive the outbreak of war. Identification of units from surviving uniform remains may not be reliable. Photographic evidence shows that German army units often did not adhere to strict uniform regulations from 1914 onwards. War raised units were formed from companies taken from a variety of regiments who may have retained their original uniform issue. Various patterns of obsolete, hybrid or stopgap equipment and clothing were issued to cover deficiencies, a process demonstrated with German no.1. As the war progressed regulation uniform items were often modified to retain older features, for example the M1915 Bluse, intended as a simplified, economy measure, frequently had cuffs and other details altered or added to. Conversely tunic decoration was often removed to hinder the identification of units by the enemy. Due to clothing shortages the Germans also repaired or modified clothing taken from casualties and reissued it to other soldiers.

During the excavation a badly corroded identity disc was recovered from the chest area and this seemed the best chance of identifying the casualty. However on cleaning it was apparent that not all the legend on the disc has survived and frustratingly it was an early pattern, which did not include the name of the individual. The only information on these discs was the regimental designation and number, the number of the company and the number of the individual on the company roll.

From the remains of the disc we now knew that the man served with a reserve infantry regiment but unfortunately the number was missing; he was in 7 Kompanie and was number 2 on their roll, so presumably enlisted or re-enlisted in August 1914. Interestingly it was known that 7 Kompanie of 121 RIR were in the trenches that later became the Heidenkopf from 10th to 13th June 1915. During these few days there was heavy fighting and it was possible that the soldier had been killed at that time. They were not in that area on 1st July 1916, which was the other period at which one would expect unrecovered casualties. It was clear that the owner was uneasy about the lack of a name on his identity disc, as he had rather clumsily scratched some details on the reverse with a knifepoint or something similar. Again the corrosion had removed some of the legend but it was possible to read the top line as "Mun ... ", the second line as "Hines", and the bottom line "Jak ...". The difficulty was in deciding what this meant. The first line could either be part of a street name, a place name or a personal name; the second line made no sense at all as it is not a German surname or an identifiable place and the bottom line could again be part of a street or place name, a Christian name or a surname. Without access to full casualty lists for 26 Reserve Division we were unlikely to progress any further. The printed history of 121 RIR, the prime candidate for our man's unit, did not contain casualty rolls for ranks below Feldwebel Leutnant. There our investigation stuck for a couple of weeks.

I was fortunate enough to make contact with Ralph Whitehead on the World War I Forum. For some years Ralph has been researching the German XIV Reserve Korps on the Somme. He was able to supply a list of casualties for 121 RIR assembled from privately published lists and the officially produced Verlustlisten. Scrolling down to 7 Kompanie I found a Jakob Hones who was killed on 13th June 1915. Re-examination of the identity disc showed that the "I" of "Hines" was in fact an "o" with an umlaut. Ralph was also able to state that Hones came from a village near Stuttgart called Munchingen, which explained the first line of the scratched legend on the reverse of the disc. It was extremely satisfying that we had identified the man and also that our methodology had allowed us to make a spot-on deduction of when he was killed and what unit he was with.

Armed with this information Volker Hartmann contacted the archives in Munchingen and received some further information on Jakob Hones, including the astonishing news that one of his sons was still alive. Ernst Christian Hones was very frail and elderly and was not able to supply any useful detail on his father, whom he probably never knew, but he was pleased that he had been found and would have a grave in a German military cemetery. We were able to get some facts from the Hones family, many of whom still live in Munchingen and we are most grateful for their help and the photographs that they supplied. From this it is possible to produce a short biography of one German infantryman.

Jakob Hones was born in Munchingen in Wurttemberg on 9th December 1880. He was one of at least three children and his profession is described in the Verlusteliste as Landwirt which translates as "farmer". The Munchingen archives however give his profession as Tagelohner which means "day labourer" or "farmhand". He probably did his military service from 1900 to 1902 and certainly served in 121 Infanterie Regiment whose depot was in Ludwigsburg. His wife was called Marie and they had six children, the last of whom was born in December 1914. Soldiers in the Reserve were liable for annual training so Jakob's military skills were probably kept up to scratch. He was called back to the colours on 2nd August 1914 on mobilisation and served with 7 Kompanie, II Battalion, 121 RIR, which was raised in Heilbronn. The second battalion was commanded by Major Otto Burger and the commander of 7 Kompanie was Oberleutnant von Raben. The German mobilisation of 1914 was an enormous undertaking, which increased the strength of the army almost overnight from about 800,000 men to over 4,000,000. It is hardly surprising that there were shortages of equipment and some men in 121 RIR had to make do with obsolete ammunition pouches. By 18th August the regiment was in contact with the French in the Vosges mountains and had suffered its first casualties. Jakob Hones probably had his baptism of fire the next day when II/121 RIR was committed to an attack near Breuschatel. Fighting continued around Nancy and Epinal until late September when the 26 Reserve Division was entrained for a move northwards as part of the series of outflanking moves that has wrongly gone down in history as "The race for the sea".

The division was unloaded from its trains at Cambrai and marched down to Bapaume. They were soon fighting the French again in the Thiepval and Ovillers area. The night of 28th/29th September was a particularly unpleasant one and although 7 Kompanie escaped unscathed 5 and 6 Kompanie both suffered. The regiment suffered 20 dead, 212 wounded and 80 missing. The casualties included Major Burger, wounded by a stray bullet. Interestingly 4 Bayerische Infantrie Division was in the line next to 26 Reserve Division. It may be at this time that Jakob did a swap and obtained a Bavarian belt. As the line became more permanent 121 RIR occupied the southern part of the ruined village of Thiepval. Their sector stretched south to the Wundt-Werk with regimental headquarters at Mouquet Farm.

It seems likely that Jakob Hones was hit and seriously wounded during the preparatory bombardment, as his full ammunition pouches indicate that he did not take part in the defence of the position. A shrapnel ball had penetrated his bread bag and a number of small shell splinters were found in the pelvis. It appears that he did not die immediately as a family story has it that his brother Christian was with him at his death. At some stage either before or after death Jakob was wrapped in a ground sheet. He may have been slung out on to parados of the trench and dragged for some distance by his feet, before being placed in the hole where he was found nearly 90 years later. The fact that the eyelet holes of the groundsheet were found round his body and that his pouches had ridden up to his chest support this interpretation. Jakob was reported as killed rather than missing, which would indicate that his death was witnessed.

Sadly the death of Jakob was only the first blow that the Hones family were to suffer in the Great War. A year later his brother Wilhelm was killed at Hill 60 in the Ypres salient whilst serving with 125 Infantrie Regiment and on 24th July 1916 Christian Hones was seriously wounded and died at the dressing station in Miraumont. Jakob and Wilhelm are commemorated, together with another Hones who may be a relation, on the war memorial in Munchingen. We had hoped that Jakob might be buried at Fricourt with some of his comrades but this cemetery is no longer open for burials. However on 26th August 2004 Jakob Hones was buried at Labry German Military Cemetery near Verdun. 14 members of his family were in attendance as well as Volker Hartmann, representing No Man's Land. By an extraordinary co-incidence a party of uniformed Bundeswehr signals personnel were present tending the graves. They were pleased to be able to provide Jakob and his currently unidentified comrade with a guard of honour. The past has an odd way of sometimes tugging at your sleeve. At some time Jakob Hones was concerned that his identity disc did not have his name on and that he would never be identified. The investigation has been a fascinating and successful exercise but most importantly we have been able to do a small service for a man long dead. He now has a grave with a cross that has his name on it."[219]

220

Into World War II, the Germans had the most extensive listing of tags for their soldiers and their prisoners. The German military identification tag was called Erkennungsmarke.[221] It is most interesting to note that the Germans did not usually put the name of the soldier on the tag. As important as personal identity was to Hitler and his war machine, individuals were required to carry all sorts of personal identification on them. Not only their Identification tags, but military documents, soldier pay books, travel passes, and family booklets.

German Identity Discs of World War Two

222

Not only to be hung around the neck or carried with them, identification was to be worn on their arms. The disk is an oval shaped disk with a perforation across the center to allow for separation. It is thin enough to be able to separate by hand, and if separated, both halves have the same information on it for identification procedures. "With the top half left on the body of the fallen soldier foe identification, the removed half was returned with his soldbuch (soldier's pay book) and personal belongings to the Company Commander, where documents were written up with details of all actions including how and where the soldier died. In most cases soldbuch/wehrpass and piece of tag were kept together often being given to the next of kin as a personal momento."[223]

"The basic field personnel record for all draft-eligible males was called a Wehrpass. It was created and issued during the first visit to a draft/recruiting office by the soldier in question, and was maintained by the individual at home until called up for duty. The Wehrpass usually contained a civilian-dress photo on the inside front cover, unless the individual was already on active duty when his draft was reinstituted. A plethora of items were recorded in each soldiers Wehrpass including unit administrative notes and records, dates of assignments, promotions, awards, battles, major injuries or illnesses, etc. Upon a soldiers discharge his Wehrpass was returned after all the field entries were transferred to the Wehrstammbuch - a series of documents covering national veterans used to document a soldiers service for claiming benefits, etc. If a soldier was killed or became MIA while on duty, the Wehrpass was sent to his next of kin by the soldier's original recruiting office."[224]

"The information on the tag varied throughout the war, but generally consisted of the designation of the individual's initial replacement unit (the unit all soldiers were inducted to before being sent to a regular field unit), a soldier number, and the soldier's blood type. Initially, all German units of Kompanie size were required to maintain complete lists of all soldiers and their Erkennungsmarke. These lists would be updated as needed once a month with any additions and subtractions based on men lost as KIA, MIA, through transfers or sick leave, or that were gained through replacements and transfers or soldiers returned from sick leave. This offical Kompanie listing was registerd with the German Armed Forces Information Office for Casualties and War Prisoners, and was kept as up-to-date as possible."

The 3d Reich made Identification tags for their prisoners. Larger than the personal tags, but similar in no name for identification, the tags hung on the neck of the prisoners.

Unit: 3rd Infantry Division, 15th Infantry, 3rd Battalion,
     Company I
Service Location: Italy; France; Germany
Highest Rank: Technical Sergeant
POW: Yes
Place of Birth: Chicago, IL

225

Joe Littell:
"One day I was walking across the compound and there was a prisoner named Mark. I don't remember his last name. Young fellow about my age, about 19. And he was carrying wood on a work detail. And he was very weak, you know. We had very, very small rations there. People were having dysentery, they were having starvation problems, and they were really having trouble carrying wood, carrying briquettes to the officers' barracks, and so forth. And this was a very serious thing.

After one month, by the way, five Americans had already died and some people were struggling and wobbling around a little bit. And Mark was one of them. He stumbled and fell and all of his wood went flying. Up to him came a German officer and said, [German insult]. Get up, you damned Jew. Well, I wasn't nearby but I heard him say something. I didn't know that until I asked Mark later what he had said. And I came up there because I wanted to see what was going on, but I also wanted this officer to know that somebody was witness to this conversation. And that officer started to kick this man, Mark. And finally Mark struggled to his feet and he picked up his wood slowly and went off in the direction of where his fellow wood detail people were.

Well, two days later Mark came back to me and he said, Joe, I've thrown away my dog tags. You know the dog tag is the identification tag that all U.S. servicemen, soldiers at least, wear around their collars, around their necks, with their name and serial number and a letter of some kind -- H or C or P -- H for Hebrew, C for Catholic, P for Protestant. And that enables the powers that be, if anything happens to you, to make sure that you're buried or given last rites of the proper service. I mean, it's just right. He said, I've thrown away my dog tag. And that's all I remember about   that.

And then a couple of days later he came back to me and said, You know, I've been thinking about this. I lay awake all night last night. I'm ashamed that I threw away my dog tag. I have renounced my Jewish faith in doing that. I didn't want the Germans to know that I was Jewish. And he said, I'm prouder of that than anything. And he said, I won't let that happen again no matter what it costs me."[226]

The German POWs had basically three shapes during WWII. There is the most frequently seen shape as with this recollection, a rectangle that breaks in the middle. Then there was a rectangular shape with softened corners that did not break in the middle. And lastly, a triangular shaped tag with no break through it.

Questionnaire Submitted:
Name of Dog Tag Owner: SEYMOUR LICHTENFELD, Veteran

Where were you first issued your Dog Tags? Ft. Benjamin Harrison, Indiana 1943

If so, where did you purchase them? Was issued a replacement set
Why did you purchase another set? Originals were destroyed during combat

Where on your body did you wear your Dog Tags? Around the neck

Do you have any special story about your Dog Tags? Yes
My outfit was surrounded for three days at the beginning of the Battle of the Bulge in Dec 1944. We were without food and ammunition and the end result was obvious if we were not killed. I am Jewish and my

dog tag had a Capital H on it for religion (Hebrew). Knowing the circumstances in Germany at that time regarding Jews, I removed my tags and ground them into the dirt at the bottom of my fox hole just prior to being captured. I had no means to identify myself as an American GI until after I was liberated by the Russians and returned to US Army control. It was then that a new pair of dog tags were issued to me for the remainder of my stay in the service.

Where do you keep your Dog Tags? I have given them to my children

Anything else you would like to share: I have written an account of my combat and prison days and it is in the Library of Congress. It is entitled "KRIEGIE 312330 – A PRISONERS STORY" by Seymour Lichtenfeld

In America, "when German prisoners were taken, the order to clean the POWs meant the removal of all their badges, documents and identity discs which were handed over to the Intelligence Corps. Bearing in mind even small pieces of metal or string could be a danger to their captors. The Soldbuchs (military id) were usually returned with the photograph removed to prevent false papers being made. But the discs were never given back."[227]

Dog Tags of the Finnish Army were much like the German ones, in the shape of an oval with perforated holes in the middle to break apart. The halves were to be distributed similarly, also. One part was to stay with the body while the other was to be given to a Finnish Officer as proof of the deceased.

The Red Army of 1930s also had dog tags. They were different from Finnish tags. They were either small flat metallic boxes with a piece of paper in it with the name and all personal information written on it, or a bakelite lipstick-shaped box with a similar piece of paper. On the piece of paper a soldier was supposed to write his full name, date of birth and home address.[228]

The Russian Army had POW tags with two styles. One was similar to a metal coin with raised information on it. The other one found is a square cardboard style with a break in the middle and information printed on both halves.

229

The Japanese Dog Tag

"Bataan Rescue producers David Axelrod and Peter Jones found many veterans -- former POWs and their rescuers -- with indelible memories of their wartime experiences. That death march was just plain murder," remembered ex-POW Bob Body. "...As you walked along you could smell, the odor was terrible from guys that had been left a day or so ahead of time, and laying in the sun, you know, and they left them people laying there. It's still hard for me to believe that this actually happened, and it is still hard for me to believe that I went through that."
"One of the duties that I had in the morning was to walk down through the [prison] barracks and take care of those men that had died, recalled former POW Tommie Thomas. "...One of my obligations was to remove his dog tags and put one dog tag down his throat as far as I could get it and I had a little forked stick that I used to push it right down to his throat. And the reasoning for that was for purposes of identification at a later date."

"Sometimes I wonder how I did it," said former POW Ralph Rodriguez of the 30-mile march after the rescue. "You have to remember, [the Japanese] were behind us, we could hear them shooting, they were trying to break through."[230]

Colin E (Col) Benson
E-mail: valiant@xxx.xxx.au, February 14, 2007 12:56 pm
Laverton Air Force Base, Victoria, Australia.

Questionnaire Submitted
Did you wear them when you were off duty? Yes worn throughout my 20 years of (Australian) air force service. Initially supplied with a chain that I changed to a leather bootlace

Did you add anything to your Dog Tag or its chain?
No, still have them 25 years after discharge from the service in 1982, and 45 years after enlistment, in 1962.

Where on your body did you wear your Dog Tags? Around my neck. In Vietnam, many Aussie airmen working with aircraft on the tarmac wore shorts and no shirt, so they had a dog tag on the lace of their safety boots. (American GIs generally were fully clothed on the tarmac, although some took off their shirts!)
Reason for wearing them where you did. If the airman was injured or killed he still had ID on his boots.

How did you feel about your Dog Tags during your service? Part of the uniform

How did you feel about your Dog Tags after you got out of the service? They are stored with my medals and memorabilia. Last week, I took them to a reunion – 45 years since I enlisted with others as RAAF radio apprentices (then aged 15 – 17).

.. .other than they are Australian – Royal Australian Air Force – dog tags. One is octagonal with two holes the other round with one hole. They each are stainless steel, engraved with initials, name, RAAF and religion.

Where do you keep your Dog Tags? In a display cabinet with my medals
Colin E (Col) Benson
Mackay, Latitude 21, Down Under

While many countries have evolved into tags that closely resemble ours, there are some that are still very unique. Austria has a different shape, and yet it seems to be a combination of many different ones. It hangs like the American tags, but breaks in the middle like the original German ones.

Austria

From an e-mail, October 3, 2007 - Andreas Krennmair <ak@xxxxxxxx.at>

Hi,

The story behind this dog tag is the following: in Austria, we have conscription system, so every man (until the age of 35) has to do military service or alternatively, civil service, for 6 resp. 9 months. I spent most of my service at one of the units that do physical examinations to find out which men are fit for service and which are not. This whole physical examination unit is part of a unit called "Ergänzungsabteilung" (roughly translates to "complement unit", i.e. the unit that is responsible for organizing and scheduling the physical exams and the subsequent conscription). One of the tasks for us servicemen was to produce the dog tags for all those who were "fit" according to the physical examination, and to tape them to each person's file. We had special machines for this, and pretty much free access. The dog tag that you can see on the picture was a product of our boredom: the "1337" is Leetspeak. A few were produced for our personal amusement, with "1337" instead of the personal ID (which is a much longer number). In the middle, you can clearly see the perforation where the dog tag is to be broken, the "A" visible on both sides means "Austria", the "Bl Gr" on the upper left side means "blood type", and the "Rh" on the upper right side means "Rhesus factor". The fields below them are embossed for a soldier "when there is time" (in my case, it was when I left the Army...). After leaving the Army, every serviceman takes his dog tag with him.

Regards,

Andreas

Andreas directed me to find the definition for "Leetspeak." It is a way to alter the language so that it intentionally plays with words in an amusing way. The image below is the specific tag he is talking about. So, if you look at the numbers upside down, you might be able to see that it looks like "leet."

The current Canadian, Dutch, and German tags all break in half to be separated at death. Hanging from a chain, the Dutch and Canadian ones are almost full size, double tags, both with the same information on each half.

Dutch Tags

Canadian Tags

However it's done, identification is too important from either the practical aspect or the emotional one. It is easily acknowledged that other countries use the identity disks for the same reason this book addresses – to identify a body or a wounded soldier and not to be unknown.

Mistakes have always been made and foreign countries have learned the same lessons in regard to burial and identification as America learned in its past. As stated throughout this book: to their government, they are for identification and collection. For the person and their family, they are for identification and memory.

Endnotes

[1] The American Heritage Dictionary (2nd college ed.). (1991). Boston: Houghton Mifflin.

[2] Jim Murphy, Boys' War, Confederate and Union Soldier's Talk About the Civil War, 1993, Sandpiper
<http://www.digitalhistory.uh.edu/learning_history/children_civilwar/child_soldie rs.cf m>.

[3]Union and Confederate Dead – Gettysburg, PA, July 1863, Images 0-233 are from The National Archives and Records Administration, Washington, DC.

[4] Jim Murphy, Boys' War, Confederate and Union Soldier's Talk About the Civil War, 1993, Sandpiper
<http://www.digitalhistory.uh.edu/learning_history/children_civilwar/child_soldiers.cf m>.

[5] Letter from John Kennedy to the Secretary of War's on May 12, 1862. It is filed under K-206- 1862 and includes a drawing of his proposed disk. The file has been reproduced as part of National Archives Microfilm Publication M221, Letters Received by the Secretary of War, Main Series, 1801-1870. It appears a copy of the response is also in file K-206-1862. The response is also found in the Secretary of War Letters Sent series in Military Book 49, A, page 168. This volume is reproduced on National Archives Microfilm Publication M6, Letters Sent by the Secretary of War Relating to Military Affairs, 1800-1809.

[6] Courtesy of Motts Military Museum, Columbus, Ohio.

[7] Harper's Weekly, October 3, 1863.

[8] MINER, AMOS B.-Age, 22 years. Enlisted, September 20, 1861, at Pitcher, to serve three years; mustered in as corporal, Co. B, October 4, 1861; discharged for disability, September 12, 1862, at Washington, D. C.; again enlisted (Regimental History says, "drafted"), August 31, 1863, as a private, same company; captured in action, May 5, 1864, at the Wilderness, Va.; died, December 1, 1864, at Florence, S. C., a prisoner of war. Courtesy Mike Brown, Blair Atholl: <http://www.bpmlegal.com/scotland/,> 76th NY: <http://www.bpmlegal.com/76NY/>, Taughannock District: <http://www.tompkinscortlandscouts.org >.

[9] Virginia. Newspaper vendor and cart in camp, 1863 November, LC-B811- 617A, LC-DIG-cwpb-01140 (digital file from original neg.), LC-B8171-0617 (b&w film neg.), Gardner, Alexander, 1821-1882, photographer., Civil War photographs, 1861-1865 / compiled by Hirst D. Milhollen and Donald H. Mugridge, Washington, D.C. : Library of Congress, 1977. No. 0238, Selected Civil War photographs, 1861-1865 (Library of Congress), Library of Congress Prints and Photographs Division Washington, D.C. 20540 USA, CONTROL #: cwp2003000238/PP.

[10] Sutler's Tent, 1864 Nov, 3b04855, LOT 4172, LC-USZ62-57024, Original glass negative no.: LC-B811-2448., Library of Congress Prints and Photographs Division Washington, D.C. 20540 USA, CONTROL #: 2004682783.

[11] Wooden Body Tag, Courtesy of the Us Army Quartermaster Museum, Ft. Lee, Virginia.

[12] Quartermaster Professional Bulletin (QPB), Defense Dept., Army, Quartermaster Center and School, DEC 1988.

[13] QPB Dec 1988, Defense Dept., Army, Quartermaster Center and School.

[14] Collecting remains of the Dead, LC-USZ62-57030 (b&w film copy neg.) , Library of Congress Prints and Photographs Division Washington, D.C. 20540 USA, LOT 4168, The War Photograph & Exhibition Company, [photographed April 1865, printed between 1880 and 1900], Creator John Reekey, photographer, No. 918. Original negative number: LC-B811-918, Civil War Photograph Collection, Print from Mathew Brady studio negative; cf. negative LC-B811-918. CONTROL #: 92505315.

[15] United States Sanitary Commission (USCC), <http://www.forttejon.org/ussc/ussc.html>.

[16] Headquarters of the United States Sanitary Commission (USSC) in 1864, photographer Mathew Brady, < U.S. Sanitary Commission building and flag, Richmond, Virginia. 1865. 111-B-147, <http://www.archives.gov/research/civil-war/photos/images/civil-war-043.jpg>, National Archives, Washington, DC.

[17] United States Sanitary Commission Records, Washington Hospital Directory Archives, 1862-1866, MssCol 3101, RG 12, NY Public Library, Humanities and Social Sciences Library, manuscripts and Archives Division, <http://www.nypl.org/research/chss/spe/rbk/faids/usscrg12.pdf> p.VI.

[18] Ibid.

[19] Courtesy of Bob Sullivan, Sullivan Press, United States Christian Commission Identification Card.

[20] Courtesy of Bob Sullivan, Sullivan Press, Maryland Bible Society Card.

[21] General View of the wrecked battleship, c1898 Digital ID: cph 3b24990 , Source: b&w film copy neg.Reproduction Number: LC-USZ62-77867 (b&w film copy neg.), Repository: Library of Congress Prints and Photographs Division Washington, D.C. 20540 USA, #9078, CONTROL #: 2002705705.

[22] Coats, Stephen D., <u>Gathering at the Golden Gate: Mobilizing for War in the Philippines, 1898</u> Fort Leavenworth, Kan.: Combat Studies Institute Press, 2006. page 160.

[23] Spanish American War Tag, Courtesy Quartermaster Museum, Ft. Lee, Virginia.

[24] *QMC Historical Studies, The Graves Registration Service in WWI*, April 1951, Number 21, Historical Section Office of the Quartermaster General, p 10.

[25] Image of remain's bottle, courtesy QM Museum, Ft. Lee, Virginia.

[26] *QMC Historical Studies, The Graves Registration Service in WWI*, April 1951, Number 21, Historical Section Office of the Quartermaster General, p 10.

[27] *QMC Historical Studies, The Graves Registration Service in WWI*, April 1951, Number 21, Historical Section Office of the Quartermaster General, p 11

[28] Military Collector and Historian, Vol XXIV, No 4. Winter 1972.

[29] Image of the 1906 tag, courtesy Quartermaster Museum, Ft. Lee, Virginia.

[30] WWI Field Kit, image courtesy Quartermaster Museum, Ft Lee Virginia.

[31] History and Museum Division, Marine Corps.

[32] General Order #294, Department of the Navy – Naval Historical Center, Washington, DC. <http://www.history.navy.mil/faqs/faq59-18.htm>.

[33] Ibid.

[34] INCO Ltd., History, www.incoltd.com.

[35] QPB, September 1988, page 23, Defense Dept., Army, Quartermaster Center and School.

[36] Image Courtesy Quartermaster Museum, Ft. Lee, Virginia.

[37] WW1 Tag, Courtesy Quartermaster Museum, Ft Lee, Virginia.

[38] Noncombatant tag, courtesy Quartermaster Museum, Ft Lee, Virginia.

[39] General Order #294, Department of the Navy – Naval Historical Center, Washington, DC. <http://www.history.navy.mil/library/online/uniform_id.htm>.

[40] QPB Sep 1988, Defense Dept., Army, Quartermaster Center and School.

[41] Image from the Tomb of the Unknown Soldier, <http://www.arlingtoncemetery.org/visitor_information/tomb_of_the_unknowns.html>.

[42] Courtesy US QM Museum archives, 1937.

[43] Burial Ceremony for the WWI Unknown Soldier, November 11, 1921, <http://www.arlingtoncemetery.net/unk-wwi.jpg>.

[44] Quartermaster Review, "Tomb of the Unknown Soldier", September-October 196.3

[45] Regulation 600-40, 1926. United States Army,. Washington, DC: War Department.

[46] Proper wear of tag, WWII, Image courtesy of US Army Quartermaster Museum, Ft. Lee, Virginia. March 22, 1942, Hyslop.

[47] WWI Tags Image, courtesy of the Quartermaster Museum, Ft Lee, Virginia.

[48] General Order #294, Department of the Navy – Naval Historical Center ,Washington, DC. <http://www.history.navy.mil/library/online/uniform_id.htm>.

[49] Ibid.

[50] WWII Tags, courtesy Quartermaster Museum, Ft. Lee Virginia.

[51] <http://www.100thbg.com/mainpages/history/history5/bowman/bowman09.htm>.

[52] <http://www.100thbg.com/splasher/toughestduty.htm>.

[53] QPB, Sep.1988, Defense Dept., Army, Quartermaster Center and School, Ft. Lee, Virginia.

[54] Ibid.

[55] Excerpt from a News Release from the United States Department of Defense, No. 1098-04, November 2, 2004.

[56] *QMC Historical Studies, The Graves Registration Service in WWI*, April 1951, Number 21, Historical Section Office of the Quartermaster General, p 10.

[57] QPB Dec 1988, Defense Dept., Army, Quartermaster Center and School.

[58] *QMC Historical Studies, The Graves Registration Service in WWI*, April 1951, Number 21, Historical Section Office of the Quartermaster General, p 10.

[59] Image Courtesy of the Quartermaster Museum, Ft. Lee, Virginia.

[60] QPB, Sep 1988, Defense Dept., Army, Quartermaster Center and School.

[61] Image Courtesy of the Quartermaster Museum, Ft. Lee, Virginia.

[62] Ibid.

[63] Ibid.

[64] QR, US Army Quartermaster, May/June 1946.

[65] Image Courtesy of the Quartermaster Museum, Ft. Lee, Virginia.

[66] Ibid.

[67] Quartermaster Review (QR), May/June 1946, Defense Dept., Army, Quartermaster Center and School.

[68] Image Courtesy of the Quartermaster Museum, Ft. Lee, Virginia.

[69] QR, US Army Quartermaster, May/June 1946.

[70] Ibid.

[71] QR, US Army Quartermaster, March/April 1953.

[72] Mortuary Affairs Center (MAC), March 2000, http://www.qmmuseum.lee.army.mil/mortuary/MA-Vietnam.htm.

[73] MAC, March 2000, <http://www.qmmuseum.lee.army.mil/mortuary/MA-Vietnam.htm>.

[74] QPB, Sep 1988, Defense Dept., Army, Quartermaster Center and School.

[75] Ibid.

[76] Arlington Cemetery, <http://www.arlingtoncemetery.org/visitor_information/tomb_of_the_unknowns.html>.

[77] QPB, Autumn 1993, Defense Dept., Army, Quartermaster Center and School.

[78] http://www.qmfound.com/14th_Quartermaster_Detachment.htm.

[79] Ibid.

[80] < http://www.jpac.pacom.mil/GulfWar.htm>.

[81] < http://www.jpac.pacom.mil/eBrochure.htm>.

[82] As told to me in a phone interview by Tom Bourlier, Director of Training, Joint Mortuary Affairs Center, Ft. Lee, Virginia.

[83] QPB, Dec 1988, Defense Dept., Army, Quartermaster Center and School.

[84] Ibid.

[85] Ibid.

[86] Image Courtesy of the Quartermaster Museum, Ft. Lee, Virginia.

[87] Dept. of the Navy Mortuary Affairs, Power Point Presentation.

[88] Marine Corps Mortuary Affairs, Sep 10, 2003.

[89] Ibid.

[90] Image Courtesy of US Army Vice President Joe Biden salutes seven Soldiers who were memorialized during a ceremony on Fort Lewis, Wash., Nov. 10. Staff Sgt. Luis M. Gonzalez, of South Ozone Park, N.Y.; Sgt. Fernando Delarosa, of Alamo, Texas; Sgt. Dale R. Griffin, of Terre Haute, Ind.; Sgt. Isaac B. Jackson, of Plattsburg, Mo.; Sgt. Patrick O. Williamson, of Broussard, La.; Spc. Jared D. Stanker, of Evergreen Park, Ill., and Pfc. Ian Walz, of Vancouver, Wash., all with 1-17 Inf., 5th Bde., 2nd Inf. Div., were killed when an IED destroyed their Stryker vehicle in Afghanistan, Oct. 27.

[91] QPB, Dec 1988, Defense Dept., Army, Quartermaster Center and School.

[92] At the time this article was written CPT Richard W. Wooley was Chief of Individual Training. Graves Registration Department (now the Mortuary Affairs Center), U.S. Army Quartermaster School, Fort Lee, Virginia.
<http://www.qmfound.com/short_history_of_identification_tags.htm>.

[93] Courtesy of
<http://www.worthingtonmemory.org/FullFrameImageMultiPF.cfm?id=929&pageNum=1>.

[94] Image courtesy of U.S. Navy photo by 3rd Class Patrick Dille.

[95] Image courtesy of US Army, Third Infantry Division.

[96] Courtesy of National Vietnam Veterans Art Museum, Chris Roberts, NVVAM Staff, March 15, 2007.

[97] Ibid.

[98] http://www.arlingtoncemetery.net/ephoisington.htm.

[99] BG Elizabeth P. Hoisington, donated collection, Us Army Women's Museum, Ft. Lee, Virginia.

[100] Ibid.

[101] Unknown Origin, sent to me with no name attached.

[102] Image courtesy of The John F. Kennedy Presidential Library and Museum is a Presidential Library Administered by the National Archives and Records Administration (NARA), Boston, MA.

[103] Image Courtesy of The John F. Kennedy Presidential Library and Museum is a Presidential Library Administered by the National Archives and Records Administration (NARA), Boston, MA. Navy identification tag for Lt. John F. Kennedy for his service in WWII. Oval silver tag attached to chain engraved: "John/Fitzgerald/Kennedy/Ensign/USNR-O/T-9/42. Courtesy of Senator and Mrs. Edward M. Kennedy.

[104] Image from the Smithsonian National Museum of American History <http://www.audiemurphy.com/smithsonian.htm>.

[105] Image from <http://acacia.pair.com/Acacia.Vignettes/The.Diary.of.Alvin.York.html>, 1917.

[106] Alvin C. York Institute, http://www2.york.k12.tn.us/, Michael Birdwell.

[107] Duck and Cover Poster, a public domain film, 1952, http://www.conelrad.com/duckandcover/cover.php?turtle=01.

[108] *Gigs and Gags*, August 3, 1945 issue, US Army Quartermasters, Ft. Lee, Virginia.

[109] *Ask Lt. Dahl*, Comic Strip, Staff Sgt. Austin M. May, US Dept. of Defense, US Air Force, Air Force 1st Lt. Kenneth Dahl, call sign "Barbie," is the star of the online Web comic strip, Air Force Blues. Creator Staff Sgt. Austin M. May, a public affairs specialist.

[110] GI Joe Doll, John F. Kennedy personal photo, Mattel Corporation.

[111] GI Joe Doll, Sailor personal photo, Mattel Corporation.

[112] GI Joe Doll, Soldier personal photo, Mattel Corporation.

[113] GI Joe Doll, Marine personal photo, Mattel Corporation.

[114] GI Joe Doll, Pearl Harbor Sailor personal photo, Mattel Corporation.

[115] Emily, accessories stock photo, American Girl, LLC.

[116] Hard Rock Barbie, personal photo, Mattel Corp.

[117] My Scene™ Sutton™ Doll, personal photo, Mattel Corporation.

[118] Medical Alert tag, <http://safetytags.com/viewProduct.php?proProId=22>.

[119] Patriotic Tags, < http://www.memorybracelet.com/>.

[120] Veteran Iraq War, Police Officer Identification Tag, personal photo.

[121] Dog Tag Silver Bracelet, <http://shimmerandstone.stores.yahoo.net/silver-bracelet2.html>.

[122] Dog Tag Bracelet, <http://www.kamikazekarate.com/cgi-local/SoftCart.100.exe/online-store/scstore/p-<132680.html?L+scstore+xsbh9567ff462c46+1171178966>.

[123] Various colored Dog Tags, <http://www.westsky.com/dog-tags.htm>.

[124] Plastic silencers, <http://www.gidogtags.com/-strse-42/dog-tag-silencers-rubber/Detail.bok>.

[125] Wine label Dog Tag, <http://www.gidogtags.com/-strse-81/Limited-Edition-Laser-Engraved/Detail.bok>.

[126] Luggage Tags, <http://www.thebattlezone.com/dogtags/lugtags.html>.

[127] Zipper pull tag, < http://www.allheart.com/ae102733.html>.

[128] Key chain, < http://www.soldiercity.com/silver-marines-dog-tag-key-chain.html?utm_source=googlebase&utm_medium=csc&utm_term=KC6001>.

[129] Key Tag flashlight, <http://www.laserengravedkeychains.com/dog-tag-flashlight.htm>.

[130] Dog Tag Thumb Drive, <http://www.dansdata.com/quickshot034.htm>.

[131] Actual Dog Tags, < http://www.petidtags.org/>.

[132] Swizz Army Knife Dog Tag, http://www.surplusandoutdoors.com/ishop/877/shopscr2678.html.

[133] Dog Tag Fitness Advertisement, < http://www.gspfitness.com/Images/title_images/Title-Header_about-us.gif>.

[134] projectak47advertisement, https://projectak47.com.

[135] Dog Tag, X Box game, personal photo, Digital Jesters.

[136] Military Challenge Coins, personal photo, (from left to right) 1st row, Darnall Army Hospital Commander Coin, US Army Chief of Public Affairs Coin, 2nd row, Vice Chief of Staff of the Army Coin, 4th Infantry Division Commander Coin.

[137] Dog Tags Movie Poster, 2008, TLA Movies, http://www.tlavideo.com/results/index.cfm?searchtext=dog+tags&v=1.

[138] Dog Tags and Cowboy Boots Movie Poster, 2009, TLA Movies, http://www.tlavideo.com/results/index.cfm?searchtext=dog+tags&v=1.

[139] Platoon Movie Poster, 1986, MGM Movie.

[140] POW-MIA Text Credit: History - AII POW MIA, News Release - US Postal Office Public Domain.

[141] Vietnam Women's Memorial Project, 1993, Glenna Goodacre, Sculptor, personal image.

[142] Ibid.

[143] Personal image of VVFW poster

[144] Frederick Hart, Three Soldiers Statue Sculptor, Vietnam Veterans Memorial, Vietnam Veterans Memorial Fund (1982). November 10-14, 1982.Washington, DC.

[145] Three Soldiers Statue, Personal Photo, Vietnam Veterans Memorial, Frederick Hart, Sculptor.

[146] Ibid.

[147] Vietnam Memorial collected personal items image, courtesy of the Smithsonian Institute, 1992.

[148] New Jersey Korean War Veterans Memorial, <http://www.state.nj.us/military/korea/index.html>.

[149] Ibid.

[150] Ibid.

[151] Information and statement about the Sculpture sent by e-mail from The University of Arizona.

[152] Image courtesy of the University of Arizona,

<http://www.union.arizona.edu/about/SUMCKeyFeatures.pdf>.

[153] Excerpt, Images in Boston, http://www.360cities.net/image/dog-tag-memorial-boston#308.50,0.00,63.7.

[154]Dog Tag Garden Memorial, Image courtesy of Old North Church (ONC) in Boston.

[155] Bruce Brooksbank, Old North Church Memorial Garden report in ONC's E-Pistle, July 29, 2010.

[156] Excerpt from < http://www.nvvam.org/index.php?option=com_content&view=article&id=218 &Itemid=54>.

[157] Above and Beyond Memorial Image Courtesy of the Chicago National Veterans Art Museum.

[158] Slave Tag, Personal Photo from Museum.

[159] Slave Tag, 1808, Ashepoo Plantation, "Patch".

[160] Slave Tag, 1814, Mansfield Rice Plantation, South Carolina, Georgetown County, "M.R.P.".

[161] 1898 Dog Tag found next to a brick foundation from a small rental house. In 1896, the house was occupied by two black women. In 1905, the house was a saloon. Guy Town, Austin's red light district. <http://www.texasbeyondhistory.net/guytown>.

[162] Cotton Bail Tag, 1836, Belle Grove Plantation, 500LB, Baton Rouge, Louisiana.

[163] Owney, Mascot of the Railway Service, 1990, Courtesy Smithsonian Museum, Washington, DC.

[164] Owney, Mascot of the Railway Service, 1990, Courtesy Smithsonian Museum, personal photo from museum.

[165] Owney, Mascot of the Railway Service,, Personal photo of Booklet from Museum.

[166] Owney Tag, Courtesy Postal Museum of the Smithsonian Museum, Washington, DC.

[167] Social Security Administration, (http://www.ssa.gov/history/briefhistory3.html).

[168] Image courtesy of the Social Security Administration, (http://www.ssa.gov/history/briefhistory3.html).

[169] Queen Victoria Tin, personal image.

[170] P-93, personal image.

[171] Al Purifoy, Mourmelon, France, November 1944. Courtesy of Mac Purifoy, son.

[172] Clicker Replica, courtesy National World War 2 Museum, New Orleans, La.

[173] Honorable Discharge Pin "Ruptured Duck" Image Courtesy of the US Army Quartermaster Museum, Ft. Lee, Virginia.

[174] http://www.americanwarlibrary.com/theduck.htm.

[175] Certificate Image, courtesy of http://www.amervets.com/replacement/duck.htm#sam.

[176] http://www.history.navy.mil/photos/sh-us-cs/csa-sh/csash-hl/hunley.htmvided as a public service by the NHHC.

[177] Confederate submarine *H.L. Hunley* (1863-1864), Inboard profile and plan drawings, after sketches by W.A. Alexander, who directed her construction. Key to numbered features also includes entries for Photo # NH 53545. U.S. Naval Historical Center Photograph.

[178] Ibid.

[179] Confederate Submarine *H.L. Hunley* (1863-1864), Sepia wash drawing by R.G. Skerrett, 1902, after a painting then held by the Confederate Memorial Literary Society Museum, Richmond, Virginia.. Courtesy of the Navy Art Collection, Washington, DC. U.S. Naval Historical Center Photograph.

[180] <http://www.mepcom.army.mil/>.

[181] Air Force Instruction, AFI 36-3026.

[182] Marine Corps Orders, MCO P1070.12, Chapter 7.

[183] Oh God, I'm Dead, Allen Clark, 1983, Texas Publishers Co. pp 54-55.

[184] <http://www.af.mil/factsheets/factsheet.asp?fsID=71>.

[185] Oh God, I'm Dead, Allen Clark, 1983, Texas Publishers Co. pp 54-55.

[186] WAAC Auxiliary M.B. Gaines, Fort Des Moines Army Post, posted Tribune, Des Moines, Iowa, October 2d 1942.

[187] Addressograph-Multigraph at "A Century of Progress", Published 1933 – Addressograph-Multigraph Corporation Cincinnati Ohio, 90 Pages. Courtesy of <www.dogtagsrus>, <graphotype.net>.

[188] Ibid.

[189] Ibid.

[190] Ibid.

[191] Ibid.

[192] Ibid.

[193] Ibid.

[194] Ibid.

[195] Ibid.

[196] Ibid.

[197] Ibid.

[198] Ibid.

[199] Ibid.

[200] Ibid.

[201] Image courtesy from Richard Clayton's personal Collection.

[202] Ibid.

[203] Personal Image Courtesy from the collection of Texas Military Forces Museum, Camp Mabry, Austin, Texas.

[204] Ibid.

[205] Courtesy from the collection at the US Quartermaster Museum Ft. Lee, Virginia.,

[206] Personal Image, Courtesy the US Army Women's Museum, Ft. Lee, Virginia.

[207] Ambrose Monell, A Century of Metals", Huntington Alloys, Special Metals Corporation.

[208] Health Information Technologies, Telemedicine and Advanced Technology Research Center (TATRC), <http://www.tatrc.org/website_pic/index.html.>

[209] Ibid.

[210] Ibid.

[211] Taken from phone interview with LTC Timothy Rapp info officer DOD med school, Detailed medicine research project manager, Readiness for Army Systems Integration HQDA, OTSG.

[212] Health Information Technologies, Telemedicine and Advanced Technology Research Center (TATRC), <http://www.tatrc.org/website_pic/index.html>.

[213] Ibid.

[214] At the time this article was written CPT Richard W. Wooley was Chief of Individual Training. Graves Registration Department (now the Mortuary Affairs Center), U.S. Army Quartermaster School, Fort Lee, Virginia. <http://www.qmfound.com/short_history_of_identification_tags.htm>.

[215] Department of Navy, Mortuary Affairs, 11 December 2006, Power Point Presentation, Military Medical Support Office, Great Lakes, Illinois.

[216] Neil C. Morrison, Museum Director, Fort Irwin, CA 92310-5029.

[217] Image of Identification papers and case, Courtesy of the Quartermaster Museum, Ft. Lee, Virginia.

[218] <http://everythingroyal.com/everythingroyalcomm.html> .

[219] Excerpts from, The Identification of a German Soldier found in the Heidenkopf at Serre, by Alastair H Fraser.

[220] Image courtesy of The Identification of a German Soldier found in the Heidenkopf at Serre, by Alastair H Fraser.

[221] German Identity Discs of World War Two, Burroughs, Michael & Burroughs, Ian. 1995.

[222] Ibid.

[223] <http://www.feldgrau.com/articles.php?ID=55>.

[224] Ibid.

[225] http://lcweb2.loc.gov/diglib/vhp/story/loc.natlib.afc2001001.05190/pageturner?ID=pm 0009001.

[226] <http://www.100thbg.com/mainmenus/pow/pow_main.htm>.

[227] German Identity Discs of World War Two, page 2, Burroughs, Michael & Burroughs, Ian. 1995.

[228] http://wfyi.org/fireandice/people_places/honoring_fallen.htm.

[229] Japanese Dog Tag, image courtesy of Richard Clayton's personal collection.

[230] <http://www.pbs.org/wgbh/amex/bataan/sfeature/sf_mail.html>.

[231] Austria Dog Tag image courtesy of Andreas Krennmair.

[232] Courtesy of <http://www.military-dogtags.com/id25.htm>.

[233] Ibid.

Bibliography

A Century of Progress. (1933). Cincinnati. Ohio. Addressograph-Multigraph Corporation. graphotype.net. www.dogtagsrus.

Alvin C. York Institute. (n.d.). Retrieved September, 2008. Birdwell, Michael. http://www2.york.k12.tn.us/.

American Folklife Center, (n.d.). Washington, DC: The Library of Congress. Retrieved 2008 from http://www.loc.gov/vets/relatedrepositories.html.

The American Heritage Dictionary. (2nd college ed.). (1991). Boston: Houghton Mifflin.

American War Library. (1988). http://www.americanwarlibrary.com/theduck.htm

Arlington National Cemetery. (n.d.) Retrieved March, 2007 – April, 2008 from http://www.arlingtoncemetery.org.

Arlington National Cemetery. (September 3 2007). http://www.arlingtoncemetery.net/ephoisington.htm.

Atkinson, R., Balog, J., Dale, B., & Black, D. (May 19, 2009). *Where Valor Rests: Arlington National Cemetery*. National Geographic .

Braddock, P. (2003). *Dog Tags:A History of the American Military Identification Tag 1861-2002*, (First Edition). Chicora, Pa: Mechling Publishing.

Brooksbank, Bruce. (July 29, 2010). ONC's E-Pistle. Old North Church.

Bruns, James H. (1996). *Owney, Mascot of the Railway Service*. United States National Postal Museum. Washington, DC: Smithsonian Institute.

Burroughs, Michael & Burroughs, Ian. (1995). *German Identity Discs of World War Two*.

Carroll, Alicia. (December 13, 2010). Everything Royal. http://everythingroyal.com/everythingroyalcomm.html

Clark, Allen. (1983). *Oh God, I'm Dead*. Texas Publishers Co.

Coats, S. (2006). *Gathering at the Golden Gate: Mobilizing for War in the Philippines, 1898*. Fort Leavenworth, Ks.: Combat Studies Institute Press.

De Trez, Michael. (1970). *The Legendary Cricket of D-Day*. Belgium: D-Day Publishing.

Digger History. (November 11, 2002). http://www.diggerhistory.info/pages-uniforms/dog_tags.htm

Fraser, A. (October 2004). *The Identification of a German Soldier found in the Heidenkopf at Serre*, http://www.fylde.demon.co.uk/fraser.htm

Friends of the Hunley, Inc. (2010). http://www.hunley.org/.

Gentile, E. (June 8, 2009). *Images in Boston*. http://www.360cities.net/image/dog-tag-memorial-boston#308.50,0.00,63.7

Harper's Weekly. (October 3, 1863). New York: Harper & Brothers.

Health Information Technologies, Telemedicine and Advanced Technology Research Center (TATRC), (n.d.). Retrieved 2008 from http://www.tatrc.org/website_pic/index.html

Knudsen, R. & Myers, R. (Jun 30, 2008). *A Living Treasure: Seasonal Photographs of*

Arlington National Cemetery. Potomac Books Inc.

Krennmair , Andreas. (June 3, 2006). *1337 Dog Tag.* [Msg 1] Message posted to http://synflood.at/blog/index.php?/archives/540-1337-dog-tag.html.

Kurson, R. (May 31, 2005). *Shadow Divers: The True Adventure of Two Americans Who Risked Everything to Solve One of the Last Mysteries of World War II.* Ballantine Books.

Library of Congress. American Folklife Center. (May 29,2007). http://lcweb2.loc.gov/diglib/vhp/story/loc.natlib.afc2001001.05190/pageturner ?ID=pm0009001

Lord, F. (1995). *Civil War Collector's Encyclopedia.* (Volumes I, II). Blue and Grey Press.

Lord, F. (1995). *Civil War Collector's Encyclopedia.* (Volumes III-V). Blue and Grey Press.

MGM. (1986). *Platoon.* Movie Poster, [Motion picture].

Military Collector and Historian. (Winter 1972). Vol XXIV, No 4.

Motts Military Museum. (1987). *Civil War Exhibit.* Groveport, Ohio. http://www.mottsmilitarymuseum.org/home.html.

Murphy, Jim. (1993). *Boys' War, Confederate and Union Soldier's Talk About the Civil War.* Sandpiper.

The National League of POW/MIA Families. (n.d.). Retrieved March, 2008 from http://www.pow-miafamilies.org/.

National Records and Archives Administration.(2006). *Using Civilian Records for Genealogical Research in the National Archives Washington, DC Area.* Reference Information Paper 110. Washington, DC: National Records and Archives Administration.

National Records and Archives Administration. (n.d.). The National Personnel Records Center, Military Personnel Records (NPRC-MPR). Retrieved October 2007 from http://www.archives.gov/st-louis/military-personnel/.

National Vietnam Veterans Museum, Chicago, Il. (n.d.). Retrieved September, 2007 from http://www.nvvam.org/.

Poole, **R.** (Oct 26, 2010). *On Hallowed Ground: The Story of Arlington National Cemetery.* Walker & Company.

Price, William H. (1961). *Civil War Handbook.* A Civil War Research Associates Series. Springfield, Virginia: L.B. Prince Co, Inc.

Priest, Karl. (n.d.). *Ghosts of the East Coast: Doomsday Ships.* The Cold War Museum. Retrieved November, 2007 from http://www.coldwar.org/museum/doomsday_ships.asp.

Shay, John. (n.d.). 100th Bomb Group. Retrieved April 2008 from http://www.100thbg.com/mainmenus/pow/pow_main.htm

Sledge, M. (May 21, 2007). *Soldier Dead: How We Recover, Identify, Bury, and Honor Our Military Fallen.* Columbia University Press.

Special Metals Corporation. *Monell, Ambrose, A Century of Metals.* Huntington Alloys.

Strout, Ben. (2003). *Fire and Ice: The Winter War of Finland and Russia.* [Movie]

http://wfyi.org/fireandice/people_places/honoring_fallen.htm

TLA Movies. (2008). *Dog Tags*. Movie Poster, [Motion picture].

TLA Movies. (2009). *Dog Tags and Cowboy Boots*. Movie Poster, [Motion picture].

Tragedy Assistance Program for Survivors. (n.d.). Retrieved November, 2007 from http://www.taps.org/.

United Services Organization. (n.d.). Retrieved March, 2008 from http://www.uso.org/.

United States Air Force. May, A. (January 2007).*Ask Lt. Dahl*. Washington DC: Department of Defense.

United States Air Force. (n.d.). Retrieved December 2007 from http://www.af.mil/factsheets/factsheet.asp?fsID=71.

United States Air Force. (October 15, 2009). Air Force Instruction. AFI 36-3026. Washington DC:Secretary of the Air Force

United States Army. (1916). General Order Number 204. (Amended). Washington, DC: War Department.

United States Army. (1926). Regulation 600-40. Washington, DC: War Department.

Unites States Army. (April 1951). *The Graves Registration Service in WWI*. QMC Historical Studies. (Number 21). Office Quartermaster General, Fort Lee, Virginia, Department of Defense.

United States Army. (Autumn 1993). *Quartermaster Professional Bulletin*(QPB), Quartermaster Center and School. Fort Lee, Virginia: Department of Defense.

United Statyes Army Center for Military History. (March, 2008). Ft. McNair, Virginia http://www.army.mil/cmh-pg/.

United States Army. (December 1988). *Quartermaster Professional Bulletin (*QPB). United States Army Quartermaster Center and School, Fort Lee, Virginia: Department of Defense.

United States Army. (1906). General Order Number 21. Washington, DC: War Department.

United States Army. (1906). General Order Number 204. Washington, DC: War Department.

United States Army Graves Registration Department (now the Mortuary Affairs Center). (December 1988). United States Army Quartermaster School, Fort Lee, Virginia. http://www.qmfound.com/short_history_of_identification_tags.htm.

United States Army. (March/April 1953). *Quartermaster Review* (QR). United States Army Quartermaster Center and School, Fort Lee, Virginia: Department of Defense.

United States Army. (May/June 1946). *Quartermaster Review* (QR). United States Army Quartermaster Center and School, Fort Lee, Virginia: Department of Defense.

United States Army Mortuary Affairs Center, U.S. Army Quartermaster School, Fort Lee, Virginia. (n.d.). Retrieved March 2007 from http://www.qmfound.com/short_history_of_identification_tags.htm.

United States Army Quartermaster. (August 3, 1945). *Gigs and Gags*. Fort. Lee, Virginia: Department of Defense.

United States Army. Regulation of 1913. Washington, DC: War Department.

United States Army. (September 1988). *Quartermaster Professional Bulletin* (QPB). United States Army Quartermaster Center and School, Fort Lee, Virginia: Department of Defense.

United States Army. (September-October 1963). Tomb of the Unknown Soldier, *Quartermaster Review* (QR). United States Army Quartermaster Center and School, Fort Lee, Virginia: Department of Defense.

United States Department of Defense. (November 2, 2004). Excerpt from NEWS RELEASE, No. 1098-04. Washington DC: Department of Defense.

United States Deptartment of Navy Mortuary Affairs. Retrieved Oct, 2008. Power Point Presentation. www.npc.navy.mil.

United States Department of Veteran's Affairs. (n.d.). *Burial and Memorial Benefits.* Retrieved May, 2008 from http://www.cem.va.gov/.

United States Department of Defense Prisoner of War and Missing Personnel Office. (n.d.). Retrieved April, 2007 from http://www.dtic.mil/dpmo/.

United States Department of Defense Military Assistant Program Casualty and Military Affairs. (n.d.). Retrieved October 2008 from http://www.dod.mil/mapcentral/casualty.html.

United States Department of Defense. (October, 1999). http://www.defenselink.mil/news/Oct1999/n10191999_9910192.html.

United States Department of Veteran's Affairs National Cemetery Administration. (January, 2009). *History and Development of the National Cemetery Administration.* Communication and Outreach Support Division. http://www.cem.va.gov/cem/pdf/history.pdf.

United States Joint POW/MIA Accounting Command(JPAC). (Retrieved June 2008). http://www.jpac.pacom.mil/eBrochure.htm.

United States Joint POW/MIA Accounting Command(JPAC). (Retrieved June 2008). http://www.jpac.pacom.mil/index.php?page=cil&size=100&ind=3.

United States Navy. (1917). General Order Number 294. Washington, DC: War Department.

Unites States Navy. (1998). General Order No. 99. Washington DC: Department of Defense.

United States Navy. (December 11, 2006). Department of Mortuary Affairs. Power Point Presentation. Great Lakes, Illinois: Military Medical Support Office.

United States Navy. (December 22, 2003). Naval History and Heritage Command. http://www.history.navy.mil/faqs/faq70-1.htm.

United States Navy. (n.d.). Retrieved November 2007 from http://www.history.navy.mil/photos/sh-us-cs/csa-sh/csash-hl/hunley.htmvided .

United States Marine Corps. (August, 1917). General Order Number 21, Washington, DC: War Department.

United States Marines Corps. (February 15, 1918). General Order Number 30, Washington, DC: War Department.

United States Marine Corps Individual Records Administration. (May 31, 2002). MCO P1070.12. Chapter 7. Washington DC:Department of the Navy

United States Marine Corps Mortuary Affairs. (September 10, 2003).
http://usmilitary.about.com/cs/marines/a/mortuary.htm.
United States Marine Corps. (October 1916). Order Number 32. Washington, DC: War
Department.
United States Marines Corps. (February 15, 1918). General Order Number 10, 6th
Regiment of Marines. Washington, DC: War Department.
United States National Archives and Records Administration. May 12, 1862. Letter
from John Kennedy to the Secretary of War's on. It is filed under K-206-1862
with drawing of his proposed disk. The file has been reproduced as part of
National Archives Microfilm Publication M221. Letters Received by the
Secretary of War, Main Series, 1801-1870. Copy of the response is also in file
K-206-1862. Also found in the Secretary of War Letters Sent series in Military
Book 49, A, page 168. This volume is reproduced on National Archives
Microfilm Publication M6, Letters Sent by the Secretary of War Relating to
Military Affairs, 1800-1809.
United States Postal Office. (March 29, 1995). POW MIA Stamp News Release
Number 95-027. Washington DC: US Postal Service.
United States Sanitary Commission. (n.d.). Retrieved October 2007 from
http://www.forttejon.org/ussc/ussc.html.
United States Social Security Administration. (n.d.). Retrieved March 2007 from
http://www.ssa.gov/history/briefhistory3.html.
United States Special Operations Command Care Coalition. (n.d.). Retrieved August
2007 from
http://www.socom.mil/care_coalition/casualty/injury.htm.
University of Arizona. Information and statement about the Sculpture sent by e-mail.
University of Houston, (n.d.). Updated February 27, 2011.
http://www.digitalhistory.uh.edu/learning_history/children_civilwar/child_sol
diers.cfm.
University of Texas. (October 1, 2001). *Austin's Guy Town.*
http://www.texasbeyondhistory.net/guytown.
WAAC Auxiliary. M.B. Gaines. (Oct. 2, 1942). Fort Des Moines Army Post, Des
Moines, Iowa: Tribune.
Worthington Memory. (n.d.) Retrieved January 2011.
http://www.worthingtonmemory.org/FullFrameImageMultiPF.cfm?id=929&p
ageNum=1.
The Wright Museum. (November, 2007). *Dog Tag and Rations exhibit.* Wolfboro, New
Hampshire.
http://www.wrightmuseum.org.
Yahoo Directory. (n.d.). Last retrieved February, 2011 from
http://dir.yahoo.com/Government/U_S__Government/Military/Veterans/Orga
nizations/.

Made in the USA
Las Vegas, NV
29 November 2024

12883149R00162